Cutting Costs

Cutting Costs

Successful Strategies
for Improving Productivity

Fred H. Neu

 PRAEGER

AN IMPRINT OF ABC-CLIO, LLC
Santa Barbara, California • Denver, Colorado • Oxford, England

Library of Congress Cataloging-in-Publication Data

Neu, Fred H.
    Cutting costs : successful strategies for improving productivity / Fred H. Neu.
        pages cm.
    Includes bibliographical references and index.
    ISBN 978–1–4408–2923–9 (hardcopy : alk. paper) — ISBN 978–1–4408–2924–6 (ebook)
1. Cost control. 2. Industrial productivity. 3. Labor productivity. I. Title.
HD47.3.N48   2013
658.5′15—dc23   2012045039

ISBN: 978–1–4408–2923–9
EISBN: 978–1–4408–2924–6

17 16 15 14 13   1 2 3 4 5

This book is also available on the World Wide Web as an eBook.
Visit www.abc-clio.com for details.

Praeger
An Imprint of ABC-CLIO, LLC

ABC-CLIO, LLC
130 Cremona Drive, P.O. Box 1911
Santa Barbara, California 93116-1911

This book is printed on acid-free paper ∞

Manufactured in the United States of America

Definitions from APICS used by permission.

To the consultants with whom I worked over the years and who were willing to share their knowledge and experience, which enabled me to be a more effective consultant, and to the memory of my parents, Frederick Wilson Neu and Mary Hooper Neu.

Contents

1. Introduction   1
   1.1 What Would Your Business Do with Cost-Cutting Savings?   1
   1.2 Purpose of This Book and What You Will Learn   3
   1.3 Understand the Importance of Cost Cutting   4
   1.4 Cost Cutting and the Bottom Line   6
   1.5 Establish Cost-Cutting Objectives   9

2. Effective Approaches and Getting a Program Started   11
   2.1 Consider Alternative Approaches   11
   2.2 Form Teams or Committees   11
   2.3 Use Consultants   12
   2.4 Set Goals for Everyone with Budget Responsibility   14
   2.5 Reduce Budgets and/or Head Counts by a Percentage   15
   2.6 Incentive Programs   16
   2.7 Supply-Chain Partnering   17
   2.8 Just-in-Time   19
   2.9 Kaizen   20
   2.10 Combine Approaches   21
   2.11 Emphasize the Need and Get the Program Started   21
   2.12 What's in It for Me?: The Employee's Viewpoint   23
   2.13 Provide Proper Tools and Training   24
   2.14 Be Cautious of Cutting Costs in Certain Areas   25

3. Methods to Identify Opportunities   27
   3.1 Utilize Multiple Methods   27

3.2 Analyze Budget Expense History   27
3.3 Study the General Ledger Chart of Accounts   29
3.4 Review Top Suppliers   30
3.5 Negotiate, Negotiate, Negotiate   31
3.6 Conduct Survey Interviews   31
3.7 Employee Suggestion Programs   34
3.8 Seek Free Advice and Services   38
3.9 Decentralize Research to Identify Better Suppliers,
     Products, and Services   40
3.10 Value Engineering   42
3.11 Perform Productivity Analyses   43

4. Apply Some Basic Common-Sense Axioms   51
   4.1 Communicate Basic Concepts and Principles   51
   4.2 Ask for It   51
   4.3 Spend Money to Make Money   52
   4.4 Obtain Competitive Bids for Goods and Services   54
   4.5 Give Incumbents the Opportunity to Keep the Business   55
   4.6 Use the Internet and Other Available Technology   56
   4.7 Establish Consistent Policies and Procedures   57
   4.8 Keep Your Eyes and Ears Open   59
   4.9 Trust Your Instincts   64
   4.10 High Volume Equals High Opportunity   65
   4.11 Time Is Money   68
   4.12 Improve Productivity and Efficiency   69
   4.13 Reduce Unproductive Time   73
   4.14 Eliminate Bottlenecks and Constraints   77
   4.15 Ask "Why?" and Do Not Accept "Because It's Always
        Been Done That Way"   78
   4.16 Invest in Improving Employee Morale   78

5. Cost Avoidance   79
   5.1 Plan, Track, and Control Budgets   79
   5.2 Establish Budget Expenditure Approval Levels   81
   5.3 Is It a Nicety or a Necessity?   81
   5.4 Product Development and Design   85
   5.5 Product Liability   86
   5.6 Determine the Effectiveness of Your Marketing
        and Advertising   87
   5.7 Preventive Maintenance   88
   5.8 Service and Maintenance Agreements   88
   5.9 Do Not Overreact to Certain Situations   89

5.10 Promote Safety   91
5.11 Security Measures   97

6. Selected Cost-Cutting Areas   99
    6.1   Raw Materials and Purchased Parts   99
    6.2   Inside versus Outside Services   100
    6.3   Temporary Plant Shutdowns   105
    6.4   Relocations, Acquisitions, and Consolidations   105
    6.5   Sell Excess Equipment   114
    6.6   Paper Usage Reduction   114
    6.7   Recycling   118
    6.8   Freight Practices   119
    6.9   Product Packaging   126
    6.10 Communications (Mail, Facsimile, Telephone, and Email)   127
    6.11 Travel and Entertainment   129
    6.12 Scrap and Rework   130
    6.13 Hire Some Mentally Challenged Workers   131
    6.14 Overtime   132

7. Quality-Related Issues   133
    7.1   Quality and Service "As They Should Be"   133
    7.2   Understand Your Quality-Related Costs   137
    7.3   Do Things Right in the First Place   138
    7.4   Inventory Control and Accuracy   141

8. Human Resources Involvement   147
    8.1   Retain Good Employees   147
    8.2   Justify All Replacements and New Hires   148
    8.3   Offer or Require a Shortened Work Week or Work Hours   148
    8.4   Early Retirement   149
    8.5   Effective Use of Temporary and Part-Time Employees   149
    8.6   Bargain with the Bargaining Units   150
    8.7   Prepare for and Manage Change   151
    8.8   Employee Benefits   151
    8.9   Policy Regarding Supplier Gratuities   151
    8.10 Avoid Recruiting Fees   152
    8.11 Reductions in Force   153
    8.12 Conduct Exit Interviews   154

9. Measure Results and Reward Positive Efforts   155
    9.1   Decide What to Track   155
    9.2   Track as Much as Possible Programmatically   155
    9.3   Set Fair Standards of Performance   156

9.4 Maintain, Monitor, Analyze, and Use Statistics   161
9.5 Evaluate Cost-Cutting Results   162
9.6 Follow-up and Accountability   165
9.7 Give Credit Where Credit Is Due   165
9.8 Performance Review Process   167

10. Concluding Comments   169
10.1 Recap of Key Points   169
10.2 Plan Your Work and Work Your Plan   180
10.3 Control the Whole by Controlling the Parts   180
10.4 Concluding Thoughts and Key Cost-Cutting Questions   183

11. Examples of Successful Cost-Cutting and
    Productivity-Improvement Efforts   185
    11.1 Brief Descriptions of Successful Cost-Cutting and
          Productivity-Improvement Projects Performed and
          Written by Various Managers and Consultants   185

Contributors   231

Index   233

1

Introduction

1.1 WHAT WOULD YOUR BUSINESS DO WITH COST-CUTTING SAVINGS?

What would you do with your winnings if you won a lottery jackpot worth millions of dollars? It is a question that is fun to think about. The most frequent answers given by past lottery winners included quitting work, buying a new home, buying a new car, and going on a great vacation trip. A really large winning amount may enable you to do all those things. Of course, the amount of the winning payout would determine what you could do, and you might have to settle for much less if your payout is not very big.

When California introduced the lottery in 1984, there were some effective advertisements geared to encourage people to buy lottery tickets. One advertisement simply asked the question, "What would you do?"—meaning, "What would you do if you won?" Another advertisement said, "If you don't play, you can't win." These messages from the California lottery advertisements can also apply to your business. Think about what your business would do if it realized big savings, or even modest savings, from a successful cost-cutting and productivity-improvement program. This should be a fun question to think about, and it might be the impetus you need to initiate a program at your business.

If you do not initiate a cost-cutting program, you cannot realize any cost savings. Moreover, you cannot afford *not* to initiate a cost-cutting and productivity-improvement program. Potential benefits of a successful cost-cutting and productivity-improvement program at your business could include the following:

By reducing costs and improving productivity, such a program provides your business with an opportunity to be more competitive. Lowering prices to meet or beat competitors' prices for similar goods and/or services enables your business to gain market share.

If expansion into larger, additional, or better facilities is deemed necessary, cost-cutting savings can help provide the funds to make it possible.

Obtaining a new system, such as a warehouse management system (WMS) utilizing bar-coding technology, can make a business with warehouses and distribution centers operate more productively and accurately.

Your business can use cost-cutting savings to invest in productivity-improvement technology, such as automation and other more efficient equipment. These types of investments provide a return on the investment (ROI) and continued longer-term cost savings.

Money saved by cost-cutting efforts can be used to raise employee wages, provide bonuses, and enable other employee incentives, all of which help increase employee morale and retention. Not surprisingly, whenever I conduct a cost-cutting seminar or give a presentation to clients, this way to use some cost-cutting savings is always the most popular option among employees attending the presentation.

I know a business that achieved small savings from a cost-cutting program. With most of the savings, it purchased new desktop computers with all the necessary software for employees using computers. The employees were also able to choose their own new ergonomic desk chair. As you can imagine, this significantly increased the productivity and morale of those employees.

If your business has publicly traded stock, informing the investment community of cost-cutting plans and successful cost-cutting efforts can result in increased shareholder value as well as attract more investors.

One of the most important things your business can do with cost savings is to fund additional research and development efforts for improving existing products and creating new products. Very few businesses can survive or grow without innovation, improving their current products, and bringing new products and/or services to the marketplace.

Your odds of winning big at playing the lottery are not good. Of course, purchasing more lottery tickets increases your chances to win. However, with the right emphasis and effort, obtaining savings from initiating a cost-cutting and productivity-improvement program at your business is almost a sure thing.

1.2 PURPOSE OF THIS BOOK AND WHAT YOU WILL LEARN

Whether you are the one to initiate a cost-cutting and productivity-improvement program in the future, or it is imposed on you, this book will help you prepare for and manage it successfully. Through the years, various descriptive buzzwords and methodology terms for cost cutting have arisen, such as "efficiency," "productivity improvement," "process improvement," "downsizing," "rightsizing," "restructuring," "process reengineering," and "lean." No matter which terms or buzzwords are used, they all result in productivity improvement and cost cutting, which help businesses operate more cost-effectively.

Unless you are a business school student and have not been out in the working world yet, it is very possible that you have already been involved in some type of cost-cutting or productivity-improvement effort in your career. You will be presented with various approaches from which to choose regarding conducting a cost-cutting and productivity-improvement program at your business. Just as important, you will learn how to plan, organize, lead, administer, monitor, evaluate the effectiveness of, and reward individuals who contribute positively to the program.

You will learn numerous ways to help identify general and specific opportunity areas for cost cutting and productivity improvement, as well as discover areas where you should avoid making cuts, except in dire conditions. No cost-cutting or productivity-improvement recommendations in the book are made that will sacrifice acceptable quality and safety levels. Many of the basic approaches, concepts, and principles used in developing a successful cost-cutting program also apply to other concerns management may have regarding areas needing improvement. Keep that in mind as you read the book. Cost cutting sometimes has a negative and, I believe, unfair connotation. All businesses need to continuously improve by becoming more efficient. Cost cutting is always important. Properly applied, these types of programs will ensure growth, employment, and satisfaction for both management and employees.

The level of explanation provided in the book is intended to be adequate for you to understand the topics discussed and to trigger ideas that help you determine which approaches and cost-cutting and productivity-improvement areas you want to pursue. Depending on your business experience, as you read the book, you may often say to yourself, "I knew that." Ideally, you will follow that with "But I am glad you reminded me of it."

The Contents listing for this book is detailed on purpose. The chapter and section titles enable you to easily find a topic of possible interest. The sections are not lengthy, so it is a book that you can easily pick up and read, then put down without losing your place. Once you have read the book, I recommend that you reread the Contents listing often to remind you of things you can do to cut costs.

1.3 UNDERSTAND THE IMPORTANCE OF COST CUTTING

At some time, cost cutting and improving productivity become important or absolutely essential to most businesses. In the extreme, a successful cost-cutting and productivity-improvement program can mean the difference between staying in business and possibly failing. Cost cutting and productivity improvement are closely related but not identical. Following is a simple general definition of productivity to remember when productivity is mentioned throughout the book: "Productivity is a measure of the output of production compared to the input of resources used to produce that output."

A cost-cutting program can be large and include an entire multicompany conglomerate, it can be small and limited to one targeted department within a business, or it can be anywhere in between. How serious a business's needs are to reduce its costs will determine how encompassing the effort will be and how drastic the cost-cutting measures are.

Sometimes, certain cost-cutting ideas may seem too unpopular, trivial, or risky for businesses that are not in desperate need for cost reduction. At other times, an idea that seems too extreme to one business may be quickly accepted by another business with financial problems in need of any and all ideas that can help it cut costs. When a business's future literally depends on cost cutting, one needs to be as creative and aggressive as possible in all areas to identify and take advantage of opportunities. Cost cutting happens continuously in both good businesses and those under pressure to survive. A business without a cost-cutting mentality and program is not as likely to be successful as one that does.

Some cost-cutting actions by big-name businesses and industry segments have been in the news and are highly visible, while others occur behind the scenes and are not known or seen by the general public.

Airlines offer highly visible examples of cost cutting. As people who have flown over the years may recognize, many cost-cutting efforts have taken place with the airlines, especially when the cost of fuel rose to all-time high levels. Airlines have typically played "follow the leader"; that is, when one airline would increase fares or frills, other airlines would follow suit. Thus, when airlines began to reduce fares and eliminate frills, other airlines did the same. For example, when one airline stopped serving free meals on domestic flights in coach class, other carriers quickly adopted the same policy. Other visible actions included eliminating free peanuts or pretzels—these free snacks have been discontinued on most airlines, at least for flights within the United States. In addition, most airlines now charge for checked baggage, which may be considered a cost reduction and/or revenue generator. Behind-the-scenes cost-cutting measures taken by airlines include reducing the number of scheduled flights to increase the number of passengers per flight. With fewer flights, fewer pilots and flight attendants are needed, and costs associated with fuel usage and maintenance are reduced as well. Some airlines overbook flights to ensure full flights. However, this sometimes results in some passengers not getting on a flight, which means they must be compensated by the airline monetarily or with a future free flight.

But that's enough about the airlines. Let's look at some other examples of cost cutting, this time involving the physical size of the product. A few years ago, the *Los Angeles Times* reduced the physical paper size, which is a smart cost-cutting move. People got used to the smaller size, and it now seems normal. Similarly, the container sizes for some ice cream brands, coffee, and some other products have become smaller.

It is never too late for cost cutting to succeed. We all know how American-made automobiles once dominated the U.S. market due to a lack of competition from foreign-made vehicles. Consumers had to deal with the inconsistent quality of American-made automobiles. However, once foreign-made vehicles—especially from Japan and now South Korea—with lower prices and higher quality entered the U.S. market, the American manufacturers started losing market share. This trend, coupled with an overall bad economic situation and recession that began in 2008, led major automobile manufacturers such as General Motors and Chrysler to receive government loans or bail-out money.

Operating costs that were excessive led to General Motors (GM) and Chrysler to make drastic cost-cutting changes in 2009, including shutting down some assembly plants. In a highly publicized move, GM phased out product lines including Pontiac and Saturn. Ford phased out its

Mercury product line. These were major actions that required in-depth analysis and planning to ensure they were the right decisions. In the case of GM, a bankruptcy was needed to shed costs. Ford saw the problem ahead of time and moved aggressively; it indirectly received benefits from the GM bankruptcy in the form of reduced labor costs and beneficial work rule changes. Regardless of where your business ranks compared to the competition, cutting costs and improving productivity are surefire ways to help move up the ladder.

Foreign-made cars did lead to a good thing for American automobile makers and consumers: it made the U.S. automakers improve their quality to be more competitive. In mid-2010, surveys showed that U.S. automakers dominated all quality categories except for luxury automobiles, with Ford at the top of the list. The foreign automobile manufacturers regained their reputation for highest quality and customer satisfaction. A customer satisfaction survey in October 2012 indicated that Japanese automakers were again ranked the highest in customer satisfaction, with the exception of the American-made Cadillac brand. The cost-cutting measures taken by U.S. automakers were not made with a sacrifice of quality. Instead, the quest by every automaker to have the highest quality ranking and highest customer satisfaction rating continues to benefit consumers.

During the editing process to prepare the book for publication, some other high-profile businesses announced major cost-cutting changes. Borders announced it was closing all 399 of its bookstores because it could not find a buyer for the business, which would result in 4,000 employees losing their jobs. Cisco Systems announced a reduction of 6,500 employees as a cost-cutting measure, Sony announced planned layoffs of 10,000 worldwide, Whirlpool announced it would lay off 5,000 employees, and Bank of America announced plans to close numerous branches and lay off 30,000 employees. The U.S. Postal Service announced planned post office location closures and layoffs of thousands. Hewlett-Packard announced planned layoffs of more than 25,000 employees worldwide. There continue to be other such examples.

1.4 COST CUTTING AND THE BOTTOM LINE

The main measure of management success is the bottom line of the profit and loss statement—that is, the amount of profit made. Cost cutting and productivity improvements result in increased profits, or, at least, they reduce losses. Cost-cutting savings begin to hit the bottom line immediately. For example, if you are able to purchase something your business uses for less money, that results in bottom-line savings.

Unless you successfully (and continually) negotiate for better prices from your current or new suppliers, increased profits may be difficult to achieve due to rising costs for personnel, equipment, materials, services, distribution, and facilities. The cost of financing capital can also have a negative impact on bottom-line profits and reduce competitiveness. Cost cutting can greatly reduce the amount of new capital that must be found and paid for.

When markets are not competitive and business is good, most businesses are more interested in the top line on the profit and loss statement—that is, the amount of revenue. Cost cutting is generally not looked upon as necessary to businesses when there is a great demand for a business's products and/or services. One of the best-selling business books of all time, *In Search of Excellence: Lessons from America's Best Run Companies*, by Thomas Peters and Robert Waterman, Jr., came out in 1982, and its emphasis was on the top line.

Increasing revenue (sales income) normally increases bottom-line profits. However, if you make 10 percent profit on gross sales, it would take $500,000 in gross sales to make a $50,000 profit. If you make a 5 percent profit on gross sales, it would take $1,000,000 in gross sales to make a $50,000 profit, and so on. If you identify and eliminate $50,000 in unnecessary expense, you begin accruing bottom-line benefits immediately, and it does not require increasing sales income.

Thus there are some distinct advantages of cost cutting and productivity improvements compared to increasing sales income to make profit, especially when a business is experiencing a decrease in demand for its products or has cash flow problems. When conditions will not support growing revenue, cost cutting can be the only way to grow profits. Cost cutting can also put great pressure on your competitors, depending on what you do with the savings.

As mentioned earlier, cost cutting begins hitting the bottom line immediately. Consider that, for most businesses, there is usually a significant time delay and cash outlay before sales income translates into profit. Some of these cash outlays and resulting delays in realizing profits may occur in many or all of the following areas:

Marketing and advertising costs, which may include advertisements on radio or television and in appropriate newspapers and other publications, Internet advertisements, brochures, mailings, show booths, attending trade shows, website maintenance, and paying to ensure the website is visited.

Sales costs for salespeople to call on accounts with proper frequency, sales literature, travel and entertainment, incentives to the sales force in terms of bonuses (push sales and marketing), and incentives to customers to buy your products in terms of rebates (pull sales and marketing).

Raw materials, purchased component parts, products purchased for resale, and supplies necessary to manufacture, package and ship your business's products.

Inbound shipping to bring in raw materials, purchased parts, and supplies. Depending on the types of parts and supplies and the locations of the suppliers, raw materials, purchased parts, and supplies could be shipped via ocean container, less than ocean container (LCL), full truckload, rail car, less than truckload (LTL), or small package carrier.

Inventory carrying (financing) costs for raw materials waiting to be used, while products are in the manufacturing process, or finished goods and replacement parts in warehouses or distribution centers awaiting sales orders.

Labor costs to manufacture products or provide service for your customers. You must pay your workforce as they are working on producing products or providing services; however, you may not be paid by your customers for quite some time afterward.

Manufacturing overhead costs.

Outbound shipping costs to deliver product, especially if you ship free to the customer.

The time required for the billing and collection process, which usually results in your business paying suppliers for goods and services long before you receive payment from customers for the products and services you sell.

All of these factors contribute to a delay in realizing a bottom-line profit from sales income. As noted earlier, when a business sector is in a downturn or stagnant period, increasing profits by increasing sales may not be possible, so cost cutting becomes a desirable option.

Another benefit of many cost-cutting efforts and productivity-improvement results is that they can be achieved without capital expense. This is of significant importance to businesses having cash flow problems or experiencing a slowdown in sales.

Finally, many cost-cutting and productivity-improvement savings are not just one-time savings. Instead, they accrue year after year because, if you had not eliminated the source of the cost, you would have continued to incur it.

1.5 ESTABLISH COST-CUTTING OBJECTIVES

By now, I hope you are convinced that a cost-cutting program is as integral to good business management as is a business's products or services. The competitive nature of business mandates that productivity continue to improve and that no unnecessary costs be ignored.

As part of the initial cost-cutting and productivity-improvement program planning, you should establish objectives, including a range of how much money you expect or want to save and what you plan to do with the resulting cost savings. This is a combination of subjective and objective considerations, and top management should be able to brainstorm and come up with some realistic expectations.

I once attended an educational presentation geared for consultants to develop an effective elevator speech. An elevator speech is how you would describe your consulting practice or the types of services you offer to someone, especially a potential client, in a quick, concise, and clear way, such as when you meet someone in an elevator. The presenter stressed the importance of using a visual image in an elevator speech to describe the results of your consulting efforts. After some deliberation, I decided on the following visual image for my elevator speech: "I help businesses save piles of money." I pause briefly and add, "Then I encourage the business to use the money wisely to make worthwhile improvements and become more successful."

You should have an elevator speech to explain your cost-cutting and productivity-improvement plan to your employees and suppliers. As example, your elevator speech could be, "We need to cut costs and save money, and I expect everyone, including you, to have ideas how to save our business money. Also, I expect ideas regarding how best to invest the saved money wisely to make us more successful."

The main objective of a successful cost-cutting and productivity-improvement program should be to save piles of money and use the savings wisely to make significant improvements to help your business become more successful. Of course, it is obvious that if your savings are great, you will be able to make big investments and big improvements. If the savings are small, you will be able to make only modest investments. In either case, use the cost savings wisely to make the biggest impact possible for your business.

2

Effective Approaches and Getting a Program Started

2.1 CONSIDER ALTERNATIVE APPROACHES

Often, a business will use a variety of approaches to address different cost-cutting opportunities. Based on my experience, utilizing various approaches provides the best results. Of the many effective approaches to cost cutting, you must decide which are appropriate and the best for your business. I use the word "business" for consistency throughout the book. In this context, a "business" could mean a publicly held company, private company, family-owned business, not-for-profit business, government entity, religious organization, or educational institution. Descriptions of some approaches for a cost-cutting and productivity-improvement program from which your business can choose are provided in this chapter.

2.2 FORM TEAMS OR COMMITTEES

You can call the group what you like, but whether it is a team, task force, or committee that you form, it can be one of the most effective approaches to cost cutting. The committee may consist of the executive level of management, or it may include a larger cross section of management. I highly recommend that you at least use a committee to oversee the entire cost-cutting effort. Committees are generally drawn from many sources and provide broad-based knowledge of the business's various facets, preliminary buy-in to the program, cost-cutting leads, communications, and "sacred cows."

Many businesses already have a mechanism in place to address issues and areas needing improvement. Two examples are quality assurance and internal auditing. If your business has such mechanisms, they may be the perfect seedbed for your cost-cutting program. They will have effective communications ability, will have formed connections to departments of interest, and will be an accredited sponsor of change.

Depending on the size of your business and the size of the program, you may need to form a main steering committee to oversee various subcommittees, cost-cutting teams, task forces, or individuals assigned to address certain areas. The teams may become very competitive and want to look good at meetings with their superiors and peers, which often leads to more ideas and better results. Chapter 3 provides ideas regarding which types of assignments could be made to the teams.

Select appropriate team leaders and members carefully, stressing the importance of choosing objective, open-minded, respected, and creative people. Especially focus on people who are reliable in getting things done and executing assignments.

Establish regularly scheduled meeting times at which substantive progress reports are due and/or to conduct problem resolution sessions should there be a need. Weekly or biweekly meetings are appropriate for the teams, and monthly meetings are appropriate for the team or subcommittee leaders to meet with and report to the steering committee.

After the teams or subcommittees develop cost-cutting recommendations, and those recommendations have been approved by the steering committee, determine whether the same or different teams will oversee the implementation of recommendations. Of course, at that time the appropriate managers of the departments impacted will also be included in the implementation of recommendations.

2.3 USE CONSULTANTS

Consider using inside or outside consultants to help plan, organize, implement, and manage portions of, or your entire, cost-cutting program. The main reasons for using outside consultants for improving productivity, cost cutting, or any other need a business may want to address include the following:

Consultants provide an expertise not available within the business.

There is expertise within the business, but there is not adequate time for those employees to devote to the effort due to the importance and time demands of their normal responsibilities.

Consultants are—or should be—objective, with no preconceived ideas of what they may find and recommend.

The business believes it has done all it can, and it needs new eyes to look at the situation.

The business needs validation of what it already believes.

It is deemed more expedient for an outsider to address cost-cutting and productivity-improvement issues due to recommendations and results that could prove unpopular and embarrassing to some individuals.

Consultants usually provide project organization and management skills to ensure the cost-cutting efforts keep moving forward.

Consultants often act as a catalyst for a cost-cutting and productivity-improvement program, even before they do anything. When the employees learn that consultants are coming in to assist with a cost-cutting and productivity-improvement program, they may suddenly become creative and come up with new ideas or voice ideas they already had but never shared.

Some management personnel and supervisory employees will be defensive and resentful of consultants for fear the consultants may make them look bad for not coming up with the cost-cutting and productivity-improvement ideas themselves. Management and good consultants can usually dispel these fears promptly. The important thing that should be emphasized is that the results are what count.

If consultants are used, management must pave the way for them, thereby helping ensure maximum cooperation from everyone in the business. Ideally, it should be a win-win situation for everyone involved.

If the cost-cutting and productivity-improvement program is a first-time effort, consultants can also help in dealing with the changes that will result from the program.

Sometimes consultants are used only to get the cost-cutting effort organized, started, and through the point of identifying the approaches that will be used.

A business may also retain consultants through the phase where cost-cutting opportunities are identified. At that point, the business may take ownership and responsibility for implementing the program.

Consultants should provide cost benefits that exceed by many times the cost of their assistance with the project. Therefore, in most instances, consultants should work with management from the beginning through the implementation of recommendations, evaluating the success of the program, helping to determine which kind of recognition should be given, and ensuring that the appropriate individuals who helped make the effort successful are rewarded.

Good consultants will not work alone, but instead will work with appropriate employees in the business to identify and achieve the cost-cutting goals.

Consultants are usually good interviewers who can stimulate and further develop ideas with the employees. Remember that two heads are better than one; thus, when you combine a knowledgeable employee with a skilled consultant, the results can be synergistic.

Lastly, another benefit of using consultants is the learning experience for the business's key staff members who work with them. What they learn will continue to be useful throughout their careers and provide ongoing benefits to the business.

2.4 SET GOALS FOR EVERYONE WITH BUDGET RESPONSIBILITY

Many businesses choose to try goal setting before considering any other method. Usually the fact that cost savings are needed is known at the outset of a program. The business may be losing money or known competition may be gaining market share due to the cost of producing its products.

Sometimes a recurring goal can be set. Several years ago, my alma mater, the University of Michigan, set a goal of reducing its costs by 2 percent annually. Consequently, the University of Michigan's budget situation is not perilous as is that of many universities.

You may instruct each member of executive management or managers with budget responsibility to identify opportunities in their respective areas of organizational control. Assigning cost-cutting goals to all levels of management or selected managers can yield positive results. As you might expect, if there are no goals, generally no actions will be taken.

If your business already uses a management by objectives or other periodic goal-setting method, cost-cutting and productivity-improvement goals must be made one of the program's highest priority goals. For cost-cutting goals, the longest time-period increment to use for establishing and measuring results is quarterly; however, a monthly increment is preferable. Yearly or twice-yearly time frames for establishing goals and measuring results are too long and not recommended.

There are five basic steps to the goal-based process for cost cutting and productivity improvement:

Step 1. Top management establishes the cost-cutting and productivity-improvement goals and program time frame and communicates them to the individuals in the business responsible for achieving them. The goals could be described in many ways, such as a certain dollar amount reduction, a percentage budget reduction, a head-count reduction, and a defined increase in productivity.

Step 2. Individuals are assigned responsibility for achieving the cost savings and productivity improvements by implementing the changes that will yield the desired results. They are expected to identify and document the results of their efforts and communicate them to top management.

Step 3. Top management and the individuals responsible for achieving the cost savings and increased productivity monitor and measure the results. Appropriate staff from the finance department, industrial engineering department (if there is one), human resources, or other departments may also be assigned to help monitor and measure results.

Step 4. Top management communicates successful cost-cutting results to everyone in the business. This is one form of recognizing and rewarding those individuals who have contributed positively to cost cutting; other rewards are typically financial.

Step 5. Top management rewards the individuals responsible for positive results on a timely basis.

2.5 REDUCE BUDGETS AND/OR HEAD COUNTS BY A PERCENTAGE

Instructing all departments to make arbitrary percentage cuts in their budgets or employee head counts can be effective. However, this approach has drawbacks that must be considered. In most businesses, there are usually some departments that operate leaner than others, due to more diligent managers who budget expenses and employee head count more tightly than other managers; the former personnel generally manage a "tighter ship."

Of course, this is an area where both objective and subjective criteria must be considered. You can identify which budgets are already under control with analysis tools such as productivity standards. Departments without measurable standards are suspect and should be directed, as a first step, to develop measurable standards.

Imposing the same arbitrary percentage budget cuts, or an equally high percentage of arbitrary employee head-count cuts, is unfair to those managers who are operating on a tight budget. They should not be expected to reduce their budgets or head counts as much as managers with what are considered loose budgets. Top management should recognize those departments that are operating leaner than other departments and impose lower percentage cuts on them.

If there is a downturn in your business's sector and the demand for your products drops, cuts can probably be made to certain variable budget items. When there is another turnaround and business increases, whatever cuts were made should be carefully evaluated to determine what needs to be restored, and when.

2.6 INCENTIVE PROGRAMS

An incentive program, such as "gain sharing," provides an opportunity for all employees to benefit from cost-cutting improvements. It is appropriate for some businesses and situations, but not all. It is appropriate when employees are receptive and positively responsive to the idea, and the business believes savings can be generated in excess of the basic need. Incentive programs serve to motivate employees by providing them with an opportunity to increase their income by sharing in a percentage of quantifiable cost- cutting and productivity-improvement savings. A business can also implement an incentive program such as gain sharing with outside consultants engaged to help cut costs.

Generally, the business sets a threshold of cost savings that the business must achieve, and the amount over the threshold is what is shared among the eligible employees. It is a good idea to show employees how cost cuts, gains in output, productivity, inventory turnover, on-time deliveries, and other changes can translate into gain-sharing–related savings.

Measuring results is critical in gain sharing. A baseline of performance must be established, with improvements then being measured against the baseline using a predetermined and published formula. Rewards are also distributed to employees and/or consultants based on a predetermined and published formula. If your business does not choose to establish a threshold of cost savings, with the employees sharing the balance, it may share all the cost savings on a pro-rata basis (e.g., 80%/20%, 70%/30%, 50%/50%, 30%/70%, 20%/80%) or however management decides. Regardless of which cost-savings formula or method is used, you must publish it to enable eligible employees to see upfront exactly how they might benefit from the program.

The program must be continually monitored and evaluated in terms of overall benefit to your business and employees, and the ease or difficulty in properly administering it must be determined. Some things to consider and questions to answer before embarking on an incentive program include the following:

Will the employees be receptive to the idea, and will it motivate them and give them an incentive to identify cost-cutting and productivity-improvement opportunities? This can be assessed by surveying the employees in departmental meetings.

How much information—especially sales and financial information—will you allow employees to see, because it may be required to measure certain results?

Do you have adequate pertinent historical data to create some "what if" scenarios regarding potential cost savings and corresponding pay-out? If you have pertinent historical data, use different formulas to predict and simulate the possible financial impact of the program assuming various levels of cost-cutting savings.

How long will the program be in effect? Will it be 6 months, or 1 year, or will it continue indefinitely?

How frequently will incentive money be paid out to employees? Monthly payments provide the most visibility, and they help give the program continued momentum.

Are there adequate controls built into the program to factor out certain things from the formula, such as price increases, cost savings resulting from some automation planned prior to the incentive program, and so forth? Such controls ensure the employees do not get an excessive windfall they should not receive.

Once these questions are answered, you can decide whether to proceed with implementing the program.

2.7 SUPPLY-CHAIN PARTNERING

For large businesses with many facilities (especially in numerous worldwide locations), products, suppliers, and customers, the supply chain can be extremely complex; however, the basics of supply chain partnering remain the same. Working with your suppliers of goods and services and your customers as partners can make your business run more efficiently and help you cut, contain, and avoid costs. Discuss your cost-cutting goals with your suppliers and customers, and create mutually beneficial strategies to achieve them. With appropriate give-and-take, this process can be mutually beneficial in helping you, the suppliers, and the customers to cut costs and become more successful.

The ideal supplier of goods would be next door to you. In this scenario, there would be no in-transit time, damage in transit should be none or very little, and there would be no cost for shipping. Of course, very few businesses are lucky enough to have a major supplier next door.

If you are happy with your suppliers' service and quality, you should try to retain them, as long as they can help you cut costs. If, however, your current suppliers are not willing to adequately participate in the cost-cutting program, then you should pursue other suppliers. Strategies to consider could include the following:

1. Your suppliers could be requested to help you carry less inventory of raw materials, supplies, or component parts by delivering those items when they are needed on a "just in time" (JIT) basis. This not only reduces your inventory levels and the related financial implications, but also enables the company to utilize less facility space.

2. For you to accomplish a JIT program, the suppliers may rightfully require a forecast and volume commitment on your part to enable this type of arrangement.

3. Request that your suppliers of parts or materials provide less costly substitute items without compromising on quality.

4. Obtain better pricing for goods and/or services based on a higher volume and/or loyalty commitment.

5. With customers, determine the feasibility of scheduling and shipping fewer and less costly larger orders, instead of several, more costly small orders.

James B. Ayers is an author of books regarding supply chain management, and he has the following thoughts about "supply chain collaboration," as he prefers to call it:

Collaboration is a popular concept in management circles with almost as many definitions as there are practitioners. One common thread is that going it alone is neither feasible nor desirable when markets, services, and products are changing fast. To be agile, companies must drop their suspicions of business partners and work together toward common goals. The required shift of attitude demands much of many executives.

Your own company costs may not be determined within your walls but at some upstream (supplier side) or downstream (customer side) trading partner. In many situations, collaboration opportunities lie in cost reduction as much as traditional arenas like product development, marketing, and coordinating production schedules. The scope of multi-company cost reduction can be wide. At one end lies broad decisions about what parts of the supply chain should be contracted out versus retained in the company, or how competition-beating channels to market segments should be designed to meet the needs of customers. At the other end of the spectrum, but no less important, lie collaborations between design and industrial engineers on product and process design. Execution at this level is particularly important to cost.

Collaboration is such a fruitful area because no cost component should be excluded. Cost categories include materials, manufacturing labor, information systems, technical and administrative, plant and equipment, material handling, logistics, and working capital.

But there are many obstacles to successful collaboration. Recent events have challenged many popular paradigms. Outsourcing to low cost foreign suppliers is no longer blindly accepted wisdom. Lessons learned include an appreciation for a flexible supply chain that can respond to inevitable changes in demand and customer tastes. Long, ponderous, ocean-spanning chains fail to respond in a timely way. As Boeing discovered with its long-overdue Dreamliner (787), suppliers may not often have their act together and do not even know it. With a million parts, a major launch was delayed for want of the fasteners needed to keep it together.[1]

2.8 JUST-IN-TIME

The *APICS Dictionary* describes just-in-time (JIT) as a philosophy of manufacturing based on planned elimination of all waste and on continuous improvement of productivity. JIT encompasses the successful execution of all manufacturing activities required to produce a final product, from design engineering to delivery, and includes all stages of conversion from raw material onward. The primary elements of JIT are to have only the required inventory when needed; to improve quality to zero defects; to reduce lead times by reducing setup times, queue lengths, and lot sizes; to incrementally revise the operations themselves; and to accomplish these activities at minimum cost. In the broad sense, JIT applies to all forms of manufacturing, job shop, process, and repetitive operations, and to many service industries as well. You should consider how JIT might work for your business.

2.9 KAIZEN

The *APICS Dictionary* describes Kaizen as the Japanese term for improvement, meaning continuous improvement involving everyone— both managers and workers. In manufacturing, Kaizen relates to finding and eliminating waste in machinery, labor, or production methods. It emphasizes quick results emanating from ideas developed and implemented within one week by a designated team of individuals focusing on a limited process area, known as a work cell. Management must arrange for the employees selected to participate in the Kaizen "event" to be available to work exclusively on the project for one week.

Kaizen methodology is often utilized as an integral component of a lean manufacturing program. Results from Kaizen can include increased productivity, increased capacity, reduced setup times, reduced lead times, reduced inventory, less floor space required, and shorter distances for employees to travel.

Some people that believe Kaizen is a good thing but do not agree that there are immediate cost savings from certain Kaizen results, unless other actions are also taken. For instance, they argue that a reduction of space requirements may contribute to productivity improvement but will not result in cost savings, unless the space is rented or sold, or if you can avoid heating it, cooling it, or using electricity there. These critics also argue that inventory reductions are not true cost savings but serve only to increase cash flow. In addition, they argue that an employee who is more productive does not necessarily result in a cost saving unless you lay a worker off or terminate him or her (I disagree with this view). I have heard some heated arguments regarding these views when they are discussed with Kaizen supporters. As is the case with most management philosophies and methodologies, there are many good books and consultants devoted to Kaizen.

When performing Kaizen events, opportunities are not just identified, but also implemented. Jerry Feingold, a successful Kaizen consultant, provided the following examples of typical results that can be achieved from conducting Kaizen events:

Project area: Aerospace industry motor assembly area.

Project results: Reduced throughput time from 34 hours per batch of 50 to 12 minutes per motor (99 percent improvement); reduced floor space from 1,657 to 890 square feet (46 percent reduction); reduced work in process inventory (WIP) from 225 to 85 (62 percent reduction); reduced conveyance distance from 880 feet to 286 feet (68 percent reduction).

Project area: Aerospace industry switch assembly cell (#1103).

Project results: Reduced throughput time from 21 days to 4 days (80 percent improvement); reduced the value of WIP from $204,000 to $54,142 (73 percent improvement).

These Kaizen project examples give you an idea of what Kaizen events can achieve. Chapter 11 includes more examples of successful Kaizen event results.

2.10 COMBINE APPROACHES

There are advantages to employing more than one of the previously mentioned approaches for a cost-cutting and productivity-improvement project. One good combination of multiple approaches might include teams or committees, the use of consultants, an incentive program such as gain sharing, supply-chain partnering, and Kaizen. Another example of combining approaches could include assigning goals for each manager with budget responsibility and reducing budgets and/or head counts in each department by a certain percentage. You could also choose to use outside consultants, as deemed appropriate, in combination with any of the other approaches described to obtain greater results. I am sure you can come up with ideas regarding which combinations would be beneficial at your business.

2.11 EMPHASIZE THE NEED AND GET THE PROGRAM STARTED

As you have probably experienced, whenever a business emphasizes the need for something important and focuses on it, positive results are generally achieved. Thus, whatever cost-cutting approaches you deem appropriate and adopt for your business, you must establish and maintain high visibility and focus on the program by making it a key company-wide goal.

It is essential that top management lead the cost-cutting and productivity-improvement program by example down through all levels of the organization. This practice of leading by example by top management must be sustained for the life of the program if it is to achieve the maximum results. If top management does not sustain the level of commitment needed, general interest may wane and the program can lose momentum and effectiveness. I have seen programs start very well with a lot of enthusiasm; however, the momentum was lost over time because of top management's lack of continued commitment. It is a good thing if and when the interest is regained by other key people involved with the program despite top management's dwindling commitment.

Fortunately, high-priority cost-cutting recommendations are usually acted upon early in a program, so not all is lost if the program momentum wanes. Unfortunately, additional good recommendations and opportunities may be lost owing to the lack of ongoing commitment.

One of the most important things top management must do is to ensure that the employees assigned directly to the program continue to have the time needed to meet those responsibilities throughout the program's life. If you are going to use teams or committees, meet with those persons selected to be members to discuss how the program will be presented to the rest of the employees. Kick off the cost-cutting program with business-wide meetings and announcements so that all employees understand the program.

I attended two memorable initial meetings with cost-cutting committees where the company president in one case and the CEO in the other case wanted to show top-down support by insisting that the committee members identify, before the meeting concluded, a cost-cutting idea that could be quickly implemented and would be visible to all the employees. The ideas did not have to result in major cost cutting, but they had to be visible and noticed by all employees. The top executives rightfully wanted to show by example that the cost-cutting and productivity-improvement program was a serious effort supported by top management.

At the meeting with the business president, after much heated discussion, it was decided to discontinue the use of an outside service that provided and maintained live plants inside the headquarters facility. A week later, after the service had been terminated and its plants had been removed, many live plants still remained around the facility. This outcome occurred because several employees had brought plants from home, or they had purchased them and brought them into their work areas. There was a concession made to provide departments with a small budget to purchase some live or artificial plants if they wanted to have them. This cost saving was not upsetting to anyone. In fact, many more employees later brought in their own plants.

At the initial cost-cutting and productivity-improvement program meeting led by the CEO of the business, someone recommended that the internal Travel Office should be discontinued. Originally the department had three full-time employees making air, hotel, and rental car reservations mainly for the sales and service staffs and executives who did most of the traveling. Over the years the department had shrunk to two full-time employees and then one full-time employee after more employees were allowed to plan their own travel and make their own reservations.

It was noted that the remaining Travel Office employee seemed to have a lot of idle time and was often observed playing solitaire on her computer. When occasionally requested to help with a special project for some department, she had the time and was willing to help. Someone indicated that she spent most of her day on the Internet, sending emails to friends and family, and writing stories she hoped to have published someday. It was agreed by everyone that the Travel Office was no longer needed and would be closed.

It was determined that the employee, who was known for having very good word processing and chart-making skills, would be transferred to an open position in another department. The employee was transferred to a department where she could use her skills and positively contribute to the business, and the Travel Department was permanently closed. Integral to shutting the Travel Department down was the development of a transportation and entertainment (T&E) policy for applicable employees to follow, which listed the approved websites, air carriers, car rental agencies and hotel chains that could be used by employees traveling on approved business.

Closing the Travel Department led to a cost savings of the employee's salary and fringe benefits. Because the employee was transferred to another department with an open position needing to be filled, instead of being terminated, there was no severance pay required. Implementing the new T&E policy and having someone in the accounts payable department audit the expense reports of those who traveled ensured compliance with the policy and resulted in greater control and additional ongoing cost savings.

In both cases of an initial meeting that resulted in a cost-cutting idea, the savings were not big, but they began accruing immediately, and they were visible to all employees. Also, everyone knew the top management and businesses were serious about cost cutting and productivity improvement.

2.12 WHAT'S IN IT FOR ME?: THE EMPLOYEE'S VIEWPOINT

The first things all employees will want to know when they hear about the cost-cutting and productivity-improvement program are "How will it affect me?" and "What's in it for me?" Employees need to know why the program will be a good thing for them individually and for the business as a whole.

Once you have decided on methods to identify cost savings and productivity improvements, communicate specifically how employees might be impacted. This communication should be done as part of the program kick-off meetings and announcements, so employees know upfront what is expected of them and how they can benefit from the program. Of course, employees are most interested in specifically how they can benefit financially from the program, so you must address this issue and let them know the different ways they can benefit financially.

2.13 PROVIDE PROPER TOOLS AND TRAINING

You cannot expect all your managers to be able to execute an effective cost-cutting and productivity-improvement program in their areas of responsibility without providing them with some help. You must provide education and training for every employee involved in working on the program, especially committee members and those conducting survey interviews. The education part includes communicating why the program is needed and what a successful program could mean to your business. The training part includes the specifics of how the employees involved will proceed with executing various steps of the program.

I was a consultant representing the users of a new system that was to be implemented at a business when the system supplier was conducting the first education and training session after the system was selected. A user asked the session leader what the difference was between education and training. The question was answered with another question: "If you had a daughter in eighth grade, would you want her to receive sex education classes or sex training classes?" Yes, there was laughter, but there was also an acknowledgment that people understood the distinction, and the difference between education and training was clear.

A good example of education combined with productivity-improvement choices is to use the analogy of a painting job around your house. You could communicate how the painting job could be done inefficiently with a small paintbrush. Then you could explain that the job could be completed more quickly and better with a large paintbrush. Next, you could show how using a roller is a better method than using a large paintbrush. Lastly, you could explain how a paint sprayer would be the best method if the job is large enough to justify it.

Develop training sessions for appropriate individuals who are responsible for leading the cost-cutting efforts. The training should include the following issues, among other things:

Preparing survey interview guides (lists of questions pertinent to the areas being reviewed) to facilitate information gathering

Determining the units of measure for the various job functions

Conducting productive survey interviews

Leading a meeting and getting a group to work together

Encouraging people with positive feedback

Ways to stimulate creative thinking

Cost-justifying cost-saving investments

Performing function observations

Setting performance standards

Evaluating productivity

Describing the dollar savings resulting from productivity-improvement and cost-cutting recommendations

2.14 BE CAUTIOUS OF CUTTING COSTS IN CERTAIN AREAS

There are certain important areas where you should be cautious regarding cost cutting, including the following:

If the cost cutting could result in sacrificing acceptable quality levels, the cost savings are not justifiable.

If the cost cutting could result in unacceptable service levels, the cost savings are more than likely not justifiable.

If the cost cutting could jeopardize safety, the cost savings are definitely not justifiable.

If the cost cutting could result in possible security risks, the cost savings are probably not worth the risks.

If the cost cutting could damage employee morale, the cost-savings ideas are almost certainly not worth it.

Lastly, do not cut costs in research and development, except in dire situations, and then only for the short term.

NOTE

1. James B. Ayers is the author of the *Handbook of Supply Chain Management*, 2nd ed., Boca Raton: Auerbach Publications, 2006.

3

Methods to Identify Opportunities

3.1 UTILIZE MULTIPLE METHODS

Cost-cutting and productivity-improvement opportunities can be identified in various ways. All of them are valid, and all of them should be utilized. This chapter contains some guidelines regarding how you can facilitate identifying the opportunities.

3.2 ANALYZE BUDGET EXPENSE HISTORY

Whether it is done by a group of top executives who meet to brainstorm ideas, or a Cost-Cutting and Productivity-Improvement Committee whose members determine good places to find ideas, looking at two or three years of budget expense history is a very good way to identify potential opportunities. Concentrate on variable expenses, because they are more controllable, and they are the costs that you need to address as your business's volumes increase and decrease.

Generate the budget expense data in various report formats to facilitate review and analysis. One format would be to display the budget expense categories in descending dollar amount order. Another format would be to display the data in descending order based on the greatest percent increase by budget expense category from last year compared to this year.

To perform proper analysis, you must include an adequate level of detail. If you review categories only at a summary level, trends such as percent change may not vary much because certain increases and decreases of subaccounts within the category may offset one another.

Do not ignore the particulars. If you look at subaccounts, trends such as percent change will be easier to identify.

For example, do not look at freight solely as a summary-level budget item. Instead, break freight expenses down into more detailed categories:

International inbound freight

International outbound freight

Domestic inbound freight

Domestic outbound freight

International inbound expedited freight

International outbound expedited freight

Domestic inbound expedited freight

Domestic outbound expedited freight

Table 3.1 is an example of a business report comparing last year's costs to this year's costs for a budget category (freight, in this example) by subaccount categories and for total freight expense. This example report enables you to compare and analyze cost trends from last year to this year. In this case, the total change for freight costs from last year to this year was an increase of $14,545, which is only a 1 percent increase in the overall freight budget. A large percent increase from last year to this year for international inbound expedited freight costs (+$69,354) and domestic inbound expedited freight costs (+$16,053) would be hidden if you reviewed freight budget history only at the summary level, because the reduction in outbound domestic expedited freight costs (–$64,925) and outbound international expedited freight costs (–$34,983) more than offset those increases.

After the business in this example analyzed reasons for the good and bad variances, it was determined that a lack of timely planning by the purchasing staff resulted in the higher cost of inbound expedited freight, which should have and could have been prevented. The procurement manager and her staff indicated they would correct the problem by better and more advance planning, thereby preventing the need to use as much expedited international inbound freight. The analysis also revealed that more timely shipments of customer orders led to the cost savings for outbound expedited freight. The broader question of using international suppliers was also discussed, and the business decided that the lower prices for offshore products more than offset the freight costs.

Table 3.1   Report Comparing Last Year's Costs to This Year's Costs for Freight Subaccounts and the Total Freight Account

Budget Subaccount Categories for Freight	Last Year	This Year	(+) or (−)	Variance
International Inbound Freight	$ 87,283	$ 98,495	$ 11,212	13%
International Outbound Freight	$ 132,668	$ 143,286	$ 10,618	8%
Domestic Inbound Freight	$ 744,298	$ 748,376	$ 4,078	1%
Domestic Outbound Freight	$ 103,290	$ 106,388	$ 3,089	3%
International Inbound Expedited Freight	$ 76,336	$ 145,690	$ 69,354	91%
Domestic Inbound Expedited Freight	$ 82,227	$ 98,280	$ 16,053	20%
International Outbound Expedited Freight	$ 73,209	$ 38,266	(−$34,983)	(−48%)
Domestic Outbound Expedited Freight	$ 238,453	$ 173,528	(−$64,925)	(−27%)
Total Account Expenses for Freight	$1,537,764	$1,552,309	$ 14,545	1%

Comments regarding analysis of this report:
The category with the biggest percentage increase change was International Inbound Expedited Freight, which saw an increase of 91% from last year to this year. We reviewed this issue and discovered that the buyers of offshore component parts were not planning ahead very well. After discussing this issue with the procurement manager and buyers, we expect to see improvements in this area, which will reduce costs.

The category with the biggest percentage decrease change was International Outbound Expedited Freight, which saw a decrease of 48% from last year to this year. This was the result of better production scheduling and timely shipment of international orders.

You get the idea. Without an adequate level of detail for reviewing costs by subaccounts, the opportunity to cut costs for inbound expedited freight would not have been seen or addressed.

3.3 STUDY THE GENERAL LEDGER CHART OF ACCOUNTS

Reviewing the general ledger chart of accounts after analyzing budget expense history is a worthwhile effort to trigger thoughts regarding areas where cost-cutting opportunities can be easily found and savings achieved. It also is an opportune time to consider revising the general ledger chart of accounts. Revising could include adding more subaccounts, deleting some subaccounts, combining some subaccounts, and

better describing what is included in some subaccount categories to facilitate better understanding and analysis of various categories.

One thing to be wary of when you add, delete, or combine chart of
accounts categories is to know how you are going to be able to make
"apples and apples" comparisons of previous years' expenses to the current year. Work with your finance or accounting staff when you want to
make these types of changes. Remember that the chart of accounts categories should mirror budget categories.

Following is an open-ended list of chart of accounts or budget categories to
review for cost-cutting and productivity-improvement ideas: salaries; direct
labor; indirect labor; employee head count; incentive plans, including piecework; overtime premiums; fringe benefits; temporary employees; retirement
or 401(k) plans to which the company contributes; sales commissions; chari-
table contributions; research and development; employee bonuses; worker's
compensation; board of directors' fees, expenses, and benefits; automobile
allowance; rents and leases; maintenance and repair (for facilities); maintenance and repair (for equipment); manufacturing supplies; tooling; distribution supplies; office supplies; training; legal fees; depreciation; educational
reimbursement; professional fees and services; travel and entertainment;
advertising; trade shows; conferences; sales promotions; customer discounts;
freight (international inbound freight, international outbound freight, domestic inbound freight, domestic outbound freight, international inbound
expedited freight, international outbound expedited freight, domestic
inbound expedited freight, and domestic outbound expedited freight); telephone and Internet; utilities (could break into subaccount categories); contracted services (e.g., waste disposal); capital expenditure projects; forms
and supplies; insurance; taxes (other than payroll); warranty repairs and
replacements; bad debt write-off; scrap; and rework.

3.4 REVIEW TOP SUPPLIERS

Look at two to three years of payment history to your top 25 to 50 suppliers, based on the dollar amounts you spent on them, to identify opportunities to cut costs. As with your budget analyses, generate the supplier
data in a variety of report formats to facilitate your review. One format
would be to display the data in descending order of dollars paid to the suppliers. Another format would be to display the data in descending order
based on the greatest percent increase of dollars paid to suppliers last year
compared to this year. Reviewing which specific products or raw materials the suppliers sell to you in descending order of dollar value is also an
effective method to help identify opportunities.

These analyses will help you identify which suppliers you should focus on to negotiate for lower prices. It can also make multiple suppliers that provide similar products or services easy to identify for possible consolidation and for obtaining lower prices through offering fewer suppliers higher volumes.

3.5 NEGOTIATE, NEGOTIATE, NEGOTIATE

Identifying reasons to negotiate for better prices with a supplier gives you added strength for the negotiations. Remember the following:

Negotiating for better prices, quality, and service with your suppliers is absolutely the most important thing, or one of the most important things, you can do.

Instruct your purchasing department to look for reasons to negotiate for lower prices on an ongoing basis and pursue those opportunities.

If you buy commodity items, the quality and specifications should be exactly the same regardless of the supplier. Request multiple suppliers to provide quotes for the business, and negotiate with the ones you want to work with for better prices.

Suppliers that are geographically closer than ones that are thousands of miles away have some obvious advantages, especially lower freight-related costs.

If you like the quality or service from a particular supplier, let the supplier know it, but tell the business you expect better pricing for it to keep the business.

When you buy large quantities of products from a supplier, that action gives you the best negotiating leverage.

If you purchase various products from a supplier and the prices for certain items are higher than you would have to pay a competitor, emphasize negotiating on those particular items.

When you know you can purchase certain items less expensively from another supplier, you have a great advantage when negotiating with your incumbent supplier to obtain better prices.

3.6 CONDUCT SURVEY INTERVIEWS

Conducting personal survey interviews with all appropriate employees and major suppliers to solicit cost-cutting and productivity-improvement ideas is generally far more effective than undertaking a suggestion program. Conducting the interviews in person is vital, however—do not consider a sent-out survey. Conduct interview surveys with employees at their workstations, because you may observe things of interest that point to cost-cutting or productivity-improvement opportunities that you would not see if the survey interviews were conducted elsewhere.

If the survey interview is conducted properly, it can provide a morale boost, as well as generate worthwhile cost-cutting and productivity-improvement ideas. Most people like being involved, and the face-to-face contact adds a personal element of inclusion in the cost-cutting and productivity-improvement program. The employees and suppliers interviewed need to be reminded of the reasons for the cost-cutting and productivity-improvement program, however, and they must understand how it will help the business and them (employees and suppliers).

The individuals selected to perform the interviews must be tactful and trained regarding how to conduct and control the interview, as well as how to handle problems that may arise. Controlling the interviews is made easier through the use of an interview guide, which is a list of questions intended to stimulate answers and prevent those being interviewed from going off on nonpertinent tangents. Table 3.2 is an example of a survey interview guide for employees that you can use as a starting point and customize for your use in each area reviewed. It will help you identify areas of potential problems and opportunities for improvement that you can explore more fully. Of course, a survey interview guide for suppliers would be different from the employee interview guide; it would be limited to the products and/or services those suppliers currently provide and possibly could provide to your business.

Regardless of an interviewer's skills, certain individuals cannot be easily controlled to stay on the subject and will take advantage of the situation to vent their feelings about whatever is on their minds regarding the business. This may include positive or negative comments about the business. An interview guide will help you control such interviews and minimize the risk of interviewees getting off track from the subject at hand. In addition, the interviewers must use their best judgment regarding when to shut off comments that do not deal with the cost-cutting and productivity-improvement program emanating from the interviews. Nevertheless, if enough people (employees or suppliers) go off on other tangents and express similar negative feelings about the business, feedback regarding these comments may help management take actions before certain concerns become even bigger problems.

Table 3.2 Survey Interview Guide

Date:	Department:	Interviewer:	Interviewee:

1. Department organizational chart with regular, part-time, and temporary employees:

2. Department purpose/goals/objectives:

3. Work hours/shift(s)/break times/overtime:

4. Are there any problems with the physical layout that prevent a smooth process?

5. Do others (departments or suppliers) cause problems?

6. Do work standards exist (e.g., units per hour, units per day)?

7. What have been the hourly, daily, and weekly production rates (are records maintained for individuals and groups)?

8. Is a backlog of available work staged at all workstations or assembly lines?

9. Do backlogs exist? How are they measured (e.g., units, hours of work, orders)?

10. Are there bottlenecks or constraints that cause problems?

11. If there are assembly lines, are there imbalanced capacities?

12. Are there predictable peak or valley work periods (daily, weekly, or monthly)?

13. Are staffing levels too high, too low, or just right?

14. Are employees cross-trained for flexibility, or are there times when some people are overworked while others are idle?

15. Are there any tasks that could be eliminated that require workers to leave the area?

16. Are there equipment problems (e.g., adequate number, too many breakdowns)?

(*continued*)

Table 3.2 (continued)

Date:	Department:	Interviewer:	Interviewee:

17. Are there any raw materials or parts shortages (manufactured or purchased) that cause problems?

18. Is quality as it should be? If no, is it too high or too low?

19. Is overtime worked? If yes, how much is there and why?

20. Are quality problems found quickly in the flow, or is there unnecessary scrap and rework caused by identifying quality problems later in the flow?

21. How is work planned, scheduled, assigned, implemented, and followed up on?

22. Which operating problems do you have, and which improvement ideas do you have?

To make your employees feel more open and cooperative, you might consider having the interviews performed by objective outside consultants. In this way, you can also give employees the option to keep some of their comments confidential. If you do give the option of confidentiality for employees, you still need to maintain proper records to ensure everyone who should be interviewed has been interviewed.

To manage interviewing a large number of employees, consider conducting some group interviews in selected areas. Group interviews of employees working in similar jobs in the same department or area can stimulate lively debate and good recommendations. You should still provide employees who want to say something confidentially the ability to do so outside the group interview.

The end result of successful survey interviews will be a list of cost-cutting and productivity-improvement recommendations to consider. These recommendations need to be reviewed by appropriate individuals or committees to be approved or rejected. Approved recommendations are put in priority order, and then included in an implementation action plan.

3.7 EMPLOYEE SUGGESTION PROGRAMS

Be aware of the advantages and wary of the disadvantages of employee suggestion programs. As previously mentioned, conducting personal survey interviews is generally a much better method to identify opportunities than such a program. Employee suggestion programs can provide some great ideas, but they require time and effort to ensure a successful program. If not administered properly, in fact, suggestion programs can cause employee dissatisfaction.

You need to appoint an employee to lead a committee overseeing the employee suggestion program. The committee should consist of a respected group of objective employees.

Following are some hints to make the cost-cutting and productivity-improvement suggestion program easy to administer:

Define the program scope, and explain what can and cannot be included. For example, if cash flow is tight, you might want to exclude any recommendations requiring capital expenditures.

Clarify who is and is not included in the program. For example, industrial engineers, design engineers, manufacturing engineers, and purchasing staff might only be rewarded for making suggestions outside their normal areas of responsibility.

Determine if measurable productivity improvements will be considered to be a cost-cutting measure. I recommend that they should be classified in this way if the productivity improvements are quantifiable in terms of cost savings. Following is an example of analyzing a productivity improvement and translating it into cost savings:

Assumptions: There were 12 employees on the day shift and 8 employees on the second shift in a work center performing the same type of work making the same part. Each employee produced 20 parts in an 8-hour shift.

An employee suggestion was made to improve productivity in the work center by ensuring there was always a backlog of available work at each workstation, which was previously not the case. The recommendation was accepted and implemented by assigning the material handlers in the area to ensure that a backlog of available work was always maintained at each workstation.

The recommendation resulted in each employee producing 25 parts in an 8-hour shift compared to the previous 20 parts in an 8-hour shift, which represented a 25 percent increase in productivity for each employee. The 25 percent increase in productivity resulted in 2 more productive work hours per employee saved each day, for a total of 40 hours (20 employees $\times$ 2 hours = 40) hours per day.

The average hourly pay rate for the day shift employees was $22, including fringe benefits, and the average hourly pay rate for the second shift employees was $24.20, including fringe benefits. The latter's higher pay was due to a 10 percent greater hourly pay rate for a shift differential. The annual cost savings emanating from the suggestion was $237,952, calculated as follows:

12 day-shift employees × 2 hours saved per day = 24 hours × $22 = $528 saved per day

8 second-shift employees × 2 hours saved = 16 hours × $24.20 = $387.20 saved per day

$528 + $387.20 = $915.20 total saved per day × 5 days per week = $4,576 saved per week

$4,576 saved per week × 52 weeks = $237,952 saved per year

The employee who made the suggestion worked in the work center, and he was eligible to receive a reward for the suggestion. The employee suggestion reward guidelines resulted in the employee earning a $10,000 reward, because that was the reward amount for a suggestion that yielded annual savings between $200,000 and $250,000.

Establish a time frame for when the employee suggestion program will begin and end. A six-month time for the program is a good starting point. If you believe the program should be extended beyond six months because worthwhile recommendations are still being made toward the end of the six months, by all means continue it for another three to six months.

Use a suggestion form to include all the data required. Table 3.3 is an example of a completed employee suggestion form, using the suggestion described in the preceding example. The entries in italics represent manual input on the form.

Kick the employee suggestion program off with group meetings, followed by posting signs, status meetings, and status emails. Place employee suggestion boxes near lunch/break areas, time clocks, or entrances/exits. Suggestions could also be submitted via email using a downloaded employee suggestion form.

Make provisions for how to handle rewards for similar suggestions. For example, the first of similar suggestions received is the one that wins, but if a similar suggestion is received at the same time, both should win and both employees should share any resulting reward. Develop clear prize

Table 3.3

ABC Company Employee Suggestion Form

Name: *James Davis* Date submitted: *6/6/2011* Time submitted: 10 A.M.

Title of Suggestion (brief description of suggestion): *Make sure there is a backlog of work maintained at each workstation in the Welding work center.*

Detail description of suggestion (Add descriptive drawings if applicable, and use the other side of the form and additional sheets of paper if needed): *Assign the material handlers to make sure there is always a backlog of work maintained at each welder's workstation.*

Description of resources required and the estimated cost for implementing the idea (e.g., employees, new equipment) and any additional comments regarding backup data to substantiate potential savings: *The material handlers who support the Welding work center deliver pallets of work to the area and pick up pallets of completed work from the area, but they do not take the work to the individual welders' workstations, and the welders move the completed pallets of work to the area for completed work. The material handlers appear to have a lot of idle time, and I believe they can take pallets of work directly to each welder's workstation and pick up completed work at the completed work station. There should be no expense involved in implementing this suggestion. It will allow the welders to make 20% or more parts each day.*

Estimated annual or one-time cost savings: *Estimated annual savings of $200,000+.*

Estimated nontangible benefits: *The morale will improve among employees who thought the material handlers did not work as hard as they should.*

Program administrator's comments regarding actions taken (e.g., date suggestion accepted, implementation assignments, date completed, reward and date given): *Suggestion accepted 6/10/2011. Suggestion implemented 6/13/2011. $10,000 reward presented to James Davis on 7/25/2011 after estimated savings were verified.*

Table 3.4   ABC Company Employee Suggestion Reward Guidelines

Guidelines regarding how employees will be rewarded for accepted suggestions:

Description of rewards for one-time savings and annualized savings

Approved Estimated Savings Range	Reward Amount ($)
$500–$2,000	$ 50
$2,001–$4,000	$ 100
$4,001–$6,000	$ 200
$6,001–$8,000	$ 400
$8,001–$10,000	$ 500
$10,000–$15,000	$ 1,000
$15,001–$25,000	$ 2,000
$25,001–$40,000	$ 4,000
$40,001–$60,000	$ 5,000
$60,001–$80,000	$ 7,000
$80,001–$100,000	$ 9,000
$101,000–$150,000	$12,000
$151,000–$200,000	$15,000
$201,000–$300,000	$20,000
$301,000+	10% of approved estimated savings

or reward guidelines, and communicate them at the time the program is announced. Table 3.4 identifies some possible reward guidelines.

Give timely feedback and rewards for accepted suggestions. Rewards should be presented to the employee making the suggestion as soon as the estimated cost savings are quantified/verified and approved. Delays in providing feedback and giving rewards to employees can cause employee dissatisfaction with the program.

Communicate information about rewards for accepted suggestions so all employees know about them. This information should include the person(s) who made the suggestion, a brief description of the suggestion, the benefits expected to be obtained by implementing the recommendation, and the reward received by the person(s) making the suggestion. Timely communication may encourage more good suggestions.

3.8 SEEK FREE ADVICE AND SERVICES

There are certain sources to help identify areas for possible cost cutting and productivity improvement that are free and without obligation.

For example, ask your current and prospective suppliers if they provide any free services that could help you cut costs or be more productive. Many trade publications are free and frequently have excellent articles that may provide ideas for improving productivity and cutting costs, so have appropriate department heads apply for publications regarding their areas of responsibility. You can also attend trade shows and conventions, and solicit cost-cutting and productivity-improvement ideas from the applicable businesses that are there to sell their goods and services.

Packaging suppliers could help design more protective or aesthetic packages and cartons, as well as make their sizes more cost-effective for shipping. Printing companies may assist with forms design. Insurance carriers may perform facility inspections and recommend ways to reduce risk and lower your insurance premium.

Some utilities may provide a no-charge analysis and suggest ways to lower energy consumption and related costs. One of my clients had multiple large facilities. Installing automatic turn-on/off switches in offices for when someone enters or leaves and installing automatic timers for turning on and off the lights in manufacturing plants and warehouses saved this company a great deal of money. Many businesses could benefit from this simple, common-sense idea.

Your telephone company may provide certain telephone statistical reports that can help with making customer service and order entry staff scheduling decisions, such as logs of calls by hour and lost call studies to show when and how many calls are lost (due to a busy signal) and how many calls are abandoned (i.e., when customers hang up before the calls are answered). Likewise, equipment suppliers may provide advice regarding productivity improvements, cost cutting, and efficiency increases to be gained by using their equipment, including custom-designed equipment and robotics.

Freight and small-package carriers will perform an analysis of your shipping practices and suggest improvements. Of course, they hope to benefit from the results of the analyses, but that outcome is acceptable if it represents a win-win situation for both parties.

Some service companies and consultants will work on a contingency basis, meaning they will be paid for their efforts out of any generated savings. Some examples include the following:

Post-auditing of freight bills to ensure they are properly discounted and you recoup excess charges

Pre-auditing of freight bills to ensure they are properly discounted and
you receive the proper discounts upfront

Auditing of telephone bills

Collecting past due accounts receivable

Utilities cost savings

Supplies-related cost savings

Freight-related cost savings

Many consultants will provide a no-cost and no-obligation analysis prior
to presenting a proposal to provide cost-cutting and productivity-
improvement services. In some cases, consultants will guarantee upfront
a minimum amount of savings that may far exceed the project cost, or will
propose payment based on a percentage of cost savings.

In addition, the Small Business Administration (SBA) or other local
area organizations partially funded by the SBA can provide free and
reduced-rate consulting assistance for small to medium-size businesses.
Your local Occupational Safety and Health Act (OSHA) office will provide free literature and consultation services to help you establish an illness and injury-prevention program.

Many states have training cost-reimbursement programs for businesses.
Such programs are intended to prevent out-of-state or out-of-country competition from taking jobs away from the state, so the training can include
many areas that improve the workforce's skill levels.

If your business plans to embark on a large education and training effort
due to a major change, such as a new computer system, identify possible
available government funding sources to help pay for the training.
Identifying, understanding, applying for, and obtaining approval for
government reimbursement programs for training takes time, so look into
this possibility as soon as you know it will be needed.

3.9 DECENTRALIZE RESEARCH TO IDENTIFY BETTER SUPPLIERS, PRODUCTS, AND SERVICES

Encourage departments other than purchasing to ask existing and potential suppliers how their goods and services could help cut costs and
improve productivity. If you do adopt this approach, you may still choose
to allow only the purchasing department to negotiate prices and terms, as
well as obligate the business regarding the purchase of all goods or

services. Line managers and supervisors should understand their area's needs better than anyone else, and they can best evaluate alternatives the various suppliers may recommend.

Do not say to yourself, "Oh no, another salesperson," when you get a cold call from a salesperson. Based on a few comments by the sales representative or answers to questions you ask him or her, you can determine whether it would be worthwhile to request more specific information from the salesperson, such as price quotes, or to schedule a meeting with the person to discuss your needs and expectations of a new supplier of goods or services. As a manager, you must be selective regarding which potential new suppliers you solicit or agree to see, because, as you know, you could spend too much time with suppliers if you are not selective.

One effective method in dealing with potential new suppliers, especially if they sell commodity-type items, is to send them a list of the items you currently purchase on a regular basis and ask them for "apples and apples" price quotes. It then becomes easy to determine who is worth seeing based on their quotes. If nothing else, this information can be used to determine whether you are getting good pricing from your current supplier, or whether those prices could be reduced.

The following example describes a cold call I received from a salesperson that piqued my interest and turned into something very worthwhile for the business where I was working. As an internal consultant at the time, I was assigned to address some areas of concern that the shipping and receiving manager at the headquarters manufacturing facility had; most importantly, he believed he was running out of space. The business shipped, via full truckloads, finished goods and replacement parts from the California headquarters to distribution centers in Texas, Illinois, New Jersey, and Georgia. The shipping and receiving manager was concerned about the space required to stage the products until it was time to call and schedule a full-truckload pickup. He also had trouble efficiently and accurately preparing a manifest for the products when the trucks were loaded.

The salesperson who called me knew I was working with the shipping and receiving manager; he was a freight broker, and he was trying to convince me that using stack trains and shipping via rail was more economical than using full over-the-road truckloads to the locations where we shipped.

I decided to meet with him, and we brainstormed the space issue. After much discussion, he agreed that his company would spot four empty stack train trailers on the dock (one for each distribution center); whenever the business scheduled a pickup, the freight broker would spot another empty stack train trailer. The term for this practice is a "drop and switch." The stack train prices were lower than the business's prices for over-the-road full truckloads, and the transit times were similar.

This change was implemented, and it enabled the shipping department to load finished goods assigned to each distribution center directly into the appropriate stack trains as product came off the assembly line, thereby avoiding the need for space in which to stage the products until a full truckload could be scheduled. In addition, it eliminated double handling of the products—once to stage the products and once to load them on the truck.

Another project I was working on at the same time was introducing bar-code data capture capabilities to the business. Working with the Information Technology Department, we obtained six bar-code readers that captured data about products as they were loaded into the various stack train trailers for each distribution center. When a trailer became full, the data were uploaded to the mainframe system to indicate that the inventory was in transit to the distribution center, and a manifest was also generated in the shipping and receiving area. I hope you can have a similarly worthwhile experience with a supplier.

3.10 VALUE ENGINEERING

Value engineering and product design are similar; however, value engineering as described here refers to a redesign of an existing product to manufacture it less expensively. You could also take this approach as if you were designing a new product. The objective and approach with value engineering is to look with creative new eyes at ways to manufacture your products differently so they can be made more cost-effectively. It is best to start with your high-volume or high-cost products. As an example, wouldn't you like to have been the person who came up with the idea to stamp the brand name on the inside of T-shirts and some other shirts instead of having to sew on a label?

The first thing to look at when you are trying to value engineer some of your products is the bill of material (BOM) to determine if some potential cost-saving changes could be made to it. Could certain purchased component parts be purchased at a higher level of assembly for less cost than buying or making component parts at a lower level of assembly? Potential benefits from buying purchased components at a higher level of assembly include the following:

The net cost may be lower than if the parts were manufactured in-house.

There are fewer part numbers to plan.

There are fewer parts to purchase.

There are fewer parts to receive.

There are fewer parts to put away.

There are fewer parts in inventory.

There are fewer parts to pick.

There are fewer parts to assemble, which is a productivity improvement that translates into cost savings.

One example of when it may be advantageous to purchase parts at a higher level of assembly is when parts are painted or plated, whether that step in the manufacturing process is performed in-house or outside. Does your business really need to finish those parts in-house, or would it result in a net lower cost to purchase the parts already painted or plated by a supplier? Another factor to consider for painted or plated parts is that the paint and plating might contain hazardous materials. You could benefit from obtaining painted or plated parts from an outside supplier at a higher level of assembly and also avoid all the potential problems associated with using hazardous materials.

Similarly, could some custom-made fasteners you currently use be replaced with standard-size, less costly fasteners (e.g., nuts, bolts, screws, washers)? You get the idea. I will not overdo this section; however, when you pursue this approach be thorough and have fun identifying potential savings.

3.11 PERFORM PRODUCTIVITY ANALYSES

You can choose from a variety of methods to determine individual and group productivity, which will help identify if you are staffed properly. Overstaffing is unnecessarily costly, and understaffing can mean you may not achieve your production goals cost-effectively or in a timely manner. If you have them, use internal industrial engineers to perform productivity analyses, especially in labor-intensive areas. If you do not have internal industrial engineers, train and use selected managers and/or use outside consultants to perform this function.

Before you can make observations of the functions performed, you need to make a list of the functions (tasks or activities) performed in each department being reviewed. One important thing to do when listing functions is to identify the proper unit of measure for each function. Units of measure could include descriptions like each (e.g., a part name or number of a product that is produced), occurrence (each time the function is performed), payment scheduled, posting, part picked, order entered, order picked, order packed. It is possible that you may want to change the unit of measure you initially selected after you observe the function being performed.

Refer to Table 3.5 for an example of a functions list to use for listing the functions performed in a department. In this case, the business wanted to use specific part numbers in the description of each function, and it wanted to use a description of the part as the unit of measure, because the business planned and assigned work based on the hours per unit required for making each part.

Conducting observations of all the job functions (tasks or activities) being performed by the applicable employees helps identify how long each task should take and enables you to set standards of performance you can use to plan work and measure performance. Observations could be made by industrial engineers who perform time and motion studies to set standards. However, if employees other than industrial engineers are trained to carefully observe functions being performed, you can set standards based on what the employees demonstrate they can accomplish, such as hours per unit that is required to weld a particular part, pick parts, or pack orders. You could use a variety of standards of performance, including units per hour produced or hours per unit produced.

The observations can also help determine whether the tasks are necessary. If they are necessary, potentially better methods may be obvious to an objective outside observer who does not work in the area.

It is a good practice to attempt to observe workers from a distance so that they do not suspect they are being watched, and to follow the observations from a distance with close observations when the workers know you are watching them. Usually employees will perform at a higher level when they know you are watching them; however, this is not always the case. Observations may also identify wasted or unproductive time and the reasons for this "lost time," which you can then try to eliminate.

After you have completed the observations, a good practice is to highlight certain things you saw that may indicate an opportunity for improvement. I always use a red pencil for this purpose. As I go back and review my observations at the end of the day, I concentrate on the comments highlighted in red pencil and document the potential improvement areas.

Refer to Table 3.6 for an example of a completed functions observation record, which is a form to use for documenting the functions you observe. The data in italics on the form represent the observer's input.

Table 3.5   Functions List

Department: *Subassembly*	Position: *Welder*		Date: 06/08/2012
Functions (Brief description of each function)	**Unit of Measure**	**Hours per Unit**	**Units per Hour**
Weld part number 115, which has 5 pieces	*Part*	*0.33*	*3*
Weld part number 117, which has 4 pieces	*Part*	*0.25*	*4*
Weld part number 119, which has 3 pieces	*Part*	*0.17*	*6*
Weld part number 121, which has 2 pieces	*Part*	*0.08*	*12*
Weld part number 123, which has 6 pieces	*Part*	*0.42*	*2.4*
Weld part number 125, which has 7 pieces	*Part*	*0.5*	*2*
Weld part number 127, which has 8 pieces	*Part*	*0.75*	*1.3*
Weld part number 129, which has 10 pieces	*Part*	*0.83*	*1.2*
Weld part number 116, which has 5 pieces	*Part*	*0.33*	*3*
Weld part number 118, which has 4 pieces	*Part*	*0.25*	*4*
Weld part number 120, which has 3 pieces	*Part*	*0.17*	*6*
Weld part number 122, which has 2 pieces	*Part*	*0.08*	*12*
Weld part number 124, which has 6 pieces	*Part*	*0.42*	*2.4*
Weld part number 126, which has 7 pieces	*Part*	*0.5*	*2*
Weld part number 128, which has 8 pieces	*Part*	*0.75*	*1.3*
Weld part number 130, which has 10 pieces	*Part*	*0.83*	*1.2*

Table 3.6 Functions Observation Record

Date: *2/12/ 2011*	Department: *Parts Warehouse*		Function: *Pick Parts*	Unit of Measure: *Part*	
Time			**Time**		
Start	**Stop**	**Total**	**Description of Observation**	**Work**	**Nonwork**	**Recoverable**	**Qty**

Start	Stop	Total	Description of Observation	Work	Nonwork	Recoverable	Qty
9:55	10:05	10	Pick parts (reasonable pace)	10			16
10:05	10:19	14	Personal talk with coworker		14	14	
10:19	10:26	7	Wait for pick lists from supervisor		7	7	
10:26	10:32	6	Pick parts (fast pace)	6			12
10:32	10:38	6	Went to restroom		6	6	
10:38	10:56	18	Pick parts (slow pace)	18			19
10:56	11:33	37	Lunch break		37	7	
11:33	11:48	15	Pick parts (reasonable pace)	15			22
Total		113		49	64	34	69

Comments: *Supervisor needs to ensure there is always a supply of pick tickets for workers, and needs to control workers better to prevent extended lunch breaks, pacing, and personal conversations. The recommended initial standard for planning purposes is picking 100 parts/hour.*

One method to evaluate productivity levels, especially in labor-intensive areas, is to conduct random periodic observations for one or two days. There are more technical and structured methods than the one described here, but this method is an effective way to accomplish what you want to. Follow these steps:

Step 1. Identify how many people are at work versus absent each day of the analysis, so you know the number of employees who should be working in each department being studied.

Step 2. Make 24 random observations during each shift (approximately three per hour, but not during scheduled lunch or break times).

Step 3. During each of the 24 observations, note how many people are working, are obviously not working, and are out of the department. Try to identify why employees were out of the department. If you determine that those employees were working on department business, include them in the working category, but also determine if they could have completed the task using the telephone or email.

Step 4. Try not to be obvious about your observations. Assign the task to three or four people if possible, so the same person is not seen returning to an area so often.

Step 5. Develop a percentage for each category (working, not working, and out of department) based on all your observations.

Step 6. Determine if the day(s) of the review were or were not "normal" work conditions for each department observed.

Step 7. If the conditions were not "normal," identify what was different. Was the work volume lower or higher than normal, were there equipment or computer problems, were work goals missed or met, and so on?

Step 8. If productivity levels appear unacceptable in certain departments, schedule in-depth analyses and evaluations to determine if the department should be given more work to perform or if the head count could be reduced.

Refer to Table 3.7 for an example of a random periodic observations report that summarizes the results of random periodic observations in an Accounting Department with 10 employees. The entries in italics represent the observer's input. They reveal that 24 tours were made that day for a total of 240 observations (24 × 10 employees), 166 employees were observed performing work (69 percent), 67 employees were

Table 3.7   Random Periodic Productivity Observations Report

Date: *5/20/2010*		Department: *Accounting*			Total Employees: *10*
Tour No.	Tour Time	Employees at Work	Employees Working	Employees Not Working	Employees Out of Department
1	8:09	10	7	3	
2	8:23	10	8	2	
3	8:51	10	8	2	
4	9:32	10	6	4	
5	9:43	10	6	3	1
6	9:58	10	6	4	
7	10:10	10	6	4	
8	10:24	10	7	3	
9	10:58	10	8	2	
10	11:06	10	8	1	1
11	11:25	10	7	3	
12	11:48	10	8	2	
13	12:52	10	10	0	
14	1:03	10	4	2	4
15	1:17	10	7	3	
16	1:29	10	6	4	
17	1:42	10	7	3	
18	2:08	10	10	0	
19	2:29	10	6	4	
20	2:46	10	6	4	
21	3:07	10	6	4	
22	3:22	10	6	4	
23	4:15	10	6	3	1
24	4:40	10	7	3	
24		240 (100%)	166 (69%)	67 (28%)	7 (3%)

Comments: *The supervisor said it was a "normal" day. It appears the department has excess capacity to perform other functions or enable some employees to be assigned elsewhere. The supervisor needs to ensure employees do not take extended breaks.*

observed not performing work (28 percent), and 7 employees were not in the department (3 percent).

Another method to determine how productive the employees in an area are is to have them maintain work logs. The purpose of the work logs is to document the various functions the employees perform each day, the number of times they perform each activity, and the time it takes to perform each activity. You can expect that employees generally will not like having to maintain logs, so you need to inform them that it is just a temporary requirement until you obtain the information you need.

This information, coupled with observations of the same functions being performed, will provide what you need regarding the time required to complete each unit of measure produced. With these two types of data, you have what you need to evaluate the productivity levels of individual employees and the department as a whole.

4

Apply Some Basic Common-Sense Axioms

4.1 COMMUNICATE BASIC CONCEPTS AND PRINCIPLES

There are some basic concepts and principles you should keep reminding yourself of—and you should also pass them on to everyone in the business involved in your cost-cutting and productivity-improvement program. These concepts and principles (basic common-sense axioms) can be introduced at the beginning of the program and continue to be communicated as reminders through the life of the program.

Students and professors can benefit from these basic common-sense axioms just like people who have been in a business-world situation for a long time. We are all students in a way for all our professional and personal lives, because we keep learning from our personal successes and failures. Also, we learn from seeing what works and does not work for other individuals and businesses.

4.2 ASK FOR IT

You have almost certainly heard and agree with some or all of these sayings/philosophies:

"Ask for the sale."

"Ask and you shall receive."

"Keep asking until you get the right answer or response."

"It does not hurt to ask." (It might be better to say, "It hurts if you do not ask.")

Apply these sayings/philosophies to cost cutting and productivity improvement, and ask for ideas from the employees in your business, as well as your business's suppliers and potential suppliers.

I recall when an employee at a business conducting a cost-cutting program made an excellent cost-cutting recommendation and was asked why she had not made the recommendation before. She responded, "Because nobody ever asked me for my opinions or to make recommendations before."

Regardless of which approaches to cost cutting you use, you need to ask for and expect cost-cutting and productivity-improvement savings ideas and cooperation from everyone associated with conducting and participating in various aspects of the program. This includes the employees who submit suggestions as part of an employee suggestion program, individuals on teams or committees, the employees assigned to conduct survey interviews, the employees responsible for implementing recommendations, suppliers, and potential suppliers. Do not forget, however, that employees are more likely to respond when you ask them for ideas if they know there is a chance for a reward of some type, especially a financial reward.

4.3 SPEND MONEY TO MAKE MONEY

A great deal of cost cutting can be accomplished without any upfront expenditure. If cash flow is tight, you should look for these types of cost-cutting measures first. With some of the money you save, you can implement other cost-cutting improvements that do require upfront expense.

Of course, there are certain investments of time, effort, and/or money that provide a worthwhile return on investment (ROI). Some potential examples of ROI projects include the following:

Automation.

Robotics.

New equipment or machinery for increasing productivity.

Programming effort to generate a routine computer report, instead of ongoing manual preparation.

A bar-coding system, which can improve data capture accuracy as well as save time.

Improved systems and procedures.

Computer-assisted design (CAD) software and equipment.

Equipment replacement or major repair. This is appropriate if your existing equipment experiences excessive down time, it does not produce the quantity it should, it costs more than it is worth to repair and maintain, or the equipment produces poor-quality products.

Outside consultants to assist with cost-cutting and productivity-improvement efforts, or any other project deemed appropriate for obtaining a positive return on investment. You are correct: I have mentioned the use of consultants often—that is, good consultants. I believe in consultants, and I have seen over my many years as a consultant and executive that a good consultant can provide valuable assistance in obtaining the desired ROI.

Security systems or staff to limit theft or damage.

Additional staff in certain areas, such as sales, research and development, and industrial engineering, which should result in increased profitable sales, new products, and improved products.

Education and training of staff to help them be more productive and perform their work more cost-effectively.

I recall a great personal investment I made when I was a new consultant. In my work, I was setting performance standards for employees, based on observing them perform their normal job functions. This activity required me to note the start time and stop time of each work step of the function, as well as the start time and stop time of any interruptions, and whether the interruptions were necessary. I tallied the number of work minutes between each start time and stop time, and then I calculated the performance in terms of units produced per hour and hours required to produce each unit of measure. This was so long ago that I used a slide rule to make many of the calculations.

I would make the observations of the employees during the work day, and then I would recap and record my calculations at home or in my motel room at night. I usually had a good meal before I started recapping and recording my calculations, but I often stayed up late finishing my work, so I would stay current and not start the next day behind.

Unlike me, most of the other consultants who were doing the same kind of work I was doing seemed to have plenty of free time for various types of fun each night. When I spoke to them about how much time they spent at night recapping and recording their observations, I was shocked at their answers, because it was far less time than I was spending on doing it.

Now to the point I am trying to make. The reason the other consultants had time for fun each night was because they all had electric calculators, instead of using slide rules to make their calculations. Needless to say, I bought a calculator as soon as possible. The calculator cost $130, and today the equivalent calculator costs about $25. At $130, my investment was worth every cent, because I had so much less stress in trying to keep current with my work, and I had a little fun occasionally at night and slept better. That calculator greatly improved my productivity and delivered a great return on my investment.

4.4 OBTAIN COMPETITIVE BIDS FOR GOODS AND SERVICES

Many people agree that obtaining competitive bids and negotiating for better prices for goods and services are among the most effective ways to cut costs. Generally, you should avoid the practice of sole-source solicitation for goods or services whenever possible.

On numerous cost-cutting assignments, I learned that clients had been doing business with certain suppliers for many years without asking those businesses to reduce their prices. To make matters worse, they never obtained competitive bids from other potential suppliers for the same goods or services.

Almost invariably, when businesses are encouraged to solicit better pricing from their existing and other potential suppliers, they achieve it. After learning they can obtain better pricing, however, some businesses get upset with their suppliers for "ripping them off for all those years." They should be as upset with themselves as they are with their suppliers for allowing this situation to occur.

Years ago when I went to my dry cleaner, the normally calm and friendly owner was angry, in a bad mood, and muttering incoherently in a Chinese dialect. When I asked him what was wrong, he told me that he just learned that his insurance agent of many years had been ripping him off. Another customer who was also an insurance agent had just given him a bid for the same insurance coverage at a savings of 22 percent. He had learned a valuable lesson: Obtaining at least three bids, quotes, or proposals for goods or services is a good tried-and-true rule. An exception to this rule occurs when the goods or services are unique and you are certain the pricing is fair and the goods or services provide benefit to your company.

Remember that the lowest price for a product does not always necessarily mean it is the best price. However, it is the best price if the products are true commodity items delivered at no freight cost to you, and you do not experience any quality rejects.

"Putting all your eggs in one basket" has both positives and negatives. When you use only one supplier, you may get the best pricing due to volume commitments. However, you may run into a bad situation if the supplier cannot perform for whatever reason, such as a strike or emergency that shuts its operation down for an extended period of time. This is something you hope never happens, but it might. It is always a good idea to have backup qualified suppliers for all your purchasing requirements.

Obtain "apples and apples" bids from suppliers to ensure objective comparisons. For example, ask these questions about all of the bids:

Are the product specifications the same?

Is shipping included?

Are items already assembled?

What is the delivery lead time?

What does the warranty cover?

What is the warranty time period?

Ask suppliers to indicate what makes them different and better than their competitors, aside from the prices that are included in the quote. Ask suppliers to cut costs or recommend alternative materials or methods that will result in accomplishing the same thing for less cost.

For certain goods or services that require a contractual agreement, be sure to get an escape or termination clause to protect you if the supplier does not perform to your satisfaction. At a minimum, you should be able to provide a 30-day written notice to end the relationship with a supplier that does not perform to your satisfaction, without adverse financial implications for your business.

4.5 GIVE INCUMBENTS THE OPPORTUNITY TO KEEP THE BUSINESS

It has always been my philosophy and policy to give the incumbent suppliers a chance to retain your business. However, if the incumbent suppliers do not provide cost-cutting recommendations or reduce their prices enough to meet or beat prices of potential new suppliers, you need to seriously consider making a change. Of course, this is if the other potential supplier(s) can provide adequate or even better quality and service.

4.6 USE THE INTERNET AND OTHER AVAILABLE TECHNOLOGY

Consider using as much up-to-date technology as you can, including the Internet and email to simplify tasks and save time and money. Remember life before the Internet? If you do, you will recognize that technology has provided many benefits of which you should take maximum advantage. Use the Internet to research potential suppliers of products and services. The various search engines can facilitate finding suppliers pertinent to your particular needs.

Many suppliers enable their customers to inquire regarding inventory availability and prices for their products as well as to place orders. One of the most common uses of the Internet is to place purchase orders. It is a much faster and less costly method than the one still used by many businesses, which is to generate multipart purchase order forms and send them by mail or transmit them via facsimile (fax) to their suppliers.

You can provide applicable employees with online training programs. Such programs are usually less costly than attending training sessions in person, and they enable workers to learn at a pace that is comfortable for them.

Advertise and sell your business's products via the Internet directly to end-user customers. Of course, this approach requires proper security control measures, and it is usually done in addition to the business's traditional method of selling to retailers, which then sell the products to end-user customers.

Utilize teleconferencing to conduct computer face-to-face meetings with key staff of your suppliers or customers in lieu of traveling for meetings. Although there will be times when face-to-face meetings are determined to be desirable or deemed necessary, you should first consider the feasibility of teleconferencing as a means to save both time and money. By the way, a teleconference can include a group of several people using a large screen, or it can be a one on one meeting using your PC.

Recruiting employees can be accomplished by using some of the premier job search websites on the Internet. There are many search websites focused on specific work areas or particular positions, such as sales, various categories of engineers, the supply chain, and IT. Narrowing down the list of potential candidates for a position is fairly easy, and then someone in the Human Resources Department can perform the necessary due diligence by checking background data for accuracy and contacting references before scheduling interviews with candidates.

Commodity items (standard items that can be obtained from various suppliers) can be purchased using a reverse auction methodology, which enables multiple suppliers to bid for the business. If you are the buying business, generally how the reverse auction works is to establish a blind reverse auction policy, which ensures that your business does not know who the suppliers are for the commodity items, and guarantees the lowest bidder will always be awarded the purchase. If your business sells commodity items to other businesses, you may want to try being on the bidding side of the reverse auctions process.

If you want to try a blind reverse auction, however, make certain that shipping costs and delivery lead times are known and considered when purchasing using this method. If you do not do so, you may experience unacceptable delivery lead times and freight costs because the supplier may be geographically far away (e.g., you are on the West Coast and the supplier is on the East Coast). One of my clients in California utilized the reverse auction method for purchasing commodity items, and it did not prove to be as good a method as the business had hoped. The buyer caused the problems, because he had not considered the freight-related costs involved. Many of the suppliers that won the business were from Alabama, Tennessee, and Georgia, and their locations resulted in higher freight costs than necessary, as well as long delivery lead times and some product damage in transit. Once we discovered the problems associated with freight, we convinced the business to change its reverse auction policy to require the suppliers bidding for the business to indicate the city and state from which the items would be shipped, and for them to ship collect using our client's preferred carrier.

Using email as a communication tool is another great example of a technology that you should use to maximum benefit. You probably use both email and the telephone, and both are important. Communicating via email internally and externally eliminates telephone tag, and avoids unnecessarily high telephone bills and delays to accomplish some tasks. It also provides a trail that communicating by telephone does not.

Tracking shipments via most major freight and small package carriers can be done on the carriers' websites instead of by telephone or email. This step is an obvious time and human resources saver for both parties.

The aforementioned are just a few examples of ways to use the Internet. I am certain you can come up with other ideas of how the Internet can be used to help your business.

4.7 ESTABLISH CONSISTENT POLICIES AND PROCEDURES

Establish appropriate policies and procedures for your business, and ensure they are clearly understood and adhered to. Policies should be developed that can be somewhat flexibly interpreted under certain circumstances to be advantageous to your business. For example, you can state that breaking of certain rules of a policy by an employee "could" result in termination, instead of stating that breaking of these rules by an employee "will" result in termination.

If your business has multiple locations performing similar functions, determine whether different policies and procedures exist at some or all the locations. If so, compare and analyze them. If there are not compelling reasons to justify the differences, select the best policies and procedures and standardize them for all locations to follow.

A good example of how following the same procedures at multiple locations can be beneficial is a situation I learned of from a friend at a major U.S. tire manufacturer. At one of the business's multiple production and distribution facilities, a policy/procedure was in place to require always using the business's own trucks, which delivered products to that location from the main business manufacturing and distribution facility, to carry some of the products that the outlying location produced back to the main facility. However, this was not done at other facilities, which used common carriers to ship the products from their production and distribution facilities to the business's main facility. That remained the case until one of the managers was transferred to one of the facilities that did not have this policy/procedure in place. When the manager made the recommendation for all facilities to follow the same backhaul procedure, it resulted in more than $1 million in annual savings for the business—and a bonus for the manager who made the recommendation.

One key policy for all employees explains acceptable and unacceptable rules of conduct (do's and don'ts), including actions that could lead to disciplinary action, including termination. Employee rules of conduct policies can range from disciplinary actions that can be taken for employees with excessive tardiness and absenteeism to punishments for employees caught sleeping on the job, fighting, or stealing from the business. Provide all regular and temporary employees with a copy of the rules of conduct when they are hired, and have them sign a document indicating they agree to adhere to the rules of conduct. This document should be included in their personnel file. In addition, post the rules of conduct on bulletin boards.

Two important policies and procedures for manufacturing and distribution businesses are the general policy and the warranty policy, which apply to the relationship with customers. The general policy should cover all points regarding the sale of your products, as well as the conditions under which products can be returned for repair, replacement, or credit by the customer. The warranty policy protects the customer for a defined period of time if your products do not perform as they are intended. Your policy will also state if the customer can return the product for credit, repair, or replacement. A general policy and warranty policy can prove to be costly if they are too loose or too tight.

Of course, consistent and fair administration of all policies and procedures is necessary, or they will be less effective.

4.8 KEEP YOUR EYES AND EARS OPEN

Cost-cutting and productivity-improvement opportunities may "drop into your lap" if you are constantly alert and open to them. An example of keeping your eyes and ears open came from one of my assignments for a client that manufactured carpets in a southwestern state. The business had seven plants throughout the state that were alike and performed similar activities, operating on two shifts. Sales were increasing, and the business was having trouble keeping up with demand. It needed assistance to help improve its productivity and output.

Most of the employees working in the plant where I was initially assigned were Native Americans, and many came to work in carpools from small towns or reservations more than 100 miles away. I was scheduled to begin interviewing employees and making observations in a department where certain styles of carpet with a pattern woven into them had an added shearing step performed by five machines. The five machines were like huge lawnmowers, and the shearing process helped highlight the patterns. The plant manager told me that I should start in another area because five of the 12 employees who worked in that department on the day shift would not be there for at least one week until the only vehicle in which they carpooled together was repaired. Fortunately, I had already put in some reports to measure performance and work output on each shift in every department in the plant.

As I began working in another area, as the plant manager requested, I noticed the work output had not decreased on the day shift in the department missing the five employees. I took the time to briefly visit with the seven employees in the department and asked how they were doing without the five employees who were in the one-car carpool. They indicated there were no problems. When I asked why there were no problems, they explained that there were normally two employees per machine; however, they devised a way to operate just fine with one employee per machine. The other two employees helped when more supplies such as yarn or special sewing thread for finishing the carpet edges were needed, or assisted when two people were required for correcting certain problems and for carrying out specific tasks such as making a changeover to a different color or carpet style.

After verifying that there were no safety or quality issues involved, we got agreement that five employees could be trimmed from that department's staff. Of more significance was the fact that this change could be made on both shifts in each of the seven plants, for a total of 70 employees. Fortunately, no one was terminated due to normal attrition and production demands that enabled the adversely effected employees to work in other departments or in the same department on a newly created third shift. When the third shift was created at each facility, the head-count savings from that cost reduction increased to 105 employees.

Another example of keeping your eyes and ears open for opportunities to cut costs and improve productivity relates to a private university that was experiencing cash flow problems. Among the many difficulties that the cash flow problems caused were partial paying of invoices to try to keep suppliers happy, which also resulted in poor productivity, errors that needed resolving, and the Purchasing Department not being able to obtain good pricing from suppliers. Processing the multiple partial payments of invoices required nine Accounts Payable Department employees.

After helping the university turn around its cash flow problems, we saw that the organization had not reduced the number of Accounts Payable employees. After further review, we learned that the Purchasing Department staff had not tried to reinstate discounts with the university's suppliers once they were able to pay invoices on time and in full. We convinced the university that we should follow up in these areas. Ultimately, the Accounts Payable staff was reduced from nine to two full-time employees and one part-time employee, who also worked in the Payroll Department some of the time. The Purchasing Department was also able to cut costs by negotiating for better discounts from its suppliers. The university was lucky we had our eyes and ears open on its behalf.

When I worked on a project for a major pharmaceutical manufacturer, keeping our eyes and ears open led to some significant recommendations for cost-cutting efficiencies. The business's products included, among other things, shampoos, denture adhesives, toothpastes, and pain relief medicine. Most of the products were processed in huge stainless steel vats, which were each staffed by two employees due to Food and Drug Administration (FDA) requirements that called for two people to check and record the temperature and viscosity of the various products at scheduled times during the production process.

The two employees were very busy at the beginning of the process, when ingredients were measured and poured into the vat, and at the end of the process, when the batch was completed and the products were put into container drums. Except for when both of the two employees needed to check and record the temperature and viscosity of the various products at scheduled times during the process, however, one appeared idle while the other was diligently watching gauges on a control panel.

After studying the FDA requirements and talking with a representative from the FDA, we concluded that one of the two employees (the one who appeared idle except at the beginning and end of the process and when scheduled checks were made and recorded) could leave the area and perform other functions instead of remaining in the area and being idle. Of course, the second employee needed to be there when the temperature and viscosity checks were made and recorded.

At first there was resistance to this idea, but after getting a good group of managers, supervisors, and employees together to discuss the idea's feasibility, we all agreed on an acceptable course of action. The course of action included identifying where else frequently idle employees could perform productive work when they were not needed in the department. In addition, we got walkie-talkies (there were no cellular telephones at the time of the project) for the employees who processed batches and used them to contact other employees when they were needed to make and record the scheduled checks. The recommendation was significantly beneficial for the business because it had three other plants that benefited from implementing this same cost-cutting recommendation.

As a side note, a funny thing happened with the walkie-talkies while we were on the project. Employees with walkie-talkies used them to warn other employees when the consultants were going into their area of the plant.

Following are some "keeping your eyes and ears open" examples of things to be alert for:

If your competitors' prices are lower for similar products, your pricing or labor and/or material costs need to be reviewed.

If an area does not suffer when employees take vacations or during periods of absenteeism, it is a probable sign of overstaffing, or at least the capacity for certain employees in the department to be assigned additional responsibilities.

Do not automatically get temporary help to cover for staff vacations, leaves of absence, or other reasons for absenteeism. If a department really needs more help, it will ask for it. You should make sure the department can demonstrate and justify the need for the temporary help.

If you hire temporary or part-time employees, observe their productivity. If they are better performers than the regular employees, learn why and set new standards of performance in the area.

I recall a company that was conducting a cost-cutting program and hired a temporary truck driver to cover for a regular truck driver's vacation. He did the required work without overtime, whereas the regular driver usually worked 5 to 6 hours of overtime each week. Needless to say, when he returned from vacation, the area manager had a discussion with the truck driver about his vacation replacement's performance. The employee rarely worked overtime again, and only for scheduled extra stops, or when there were major traffic problems.

A true story that applies to me is similar to the truck driver story described previously. This story was described by my late father as the time when I became an "efficiency expert," as he called it. For three of the four summer vacations when I was at the University of Michigan, I operated a large bulldozer for a construction business. My father was the general manager of the business, and he was also named Fred Neu. We had different middle names, so I was not technically a junior and I was not called Junior. The first summer, before I started operating a bulldozer, I had to fill in for a man called the fuel man who was on a two-week vacation and who drove a fuel tanker truck that contained #2 diesel fuel; it had a smaller tank, called a pup, behind it that contained gasoline. The business had a master mechanic who was in charge of maintaining all the business's heavy construction equipment used on the construction project sites and the business's fleet of trucks and pickup trucks.

On my first day of work, at 7 A.M. sharp, the master mechanic gave me the keys to the fuel truck, the fuel pump gauges, and a list of the equipment and trucks that should be at each of the five current active construction sites. Each piece of equipment and truck had a number assigned to it, and the number was painted on the cab of the equipment or truck. There were also 150-gallon gasoline tanks at each site, and they all had numbers painted on them. The master mechanic gave me a book with pages containing columns that I was to use for indicating the date, equipment number, truck number, or tank number, as well as the number of gallons of #2 diesel or gas I put into each vehicle or gas tank.

To learn where the construction job sites were, I was told to follow a man they called the "grease monkey" on the first day. The grease monkey's job was to change engine oil, lubricate, and grease the various pieces of equipment and vehicles as appropriate. I followed him out of "the yard," as it was called, and I was shifting gears without grinding them too much. The grease monkey stopped at the first diner we came to. I parked the truck and followed him inside. We sat side by side at the counter, and he said, "The first thing you have to learn is to take a lot of breaks." He was sipping from a cup of coffee that the waitress brought to him, because he was obviously a regular customer there and she knew him and what he wanted. He asked me my name (remember my father was the general manager of the business and we were both named Fred Neu), and I said, "Fred Neu"—to which he responded by spitting out his mouthful of coffee on his doughnut and the counter. We hurried out of the diner, and once we were at the first construction site, I was pretty much on my own to locate and fill up each piece of equipment, truck, and gasoline tank.

When we were finished fueling, oiling, lubing, and greasing all the equipment, trucks, and tanks, we returned to "the yard." The master mechanic hurried out to greet us. He asked me, "Did you have any problems? Why are you back here so early?" Apparently, the regular fuel man usually did not return to "the yard" until 2½ hours later than I did, including 1 overtime hour. The master mechanic carefully checked my book to be sure that I had fueled every piece of equipment, truck, and tank. He verified I had, so he said, "Fine job, Fred. Your father would be proud of you."

I had my truck, the #2 diesel tank, and the gasoline tank filled up to be ready for the next day. Because I still had 2 hours to go before the end of the shift, I was assigned to drive a huge farm-type tractor that had a big electromagnet attached to the back of it over the roads and parking spaces around "the yard" to pick up any nails and sharp pieces of metal that could damage tires. Apparently, many asphalt truck drivers, visitors to the headquarters building, and even employees frequently had flat tires when driving around "the yard." That assignment was fun and productive, because the magnet picked up numerous nails and sharp pieces of metal that would have surely damaged many tires if they had not been picked up. As I still had 1½ hours to go before the end of the shift after that assignment, I was allowed to learn how to operate all the heavy equipment in "the yard," including bulldozers, road graders, forklift trucks, scraper pans, and cranes.

To end the story, from then on, the grease monkey was assigned the duty of driving the tractor with the electromagnet behind it around "the yard" every day when he returned from his oiling, lubing, and greasing job, which was about 2 hours earlier than he had returned prior to my fill-in duty. When the fuel man returned from vacation, he was assigned the very dirty, undesirable job of cleaning various parts with gasoline that had been removed from equipment and trucks; he now had the time to carry out this task when he returned from his fueling job every day. The parts he cleaned were used to repair or rebuild equipment or truck parts such as engines and brakes. The good news for the fuel man was that he was trained how to make truck and equipment repairs, which led to a promotion and more money for him.

> If an area works little or no overtime, it probably has capacity to perform additional work, or it may be overstaffed.
>
> If you subcontract the same type of work to different businesses, compare them to determine which businesses are the better performers. Take appropriate action to use the best one, but retain the other(s) as backup.

If you keep your eyes and ears open, and look and listen well, you may find many other worthwhile opportunities.

4.9 TRUST YOUR INSTINCTS

If you feel there are opportunities to cut costs and improve productivity, you are probably right. Remember these sayings/philosophies:

"Where there's smoke, there's fire."

"Trust your instincts."

"Listen to your sixth sense."

When I first began working for a durable medical equipment manufacturing business as a consultant, I was instructed to take a tour of its four regional distribution centers (DCs). After I completed the tour of the DCs, my first project was assigned to me by the company's chairman of the board. He personally knew many of the company's customers, who were owners of durable medical equipment retail stores. He said that many of them complained to him about how long it took to get delivery of a wheelchair when they requested it in a color that was not a standard inventory color. These "special chairs" were promised to be delivered in 3 weeks; however, delivery was taking 5–6 weeks. A "special chair" was defined as a nonstandard configuration of standard component parts. These items were produced at the business's main manufacturing facility.

My tours of the DCs indicated that the warehouse workers were idle at least 30 to 40 percent of the time and had excess capacity to do much more work. My instincts told me that the process of making "special chairs" should be moved away from the business's main manufacturing facility, with the "special chairs" instead being assembled at the company's regional DCs closest to the customers ordering them. We made this change, and it reduced the turnaround time from 5–6 weeks to 2 days. This was accomplished by stocking certain upholstery and other component parts at the regional DCs, where the stock chairs were converted to become "special chairs." Initially, the only "special chairs" involved a change in the upholstery color, but the program was quickly expanded to include customer requests for nonstandard wheels, arm rests, leg rests, or foot rests. It was a win-win situation. The chairman of the board was happy, I was happy, the customers were happy, and the DC managers were happy because their workers were more productive than ever before.

You can have good instincts when you are a student or just starting out in the business world. However, as you progress and grow professionally with added experience, you will trust your instincts more and more, and you will pursue, instead of ignore, potential opportunities to make improvements.

4.10 HIGH VOLUME EQUALS HIGH OPPORTUNITY

Small material savings on each unit produced can add up and achieve big cost savings when high volumes are involved. Likewise, small labor savings on each unit produced can add up and achieve big cost savings when high volumes are involved. Whenever you consider changing a product design (value engineering), determine if using less expensive materials and/or modifying the manufacturing process to require less labor to manufacture the product can cut costs significantly when high volumes are concerned. "You can make a million dollars one dollar at a time" and "Watch your pennies and the dollars will take care of themselves" are old sayings that apply to these kinds of high-volume opportunities.

Remember, your Purchasing Department can usually obtain better pricing and discounts on high-volume commitments to suppliers. You do not necessarily have to take delivery of all the items you commit to at one time, but can instead have the supplier keep in inventory adequate minimum-maximum levels from which you can take delivery as required on a JIT basis.

If you ship from multiple locations, you can probably negotiate national account discounts with freight carriers based on the combined volumes of all your locations. If you have enough employees who travel frequently, you can negotiate with some car rental agencies and hotel chains for discounts.

When feasible, conduct group training, seminars, or workshops to obtain a lower price than if you paid for several separate smaller sessions. I am sometimes requested to work one-on-one with a manager or supervisor to cover topics that I include when I conduct group seminars. I point out to the business how much more costly the one-on-one sessions are compared to the group seminars. This sometimes results in me conducting group seminars, but sometimes the business believes the one-on-one sessions are a better choice.

A previous client manufactured Styrofoam packaging for one of the largest fast-food chains. The business produced millions of the packages each week. It also manufactured Styrofoam egg cartons, meat trays, and avocado trays for grocery stores.

Samples from the rolls of Styrofoam sheets used to make the packages were weighed after the rolls were completed. If the weight of the rolls was too high, it was too late to do anything about it. The weights always resulted in each egg carton, meat tray, avocado tray, and fast food container being 3 to 4 grams over the specification weight. We determined that if the business could consistently meet the proper specification weight for all packages without going over the limit, it would realize more than $650,000 annual savings in raw materials costs at that facility, and other facilities might benefit from the same thing. We worked with the client to identify the proper step in the production process for weighing samples of the Styrofoam sheeting to ensure the packages it produced were the proper weight, and not unnecessarily over weight.

A side benefit of our review that resulted in ensuring the proper weight of the Styrofoam sheeting was that we discovered another way to improve productivity in the process of making the egg cartons, meat trays, avocado trays, and fast-food containers. The temperatures and cycle times of the machines used to stamp out the products could be controlled by the machine operators. Most of the machine operators turned the temperatures down as far as possible so that the cycle time to make each part was slowed down. This practice enabled the machine operators to not work as hard, because they needed to stack completed products less frequently. We got approval from the plant manager to put locks on the control panels of the machines so the optimal temperatures and cycle times to obtain maximum capacity were never changed.

Another example of the "high volume equals high opportunity" equation involved a client that imported millions of sports shoes each year into the United States, Canada, and Europe from offshore Pacific Rim sources. We noticed that the business was using only two sizes of shoe boxes as part of an effort to standardize its operations, even though it made shoes for infants, children, men, and women. The two sizes of shoe boxes resulted in the following problems when they were used for small size shoes:

There was wasted space (air) in the shoe boxes that contained smaller size shoes.

Some shoe boxes that contained smaller size shoes were damaged more easily and had to be replaced because they had collapsed when other pallets of shoes were stacked on them.

Shoes were damaged due to boxes and cartons being damaged, and there was scuffing of leather shoes, resulting in the Quality Assurance Department rejecting them.

There were added labor and supply expenses to rebox the shoes removed from damaged boxes.

Damaged outer cartons had to be repaired or replaced.

The unnecessarily large cartons increased use of warehouse space.

The unnecessarily large cartons resulted in a higher than necessary unit cost per pair of shoes to transport them by ocean container.

There were higher than necessary costs to ship customer orders containing smaller shoe sizes.

We convinced the client to increase the number of sizes of shoe boxes from two to four. This change was made only after soliciting input and acceptance from key customers, warehouse management, and the Purchasing Department to ensure the sizes would be acceptable. The change from two sizes to four sizes of shoe boxes resulted in the following outcomes:

Lower overall packaging costs

Almost total elimination of damaged shoe boxes, cartons, and shoes

An increased quantity of pairs being shipped in each ocean container, which lowered the transportation cost per pair of shoes

More pairs of shoes being warehoused in less space

More pairs being shipped in smaller packing cartons when a customer order included shoes for children and/or infants (there was not a high volume of infant shoes)

Lower outbound freight costs for customer-order shipments

Generate and review reports related to your suppliers to identify high-volume purchased products and/or raw materials you should study for cost-cutting opportunities. Generate and review reports of products you produce to identify the high-volume items you should study for cost-cutting opportunities. Brainstorm with the appropriate employees involved in your cost-reduction and productivity-improvement efforts to identify where other "high volume equals high opportunity" possibilities exist.

4.11 TIME IS MONEY

It is common sense to say, "Do not spend time on activities that are not worthwhile, because it is a waste of time and money that could be spent on productive activities." For example, ensure that your invoicing and collections methods minimize days outstanding. Negotiate extended payment terms with suppliers if deemed feasible, and negotiate additional discounts for quick invoice payment. Maximize inventory turnaround of your products. Rotate stock on a first in, first out (FIFO) basis. Carrying inventory too long can result in excessive carrying costs, damage, deterioration, and/or obsolescence.

Process and ship customer orders as quickly as practical. This practice not only makes for happier customers, but you can also invoice your customers and receive your payments sooner. An exception to this is when some retail customers give you a delivery window that you must honor, or possibly pay a penalty for an early or late delivery.

Make sure that traveling sales and service personnel use their time productively. This especially applies when overnight travel is involved, but also applies to local travel. Plan driving trips to avoid wasted time and cost due to backtracking, especially when out-of-town travel is involved. Wasted time means other existing and potential customers/clients cannot be visited. Help the sales staff to analyze their customers to determine the frequency of visits required to maximize potential sales, without wasting time and money. Some examples include the following:

Make weekly instead of twice-weekly visits, or monthly instead of twice-monthly visits.

Conduct a short visit at the customer's facility instead of taking contacts out for a long lunch, especially when the customer is not highly profitable, or is seen as not potentially highly profitable.

Telephone the customer and schedule an appointment, instead of showing up in person without an appointment, which may result in a wasted visit if the contact cannot meet with you.

If only some in-person visits are deemed necessary, consider alternating in-person visits with telephone calls or email messages.

After the frequency and types of sales calls necessary to keep or increase sales from customers are determined, make a spreadsheet like a calendar, indicating all customers and the dates when they should be contacted, as well as whether they should be contacted in person, via telephone, or via email. Use this information to make yearly, quarterly, monthly, and weekly calendars to be a reminder and record of your sales calls. Salespeople for a business I worked with in the Los Angeles area were genuinely happy after we developed calendars for each of them, because it gave them time to obtain new customers, which resulted in more sales, and more sales meant more commission money. Before developing the calendars for each salesperson at this business, we temporarily implemented the use of daily logs for each of the salespeople to maintain. The logs required them to record where they traveled each day, how many miles they drove to each appointment, and how long they spent with each customer and potential customer. The logs revealed that one salesperson was not traveling very much, and he was instructed to increase the number of customers and potential customers he visited each workday. The log of another salesperson indicated that she could plan her trips to be far more efficient. One day per week she was visiting customers in West Los Angeles and Santa Ana, and another day each week she was visiting customers in Santa Monica and Anaheim. West Los Angeles and Santa Monica are geographically close together; Santa Ana and Anaheim are also geographically close together. It was easy to convince the salesperson to visit customers and potential customers in West Los Angeles and Santa Monica on the same day, and to visit customers and potential customers in Santa Ana and Anaheim on another day. The changes in travel schedules for both of these salespeople resulted in them going from receiving the sixth and eighth highest commissions of the 13-person sales force to receiving the third and fourth highest commissions.

4.12 IMPROVE PRODUCTIVITY AND EFFICIENCY

As a reminder, I provided the following basic and simple definition of productivity previously in this book: "Productivity is a measure of the output of production compared to the input of resources used to produce that output." The Association for Operations Management was formerly known as the American Production and Inventory Control Society;

although its name has changed, the organization retained the APICS acronym. Following are the APICS definitions of productivity and efficiency:

Productivity (*APICS Dictionary* definition):
Productivity is an overall measure of the ability to produce a good or a service. It is actual output of production compared to the actual input of resources. Productivity is a relative measure across time or against common entities (labor, capital, etc.). In the production literature, attempts have been made to define total productivity where the effects of labor and capital are combined and divided into the output. One example is a ratio that is calculated by adding the dollar value of labor, capital equipment, energy, and material, etc., and dividing it into the dollar value of output in a given time period. This is one measure of total productivity. In economics, productivity is the ratio of output in terms of dollars of sales to an input such as direct labor in terms of the total wages. This is called single factor productivity or partial factor productivity.

Efficiency (*APICS Dictionary* definition):
Efficiency measures how well something is performing relative to existing standards; in contrast, productivity measures output relative to a specific input, e.g., tons/labor hour. Efficiency is the ratio of (1) actual units to the standard rate of production expected in a time period or (2) standard hours produced to actual hours worked (taking longer means less efficiency) or (3) actual dollar volume of output to a standard dollar volume in a time period. For example, (1) if the standard is 100 units per hour, 800 units should be produced during an 8-hour shift (this standard example takes work breaks into consideration). (2) If efficiency is measured in hours and it took 8.21 hours to produce 8 standard hours; the efficiency is 8/8.21 converted to a percentage or 97.5%. (3) The work is measured in dollars and produces $780 with a standard of $800; the efficiency is $780/$800 converted to a percentage is 97.5%.

I sometimes explain that improved productivity is achieved in the following situations:

You achieve less output than before but with even less input than before as a percentage.

You achieve the same output as before with less input than before.

You achieve more output than before with the same input as before.

The best: you achieve more output than before with less input than before.

Performing productivity analyses helps provide a basis of information you can use to improve productivity and efficiency. You must first determine if all functions performed are needed and contribute to the business or department goals and objectives. If you determine that some functions are not needed, eliminate them. If the functions are needed, determine if they can be simplified or performed more efficiently. You may be saying that this sounds good, but is difficult to achieve. That may be true in many cases, but not all cases, so give it a try.

Identify any duplicate, overlapping, or fragmented functions that exist and that could be performed more efficiently if they were combined or centralized. This recommendation is often applicable when a business acquires another business and centralization of certain functions is feasible.

Do the managers and supervisors have the proper spans of control, based on how complex the work performed by their subordinates is, as well as the physical area covered? Can some managers and supervisors assume greater responsibility, or do you need additional supervisors to improve control, quality, and productivity?

Are employees adequately cross-trained to ensure flexibility and prevent some staff from being overworked, while others are less productive or idle when the work mix changes? Cross-training employees to perform as many jobs as practical in each department will provide flexibility so that the business can assign employees to different functions as needed when requirements within the department fluctuate, as well as when some employees are on vacation or absent for any reason. You need to indicate which employees are cross trained as well as the specific job functions on which each employee is cross-trained. Refer to Table 4.1 for an example of flexibility/cross-training lists. The example list compares the employee names against job functions; however, you may choose to make a list comparing each employee to the other employees in the department. The entries in italics on the form represent the entries made by the preparer—in this case, the department manager.

Are you getting a fair day's work from all your employees? A credo I tried to instill in the organizations I managed was, "Do as much as you can, as fast as you can, as long as you do it safely and accurately." Improving productivity is easier said than done, but the effort involved in addressing these areas is worth it and will provide valuable results. Establish

Table 4.1   Flexibility/Cross-training List (Employee to function)

Employee Names	Pick Parts	Pack Parts	Audit Orders	Load Trucks	Prepare B.O.L.
Department: *Accounts Payable*			**Date prepared:** *6/20/2011* **Job Functions**		
D. Jones	X	T	T	X	T
A. Taylor	X	X	X	X	X
C. Chandler	X	X	X	T	N
R. Boyer	X	X	N	T	X
S. Davis	T	T	T	X	N
F. Stanton	X	N	X	T	X
P. Simmons	X	T	N	X	T
N. Platt	X	X	X	X	X
B. Ross	X	X	X	T	N
T. Flanagan	X	X	N	T	X
J. McCoy	X	T	T	X	X
S. Allen	X	N	X	T	N
B. Brower	X	X	T	X	T

Instructions: Enter a check mark (X) if cross-trained. Enter T if trainable. Enter N if it is not practical for this employee to be trained to perform this job function.

quantitative and qualitative standards and measure the performance/productivity of individuals and departments against them wherever possible. Monitoring employee performance can also point out barriers that prevent employees from achieving maximum performance, such as equipment problems or lack of available work to perform.

Inform employees and departments what is expected of them, and then measure performance and provide appropriate feedback on a timely basis. Timely feedback may be weekly, daily, or even hourly depending on the work involved and control required for ensuring the proper quantitative and qualitative results are achieved. As performance is measured, the feedback could be in the form of praise, counseling, education, training, demotions, promotions, reassignments, or terminations.

Controlling absenteeism and tardiness will improve productivity. Obviously, if employees are not at work, they cannot contribute or be productive. For example, limit the number of employees in a department who go on vacation at the same time. This should be a Human Resources Department rule for the business to follow. Generally do not allow vacations at traditionally busy times for the business.

Consider providing small incentives and rewards for departments that experience perfect attendance and no tardiness each quarter, such as free snacks at break time for a day or week. Maintain charts indicating absences and tardiness by individual. This system provides peer pressure because workers want their snacks, and it can show you if any employees are taking Mondays or Fridays off to stretch their weekends.

Make certain employees understand the business's disciplinary policies regarding absenteeism and tardiness, and assure the policies are properly administered. Employees will often straighten up when they are given a warning regarding absenteeism or tardiness and never repeat that behavior. If they do continue their excessive absenteeism and tardiness, it is probably best for the business if they were ultimately terminated.

4.13 REDUCE UNPRODUCTIVE TIME

Without proper controls of workloads and employees, you can experience a lot of unproductive or "lost" time. The term "lost" time is a good one, because once you have lost the time, you can never get it back—it is lost forever. The major areas where I have frequently seen unproductive time are at the beginning of a work shift, at break times, at lunch time, and at the end of a work shift. Without proper controls, the start-up is slow, breaks and lunch periods are extended, and many people stop working too early before time to quit.

A business that controls this kind of unproductive time does so mainly by educating and training supervisors and requiring them to get to work before the shift begins and to have work available at each workstation for each employee. Maintaining an adequate ongoing backlog of available work at each workstation is an essential element to avoid unproductive time. If there is nothing to work on, employees cannot do any work. The available work could be parts needing to be machined, pick lists for customer orders to be fulfilled, invoices for Accounts Payable employees to process, component parts to be welded together, returned products to be analyzed and repaired, telephone messages from customers needing to be called back, parts requiring painting or plating, reports to be reviewed, raw materials to be weighed and put into inventory, purchased component parts to be quantity verified and put in the proper location, or parts of garments needing to be sewed together. You get the idea: whatever the type of job, the supervisor should place a backlog of available work at each employee's workstation at the start of the shift and ensure there is always a backlog of available work throughout the shift. Employees working on a piecework incentive system will be upset if they do not have available work at their workstations at the start of the shift, because that means time wasted when they could be making more money.

Another thing supervisors should do before the shift starts is to turn machines on so they are warmed up and ready to be used. It may seem "old school," but I have seen some businesses effectively use an alert bell that sounds 3–5 minutes prior to the start of the shift, followed by a different buzzing sound when the shift actually starts and when work should begin. This alert bell enables employees to get ready and be at their workstations to begin working on time. Again, the employees on a piecework incentive system are usually very eager to get to work and start to make extra money.

Mismatched capacities in an assembly line or workflow process can result in lost time when one step in the process takes more time than the next step(s), and this bottleneck causes some employees to be idle while waiting for something to work on. Assign someone to review the individual work functions performed in the assembly line or workflow process to determine if there is unproductive time that could be eliminated through better balancing and redistribution of the tasks being performed. This is best accomplished by making observations of each function to determine the units per hour or hours per unit it requires to perform each function. One very effective approach is to make a chart indicating the current units per hour rate for the entire assembly line or process flow as a straight diagonal line from left to right. Then indicate the units per hour rate for each employee on the assembly line or in the process flow. Refer to the assembly line example in Table 4.2.

Table 4.2   Toy Car Assembly-Line Units/Hour Productivity Analysis

Units/Hour	Worker 1	Worker 2 & 3	Worker 4 & 5	Worker 6	Worker 7	Worker 8
		(2 & 3 combined)				
18		O			O	
17			(4 & 5 combined)			
16			O	O		
15	Proposed assembly line speed: 15 units/hour					O
14	O					
13						
12	Current assembly line speed: 12 units/hour					
11						
10						
9		O O				
8			O O			
7						
6						
5						
4						
3						
2						
1						

Worker 1	Worker 2 & 3	Worker 4 & 5	Worker 6	Worker 7	Worker 8
(Place car body on chasis on Assembly Line)	*(Place rear wheels on rear axle)*	*(Place front wheels on front axle)*	*(Place on front lights)*	*(Place on rear lights)*	*(Place on antenna)*

Analysis comments:

The assembly line speed can be increased from the current 12 units/hour to 14 or 15 units/hour if the following assembly-line balancing actions are taken:
  • *Assign Workers 2 and/or 3 to assist Worker 1 with placing the car body on the chassis.*
  • *Assign Workers 4 and/or 5 to assist Worker 6 in putting on the front lights.*
  • *Assign Worker 8 as needed to assist Worker 7 in putting on the rear lights.*
This represents a 17% to 25% increase in productivity.

Upfront efforts to ensure that good work-planning and assignment techniques are used will help prevent unproductive time. There are many instances where higher skill-level and higher-paid employees perform work that should be performed by less-skilled and lower-paid workers. Obviously, if you redistribute the work functions to ensure the less-skilled and lower-paid employees perform the functions requiring less skill, you will realize cost savings.

Consider this example: a business that repairs computers and printers paid its repair technicians more than any other hourly workers. The repair technicians spent an excessive amount of time away from their workstations on activities other than repairing computers, such as selecting the next computer to repair, borrowing tools, going to the customer service department to have a question answered (e.g., what is the computer password, does the customer want the defective hard drive returned), taking the repaired products to the quality area for inspection, and waiting to ensure they received credit for the repair on the production board. Waiting to ensure they received credit for the repairs they completed was important to them because they were evaluated on that basis. By assigning lower-paid employees who were performing expediting functions to also perform material-handling functions, the business improved the productivity of its repair technicians by more than 200 percent.

A similar example involved a machine shop where highly skilled and highly paid workers moved the pallets of work they had completed to the next workstation. It proved far more cost-effective to assign a few material handlers to move pallets of completed work to the next workstation to ensure an available backlog of work for all machine operators. The job-routing instructions were updated to include these material movements.

Another example comes from a machine shop where highly paid and highly skilled machine operators were called on to make pickups and deliveries in the city where they were located on a regular basis. The workers used their own vehicles, so the company paid them for mileage and considered it a little bonus for them to get a break from machining parts. After it was pointed out how much money the business could save by using a local delivery service or small package carrier to make these types of pickups and deliveries, the company discontinued the practice of having the machine operators perform this function. It turned out that most of the machine operators did not like doing this task anyway.

4.14 ELIMINATE BOTTLENECKS AND CONSTRAINTS

As the old wise saying goes, "A chain is as strong as its weakest link." In Eliyahu Goldratt's best-selling business book *The Goal*, a slow-walking young boy, Herbie, who led the way on a hike, demonstrated the weakest link. The slow leader dictated the speed of the entire group. Once Herbie, the leader, was replaced with a faster young boy, the weakest link no longer slowed down the entire group. In a business situation, the slowest boy would probably be assigned to a job that would avoid such a constraint. Constraints and bottlenecks prevent you from operating efficiently.

It is especially easy to identify the weak link on an assembly line or in a process-flow type of operation. When a product or process involves numerous separate steps in a flow sequence, you can easily determine which step takes the longest time by performing observations, performing time and motion studies, or having workflow logs maintained at each step. You can also identify a constraint or bottleneck by performing observations of each step in a process flow until you see which employees are idle or slowing down and pacing due to lack of available work flowing to them. Obviously, the earlier the constraint or bottleneck occurs on the assembly line or in the process or flow, the more unproductive time will occur downstream in the process if it is not eliminated.

Your biggest constraint or bottleneck may be a piece of equipment that does not produce fast enough; a slow, poor-performing employee; or an imbalance in the workloads that results in one operation being slower than the others. Once you have identified and corrected the biggest constraint or bottleneck, your unproductive time will decrease and performance will increase. You can then work on your second biggest constraint, which has become your new biggest bottleneck, and so on, until you have eliminated all the constraints and have a smooth-flowing operation.

Whenever I think of bottlenecks and constraints, I think of the classic *I Love Lucy* episode when Lucy and Ethel worked on the assembly line packing boxes of candy. You can probably recall how hilarious it was to see Lucy and Ethel doing their best to keep up with the flow of pieces of candy from the conveyor belt and pack them in boxes. Because their best was not good enough, they tried stuffing candy in their mouths and eating it, as well as stuffing pieces of candy in their uniforms to hide them. This episode may have been a situation comedy TV show but it taught valuable, serious lessons about productivity, line balancing, and staffing requirements.

4.15 ASK "WHY?" AND DO NOT ACCEPT "BECAUSE IT'S ALWAYS BEEN DONE THAT WAY"

Almost everyone has experienced a situation when they questioned why something was done in a certain way because it seemed inefficient, and this answer was given: "Because it has always been done that way." Never hesitate to ask, "Why do you do it that way?" when you believe there may be a better way to do something. You do not have to know what the solution or the better way is, but you do have to get the right person or persons involved to study the situation to determine if there are better options. Almost every time I asked why a task I observed seemed inefficient the way it was performed, and the answer was "Because it has always been done that way," after some effort an easier and more cost-effective way was identified to accomplish the tasks.

4.16 INVEST IN IMPROVING EMPLOYEE MORALE

If you are a manager or supervisor, put yourself in your employees' shoes to imagine how a little something unexpected, such as occasional free doughnuts at the morning break or cookies at the afternoon break, would make you feel. If you know of health-conscious employees who may not like doughnuts or cookies, get them something else. Wouldn't you feel appreciated by your boss and the company? You might work harder (at least for a while) and become a more loyal employee.

The Human Resources Department may provide a budget for this doughnuts or cookies idea; however, if it does not, you should consider making this investment out of your own pocket. Of course, the best thing a manager or supervisor can do is give a literal or figurative pat on the back when an employee or department does a good job, but the doughnuts and cookies also help boost morale.

In certain areas, such as the shipping department, freight carriers may provide pizza during the month-end week when many businesses have a push to get product out and invoice customers to "make the numbers." If asked, the sales representative for your major freight carrier will probably be glad to help make his or her customer's employees happy by providing pizza occasionally. Do not hesitate to ask the major supplier of goods or services in any department to do something like this during the month-end "crunch" time." The employees will appreciate it, and the supplier will probably notice that some employees will show their appreciation and improve their cooperation and working relationship.

I strongly urge you to try something like this and see what happens.

5

Cost Avoidance

5.1 PLAN, TRACK, AND CONTROL BUDGETS

By taking certain precautionary steps, you can avoid many unnecessary costs. Preparing and monitoring budgets is a good example. Allow adequate time for your business's budget process, including initial preparation, review, revisions as needed, and approving the final budget. "Haste makes waste" really applies when preparing budgets is concerned. Refer to the previous year's budget, but use the zero-based budget concept to look at all items with new eyes and justify each and every line item when preparing budgets. Control the whole by controlling the parts by monitoring budgets in detail.

Each level of management should review the planned and actual budgets for the department(s) for which they are responsible on at least a monthly basis. The sooner you identify expenses as being higher than budgeted, the sooner you can determine why and possibly correct any bad situations. Closely analyze both controllable and variable budget items.

Understand certain expenses that may be allocated to your department(s), as well as the basis for those allocations. Some examples include the expenses assigned to the Information Systems, Facility, Maintenance, Security, and Janitorial Departments. Certain allocations may be based on the square footage of your area, number of employees in your department (s), estimated usage of the services being allocated, or other factors. If you believe you are being unfairly charged, request a review; you might also seek to have the allocation method for your department(s) changed.

Especially look for negative trends in your budget actual expenses, but analyze and be prepared to explain to your superiors both positive and negative trends and variances.

Provide all departments with needed assumptions that will have an impact on the budget, such as the sales forecast by month, product price increases, new product introduction schedules, and proposed salary increase percentages. If any major assumptions change during the year, such as a significant increase or decrease in the sales forecast, require certain departments with variable budgets that are affected to revise their budgets. Many departments could be affected by a major change to the sales forecast, including, but not limited to, the following: Production, Planning, Procurement, Warehousing, Accounts Payable, Distribution, Customer Service, and Accounts Receivable.

As a manager with budget responsibility, make certain you understand all the budget line-item categories included in the chart of accounts and budget. If you believe that your department's chart of account categories are inadequate and you think you could improve your control by revising them, request that the Accounting Department make changes. This could simply include some clarification, the combination of some subaccounts, or possibly the addition of more detailed categories (subaccounts). Explain to the Accounting personnel your reasoning and state why it would also be beneficial for their analyses.

The following excerpt was provided by James B. Ayers:

Know When to Take a Snapshot: A Case for Activity-Based Costing

Companies have to regularly report their financial condition to a variety of stakeholders. This responsibility is like filming a business "movie," a continuous process. It's tempting to use movie data to make critical financial decisions.

Company movies are an obstacle in making important financial decisions. One client, a producer of a large variety of household furniture products, faced such a dilemma. Its highest volume product appeared, according to the company movie, to be the most unprofitable. This was because the rules baked into GAAP (Generally Accepted Accounting Practices) burdened the product with overhead markups. The markups were a necessary convenience for "absorbing" production overhead and G&A (General and Administration) costs. But the no-problem high volume "runner" product was simple to make, requiring little fuss and need for overhead support. So the picture of the product's profitability was faulty. An activity-based cost, which removes these allocations, produces a superior "snapshot" view. This entails a bit of analysis, but can be critical in reaching good decisions for a product like the runner. Activity-based costing should be a capability in businesses that deliver a variety of products or services. Adoption should avoid creation of a parallel financial reporting movie. This has happened to many companies applying the approach. As-needed snapshots are appropriate and vital, and worth the price of putting them together.

Product proliferation raises the stakes. Inevitably some products are more profitable than others. People inside the business receive conflicting information or none at all. Often, the finance department is the least likely to want to deal with "snapshots" that compete with their official line. It is up to stakeholders like marketing, sales, and operations functions to demand that a trusted party take the snapshots.

5.2 ESTABLISH BUDGET EXPENDITURE APPROVAL LEVELS

Most businesses have expenditure dollar limits for individual purchases that can be made by each manager. If a proposed purchase exceeds the allowed amount, the manager must first receive prior approval from his or her superior. If you do not already have this type of policy control in place, establish a policy and procedure for expenditure-approval levels and obtaining prior approval before making purchases above the allowed amount.

5.3 IS IT A NICETY OR A NECESSITY?

This is one of my favorite topics. Every manager must ask the question, "Is it a nicety or a necessity?" whenever someone in the organization wants to spend money or effort on something new. Although money for the item may be in the budget, challenge and review all expense requests to determine if the goods or services being requested are really needed. Get people in the habit of asking, "Is it a necessity or only a nicety?" to help them decide prior to requesting, approving, or disapproving an expenditure.

Most people need to watch their budgets closely in their personal lives at some point in their life. The best way for an individual, couple, or family to control their expenses is to closely examine how they currently spend their money and determine which expenditures are niceties and which are really necessities. In addition, prior to spending money on anything new, they must make the same determination.

Certain items are usually inarguable necessities, such as payment of the utility bills to keep the electricity, water, gas, and telephones working. If times are financially tough, the amount of electricity, water, gas, and telephone usage may be reduced by taking certain steps to save money, but the basic items are necessities.

It is very interesting to see how some individuals view certain expenditures as absolute necessities while someone else would consider the same things as unnecessary niceties. When I went through the iteration of carefully documenting and analyzing how I spent my money for a three-month period, the review verified what I thought, which was that I spent a lot of money at restaurants.

An example I recall that demonstrates a good decision-making process is a business that retained a service that provided rugs, dust mops, and brooms for its warehouses. These items were replaced every two weeks by the supplier, and there was a monthly fee for the service. When the supplier of the service was requested to suggest how it could help the company cut costs, the supplier recommended that it provide some smaller rugs and fewer rugs.

The business decided to contact other potential providers of the same kind of rug service. A potential supplier that provided a similar service was more creative and flexible than the incumbent supplier because it wanted the business. It offered the same service as the other vendor at a lower cost. The vendor also offered to not exchange rugs as often unless the weather was rainy, because the rugs would not be as dirty as often; this would lead to an even lower cost. Another potential supplier that sold products similar to those being provided by the service companies demonstrated how purchasing its items would be more cost-effective than utilizing the rug service.

Someone suggested using the "necessity or nicety" approach to determine whether the service was a necessity. The service was considered a "nicety"; however, some items were considered a necessity. The company opted to discontinue the current service and instead purchased a few rugs, mops, and brooms, because that approach seemed to be more cost-effective and made the most sense to the business.

A non-business-related experience I had that brings the point of "nicety or necessity" home was with a young married couple who were friends of mine. They were going through the iteration of trying to reduce their expenditure levels to save extra money because they had learned that they could expect the arrival of their first child in six months. I suggested that the couple carefully document and review how they spent their money for three months and determine which expenditures were necessities and which might be considered niceties.

They had some heated arguments regarding some of their ongoing expenditures. They found that they spent a lot of money in the following areas:

They saw many new films as soon as they were released and at the movie theaters.

They ate dinner at restaurants at least four or five times each week.

Both of them worked, and they went out to restaurants for lunch every work day.

He bought several magazines each month at the grocery store, and she thought he did not always read them.

She had her nails and hair done professionally each week.

He got a haircut every two weeks.

They both had health club memberships at different clubs near where they worked.

The hair and nail appointments, haircuts, magazines, and restaurant lunches did not seem that expensive to the couple—until they looked at what it cost them over the period of an entire year. The husband suggested that his wife should have her nails done less frequently or try doing them herself. The husband also suggested that she cut her hair, or get a permanent to reduce the need to go to the hairdresser each week. The areas the wife targeted as niceties instead of necessities in her husband's spending habits were the magazines she thought he did not read, and his purchase of lunch from restaurants every day when at work; she also thought he should consider buying a haircutting kit so he could trim his sideburns and clean the back of his neck to enable him to go to the barber/hair stylist less frequently.

The husband agreed to buy fewer magazines and get yearly subscriptions for his favorite magazines instead of buying them at the grocery store, which was a good savings. He also agreed to prepare his lunch at home and take it to work at least three times each week, which was also a good savings. Lastly, he agreed to buy a haircutting kit so he would not have to get his hair cut as often. The wife agreed to take her lunch to work at least three times each week, and she encouraged some of her work friends to do the same thing.

The couple agreed to change the frequency with which they saw new movies at the theaters. Instead, they began renting DVDs after the movies were released for sale or rental to watch them at home. They concluded that when their baby arrived, they would not be able to go to the movie theaters for a while anyway, so they could get used to watching the films at home. Because they liked watching movies so much, they eventually decided to get unlimited DVDs for viewing on their television from the major company offering that service for a monthly fee. This saved even more, plus it had the convenience of having the DVDs mailed to their home. Later, the couple started using a service that allowed them to view unlimited movies with a system attached to their television, so receiving and exchanging DVDs through the mail was no longer necessary.

They also decided to reduce the frequency with which they ate dinner out at restaurants. The movies and restaurant dinners were often on the same night. They agreed to drop both of their health club memberships, and to walk and work out at home instead.

Once the couple became accustomed to the cost-cutting changes, they were happy with the savings and were proud of themselves. By the way, the wife kept getting her hair and nails done each week. No surprise there, because that was an absolute necessity for her. Once the baby arrived, they went through the "necessity or nicety" iteration a few additional times to determine where they could cut some more costs.

A recent experience I had relates to the subject of "necessity or nicety." It reminds me of the old saying about beauty being in the eye of the beholder; necessity is also in the eye of the beholder. I will recall this experience for the rest of my life. Two of my good old friends have vineyards on their property and they make wine. They conduct wine tasting and evaluating parties to see which of their wines people like the best. On one such occasion, they had 18 people tasting and evaluating eight different varieties of their wine. Because the test is a "blind" test, they cover the label on each bottle by placing a number over each label. When my friends asked the group to evaluate (rank) bottle number 1, they asked how many people ranked it as their favorite wine of the eight tasted, and six people raised their hands. When they asked how many people ranked bottle number 1 as their least favorite wine of the eight tasted, six people raised their hands. If that response does not prove that beauty (or good wine in this instance) is in the eye of the beholder, nothing will.

On one project for a private university that was having severe cash flow problems, I was assigned to be the vice president of finance and administration on an interim basis. I had already managed a successful cost-reduction project for the organization.

All university employees, including faculty and administration, were informed of the cash flow problems and asked to be more careful about expenditures. My duties mainly consisted of reviewing how much money the university received each day, and approving expenditures based on the need and cash available. In addition, I reviewed every purchase requisition and funds request. Following the "nicety or necessity" philosophy, I approved and processed only requests that I knew were vital and refused all other requests. I figured that if the expenditures were really needed, the requestors would fight for them. When faculty members and administrators occasionally fought for their expenditure requests, it gave me the opportunity to discuss their requests, and sometimes they won the fight, but mostly I won.

After seeing numerous requests for various types of office supplies, I borrowed a method I learned from a consulting boss I had years before, which was to open all the desk drawers in each office to see how many pens, pencils, pads of paper, and other supplies were there. (You may want to try this step at your business if your cost-cutting needs are great.) It is universally believed that most employees take some office supplies home from their employer for personal use. That was also probably the case at this university. The review of the contents of desks yielded more than enough office supplies to preclude the need to purchase them for more than a year. We allocated what were believed to be adequate supplies for each department, and put all the excess in the Finance Department to be distributed later, as necessary, when requested by departments.

5.4 PRODUCT DEVELOPMENT AND DESIGN

By designing your products to be made as cost-efficiently as possible, be safe for consumers, and have little likelihood of requiring repair or replacement during their warranty period, you will avoid unnecessary costs. Of course, this is more difficult for businesses that manufacture potentially "dangerous" products with explosive components, such as a business that manufactures air-bag detonators.

I attended a new-product planning session for a footwear manufacturer that had a goal of making improvements to its process. After some productive discussion, it was noted that it cost the same amount of time and money to develop a "loser" (not likely to be a high-sales-volume or profit-making product) as a "winner" (likely to be a high-sales-volume and profit-making product). Each year the business developed the same number of new models of shoes. Company personnel agreed that their experience had enabled them to determine which products would likely be "winners" and "losers," but they went ahead and developed the losers anyway, because they believed they always needed to introduce a certain number of new products. In some cases, the only differences between a "winner" and a "loser" were the materials or colors used. The business decided to utilize a focus group of good customers to help make the final decisions regarding which products to develop and introduce each year. This proved to be a great cost-avoidance method for the business.

5.5 PRODUCT LIABILITY

This topic goes hand in hand with the previous section regarding product development and design. Generally, you should try to avoid product-liability problems that could lead to legal costs and damage your business's image by designing and producing safe products. You should also assure you are not infringing on patents before developing products for sale.

Include documentation and labels regarding the proper use of your products (e.g., do's, don'ts, and warnings). It is very important that these disclaimers be thorough and worded properly. Even makers of products that you might think of as harmless, such as stuffed dolls and animals, have been involved in product liability lawsuits because of the stuffing material or plastic wrapping used. Your disclaimers will help you prevent lawsuits, but you cannot be certain they will stop such litigation altogether. Because of this risk, you need to obtain the proper product liability insurance to prevent or limit your financial exposure should you lose a lawsuit.

Train your customer service employees how to respond to customer complaints on the telephone. Some basic guidelines are provided here:

Listen carefully.

Obviously, if a customer indicates that someone was injured or even died using one of your products, or the customer threatens a lawsuit, the problem needs to be handled by your resident expert at resolving such matters as quickly as possible.

Write down all the customer's comments.

As you listen, try to determine what the customer wants done to resolve the situation.

Remain as courteous as possible during a conversation with the customer.

If one or more individuals in the business are specially trained to talk with customers who have a potentially serious problem, transfer the customer to one of those individuals, or ensure the customer receives a speedy callback.

Be very careful what you say and commit to doing.

Do not promise anything over the telephone or via email aside from promising that someone who could better deal with the customer's concerns will call the customer back as soon as possible.

It is more of an art than a science to determine how to respond to each customer complaint. You want to correct all problems fairly and at the least cost, as well as avoid potential lawsuits if possible. Free products, repairs, or service (even for certain out-of-warranty products) may be justified and the prudent action to take to avoid litigation.

There may be instances when your business believes it must face and fight a lawsuit in court to resolve a product liability issue rather than settle the problem in other ways if it reaches that point. The company may deem that winning such a case may help it avoid future similar lawsuits, or at least will help the business determine how best to handle similar possible future situations.

5.6 DETERMINE THE EFFECTIVENESS OF YOUR MARKETING AND ADVERTISING

You have possibly heard people half-jokingly (and half-truthfully) say that they knew that half of their advertising budget was worthwhile, but they did not know which half. Performing surveys, using focus groups, and soliciting feedback from the buyers of your goods or services can help you understand what the major motivators are for them when making buying decisions. This information includes in which publications buyers saw your products and what influenced them to buy one of your products. If the feedback is fairly consistent among various buyers, it should help you with future marketing and advertising decisions and strategies.

One thing some companies do to create sales that can cloud the issue of what motivated the sale is to employ push and pull incentives at the same time. If discounts or added benefits are offered to customers as buying incentives, and sales incentives such as bonuses or higher commissions are offered to the sales staff at the same time, you may not know for certain which incentives worked. Generally, it is best to use these incentives separately instead of together.

I am not professing to be an expert in marketing or advertising, but you probably understand what I am saying you should strive to do.

5.7 PREVENTIVE MAINTENANCE

The following sayings are applicable to preventive maintenance programs:

"A stitch in time saves nine."

"An ounce of prevention is worth a pound of cure."

"Spend a dime now instead of a dollar later."

Develop a preventive maintenance (PM) plan for all your key equipment (expensive and/or vital for production) and for your facilities. The main benefits of a PM program for key equipment include minimizing down time due to unscheduled maintenance and reducing long-term repair costs. Where feasible, train and assign certain equipment PM tasks to be performed by the applicable machine operators.

Some PM can be safely performed even while the equipment is running, such as maintaining proper oil levels; however, most PM tasks require equipment to be shut off. I have seen machine operators who produced parts on multiple machines and, depending on which types of parts were being produced, performed PM tasks on one machine as the other machines ran, as long as those machines did not require their constant attention. In contrast, for certain major equipment that requires several consecutive days of PM each year, the organization may consider scheduling a plant shutdown and vacation for all employees except those performing the PM activities.

From the parking lots to the roofs, consider all areas where a PM plan will save money in the long run. Have a supply of key parts on hand to avoid down time of critical equipment, unless you know you can get those parts very quickly from a supplier. Develop a PM plan for both your owned facilities and leased facilities if you are responsible for their maintenance; this could include manufacturing plants, warehouses, and offices. Remember the old advertisement quote: "Pay me now or pay me later."

5.8 SERVICE AND MAINTENANCE AGREEMENTS

Evaluate the possible advantages of service and maintenance agreements. Negotiate for long-term free or low-cost service and maintenance when purchasing new equipment or computer systems, because that is when you have the most negotiating strength for these items.

Review your history of paying for service and maintenance, and compare the annual cost of a service and maintenance agreement with the estimated cost of paying for service and maintenance as you need it. Some things to consider include these issues:

Are there minimum charges for a service call?

What are the hourly rates charged for service calls and repairs?

Is there a charge for travel time?

Are parts included with repairs?

Is labor included?

One advantage that you have with a service or maintenance agreement is a more predictable budget. Some businesses have service and maintenance agreements that provide free labor and parts to repair certain types of equipment, provided you purchase the supplies used for the equipment from the supplier. For example, with label printers, the supplier may provide free service and print heads if you purchase the labels from that business. However, some businesses believe it to be more cost-effective overall to buy labels at a lower price from another supplier and to pay for maintenance and service on an as-needed basis.

This is another topic I will not cover in much depth. You must determine which equipment and systems should be evaluated to determine whether service or maintenance agreements are feasible and what your best course of action is.

5.9 DO NOT OVERREACT TO CERTAIN SITUATIONS

Sometimes an unnecessarily costly practice originates from overreacting to a specific situation or problem in the past. An example is a business that used far too much tape to seal its packing cartons. According to the employees who packed the products, this practice resulted from a few isolated customer complaints that had reached the ear of the business's president several years before. Some cartons had been over-packed with heavy items, and the cartons had burst open, spilling and damaging the products. As a result, the president required that employees use 24 or more strips of 2-inch-wide packing tape to close the shipping cartons. Instead of overreacting to this situation, the proper course of action would have been to carefully analyze the situation and evaluate various remedies to fix the problem. After determining that the taping procedures were costly and not necessary if employees were trained to pack cartons properly, we convinced the business's president that it was acceptable to use 3-inch-wide packing tape and only 2 to a maximum of 6 strips of tape per carton.

The unnecessary overreaction had cost the client considerable time, labor, and materials over a period of years until we convinced it to make the change, which corrected the situation.

Another overreaction was the client that produced Styrofoam packaging for one of the United States' largest fast-food chains. Due to a one-time customer complaint about the cartons being flimsy and under standard, the plant manager decided to make all the cartons thicker. The one-time problem had been the result of an isolated bad production run, and one roll of rejected Styrofoam that was too thin and was used by mistake. The quality control manager could not convince the plant manager that the problem had been an anomaly and was corrected. Although the extra thickness resulted in the use of only a few more grams of Styrofoam per carton, the amount of material added up quickly due to the millions of cartons made each week. The problem was exacerbated because the plant manager decided to make all of the business's products with this added thickness, such as its egg cartons, avocado trays, and meat trays (used in the meat departments of supermarkets).

Do not overreact and "throw people at a problem" without first determining whether productivity could be increased instead of adding more personnel or labor hours. Also, make certain you go back and review a situation/problem you felt you needed to throw people at to ensure it is not a permanent situation.

Following are some words of wisdom on the subject by James B. Ayers:

Forsake "Whack-a-Mole"

There is a game for children and those who want to be children called "Whack-a-mole." Found at carnivals and charity events, the player guesses from which of several holes the "mole" will appear. The player gets points if he or she is quick enough to hammer the mole before it ducks underground.

Many executives play a similar "game" when it comes to cost control. Like "Whack-a-mole," the so-called "management" approach is totally reactive. A cost goes out of bounds somewhere; the executive team whacks the cost like the child wielding his or her hammer. The "hammer" in this case is usually a short-term mandate to lower the costs under question—across the board reductions, travel cuts, more approval levels for expenditures, delayed hiring, called-off conferences, an overtime freeze, and other discretionary cost reduction. Such pressure is driven by management mandates to "meet the numbers."

What is missing is an understanding of the root cause for whatever cost has poked its head out of the mole hole. This short-term cost cutting fails to address the root causes that are at work. B addressing root causes can include, among other things, cost a____ ing that hides the root cause and management failure to recognize that costs are a consequence of process design or execution. As such, it is the process that needs management attention, not the symptoms in the form of costs.

Breaking free of the Whack-a-mole game requires adopting a "process-centered" paradigm, and forsaking the "budget-centric" paradigm. The first step is identifying the processes needed to keep the company going and assigning costs to those processes. This is done easily using current budgets built around the organization structure. The approach enables the organization to move from reactive to proactive by enabling decision-makers to look past budgets toward the health of company processes. This attention should lead to real, lasting cost reduction without sacrificing service to customers.

5.10 PROMOTE SAFETY

Working safely is an obvious area where you can avoid unnecessary costs. Employers and employees are responsible for maintaining a healthful and safe work environment according to federal and state Occupational Safety and Health Administration (OSHA) guidelines. If you do not have one, implement an illness and injury prevention program to ensure your business is working safely and in compliance with OSHA requirements. Establish a Safety Committee, and appoint one employee to administer the safety program. Consider retaining a consultant experienced in implementing illness and injury prevention programs to help you meet OSHA requirements and develop procedures for maintaining the program in proper compliance.

Develop and publish a list of health, housekeeping, and safety rules for each facility. See the following pages for a list of items to consider for inclusion in a list of these rules for your business.

Items to Consider for a List of Health, Housekeeping and Safety Rules

General Safety Rules

Do not block exit doors, roll-up doors, aisles, fire extinguishers, electrical panels, meters, or traffic lanes.

Be careful when near employees who are operating a forklift or electric cart, especially at corners of aisles and doorways.

Do not stack cases of product more than 12 feet high on the floor.

In case of an emergency that requires evacuating the building, such as a fire or earthquake, use common sense and walk quickly (do not run) to and out the closest safe exit.

Do not stand pallets on their sides, because they could fall over and injure someone.

Always turn off the power source and follow lock-out/block-out procedures when machinery is being repaired.

Lifting Safety

Avoid risk of injury when lifting, pulling, or pushing.

If possible, avoid lifting alone anything that weighs more than 50 pounds.

If you believe something is too large or heavy to move alone, ask for help.

Use the correct lifting technique. Stand with your feet apart, squat with knees bent, tuck in your chin, grasp the object securely with both hands, keep your back as straight as possible, and slowly push up with your legs.

Use equipment or movable stairs when reaching for an item that is over your head.

If using movable stairs, lock them into place prior to climbing on them.

Safety Hazards, Accidents, and Injuries

Report unsafe conditions, accidents, and injuries, no matter how minor, to your supervisor immediately.

Housekeeping

Throw trash in cans and boxes provided for that purpose.

Keep the restrooms clean.

Inform your supervisor if the restroom needs to be cleaned or needs supplies.

Do not spit on the floor, because someone could slip and fall.

Do not eat or drink at your workstation. Spilling coffee, tea, soda, and water is a major cause of costly damage to personal computers.

No smoking inside the buildings.

Operating Material-Handling Equipment (e.g., forklift t.
pickers, reach trucks, electric pallet jacks, electric carts)

Drive equipment only if you are licensed to do so.

Drivers must carry their license with them to operate equipment.

Inspect your equipment at the start of your shift to assure it is safe. This is especially true for equipment with brakes, which you can test carefully without operating it in such a way that you could cause an accident.

If you do not have one, develop a vehicle checklist and require employees to complete it as part of their daily inspection.

• Report any unsafe equipment to your supervisor immediately.

Always use the seat belt on sit-down equipment or the safety belt on stand-up equipment.

Do not let riders on your equipment.

Do not stand on the forks of forklift trucks or pallet jacks.

Keep your arms, body, and legs safely in or on the equipment.

Always be alert for pedestrians.

Do not ever drive faster than a safe speed.

Be careful not to damage company property, such as racking and walls.

Be careful not to damage products, such as by putting a fork hole in a carton. Some businesses penalize employees when they do so, especially if expensive product is also damaged by the fork.

Report any damage immediately if and when it occurs.

Look in the direction you are traveling.

Drive in reverse if the load blocks your vision when you drive forward.

Sound the horn as you approach corners, in tunnels through racking, at ends of aisles, and before traveling through roll-up doors.

For propane-powered equipment, when changing propane tanks, be certain the valve connection is tight. If you smell propane, shut off the engine. If it is not a tight connection and you cannot tighten it, change the propane tank.

For electric equipment, be careful not to under-fill or over-fill the water in batteries when they need to be filled.

Keep the forks of forklift trucks as low as possible.

Move a load only when it is secure.

When leaving equipment unattended, shut off the power and set the brakes.

Ergonomics is an area that has received more attention in recent years, including from OSHA. Following is an excerpt from an OSHA article regarding ergonomics:

Ergonomics is the science of fitting workplace conditions and job demands to the capabilities of the working population. Effective and successful "fits" assure high productivity, avoidance of illness and injury risks, and increased satisfaction among the workforce. Although the scope of ergonomics is much broader, the term here refers to assessing those work-related factors that may pose a risk of musculoskeletal disorders and recommendations to alleviate them. Common examples of ergonomic risk factors are found in jobs requiring repetitive, forceful, or prolonged exertions of the hands; frequent or heavy lifting, pushing, pulling, or carrying of heavy objects; and prolonged awkward postures. Vibration and cold may add risk to these work conditions. Jobs or working conditions presenting multiple risk factors will have a higher probability of causing a musculoskeletal problem. The level of risk depends on the intensity, frequency, and duration of the exposure to these conditions. Environmental work conditions that affect risk include intensity, frequency and duration of activities.[1]

Many businesses are aggressively pursuing ergonomic improvements to help workers perform their jobs more easily and prevent injury. A few examples include adjustable-height workbenches so workers of different heights do not have to bend or reach as much to work on a product being made; special computer keyboards to prevent carpal tunnel syndrome; chairs that enable a worker to easily adjust the height so the worker's feet can touch the floor; and cushioning gloves to use when performing work with a tool that vibrates a lot.

Contact OSHA and request the required forms and guidelines regarding compliance measures. This information is free, and I have been assured that asking for it will not trigger an audit. If you are not in compliance with OSHA requirements, in the extreme, OSHA could shut down your operation if it finds major problems during an audit, which is an unscheduled inspection check.

Provide initial safety education and training to newly hired employees prior to beginning work. Provide ongoing education and training to all existing employees regarding working safely, including conducting monthly safety meetings for all employees (one of the OSHA requirements). Expand the definition of safety to include the following one I developed years ago: "You do not get hurt, your coworkers do not get hurt, the products do not get hurt, the equipment does not get hurt, and the facility does not get hurt."

Whenever I conducted monthly safety meetings as part of an illness and injury prevention program consulting assignment, I always had eight large candy bars with me. I used the candy bars as rewards when employees answered safety-related questions I asked. Questions included, "What is one of the main safety concerns at this facility?" (I asked this question until all concerns had been identified) and "What is our definition of safety?" (the answer to that appears in the previous paragraph). The first person to raise his or her hand and answer a question correctly was given a candy bar. On one occasion, an employee came up with a safety concern I had not thought of, so I did not have a candy bar for her. I did not have a dollar bill with me, so she won $5 for that answer. These rewards helped get the employees' attention and responses.

The key education and training areas regarding health, safety, and housekeeping depend on your type of business. Manufacturing operations and businesses that use and/or produce hazardous materials obviously have more areas of concern than a warehouse or distribution operation with nonhazardous materials. Following is an open-ended list of education and training areas for you to use as a starting point:

Forklift driving training and rules, followed by testing and licensing operators

Proper lifting techniques

Using appropriate guardrails on equipment

Emergency evacuation procedures, including understanding the posted floor plan layouts throughout the facility indicating the locations of all exits and pointing out the closest exit to each posted floor plan

Handling and disposal of hazardous materials

Stacking and storage of product and supplies

CPR and first-aid procedures

Fire extinguisher training (This training should be provided at no cost by the supplier of your fire extinguishers, and it is helpful for your home protection as well. You hope you never have to use any of your fire extinguishers, but you need to have your employees trained in case they are needed.)

Ergonomics and training to prevent repetitive motion injuries

How lost time, work-related injuries, and worker's compensation claims cost the company, and could even rule out pay increases— which will get employees' attention

Perform routine health, safety, and housekeeping inspections using the following guidelines:

Assign individuals to inspect areas other than their own.

Monthly or more frequent inspections are recommended.

Generate a report of inspection findings.

Provide immediate feedback regarding problem findings emanating from a safety inspection to the appropriate manager, and send a copy of the report to the safety committee leader.

Discuss corrective actions taken at the next safety committee meeting.

Consider giving group incentive rewards for working safely and without lost work-time injury accidents. This provides peer support/pressure.

Display the number of days without a lost work-time injury where it is visible to everyone, such as on a safety bulletin board or at the main entrance to the facility. Rewards for the entire facility working safely without accidents should become progressively larger through at least a one-year period. After one year, determine how to proceed. The rewards could continue to be greater, or you could start anew.

Incentive rewards could begin with something like free doughnuts at break time one day after the first month with no accidents and continuing for three months, free beverages and doughnuts one day after the fourth month with no accidents and continuing for three months, free lunch one day each month on the seventh month through the 12th month, cash prize drawings for one to three employees each month after one year, and so on. Yes, you are right about me being big on using doughnuts as a reward. The cost justification of rewards is easy to see if you keep in mind the cost and problems associated with a lost work-time injury accident.

Investigate and challenge "questionable" worker's compensation claims. At one client's warehouse facility, we analyzed the tangible and intangible costs associated with a minor injury accident that occurred while we were there. A forklift driver was injured when stacking show booths crated in plywood containers that were 4 feet wide by 8 feet long by 6 feet high. While stacking one container on top of the other, the driver struck a hanging overhead fluorescent light fixture, which broke, and a piece of falling glass slightly cut his head.

The accident was a distraction, resulting in nine employees coming to see what happened.

The cleanup of the broken fluorescent bulb took time and effort.

The injured employee's supervisor drove him to and from the company's urgent care provider, which took 3 hours total. The employee had to go back for a checkup in 3 workdays, then again one week later.

You can see that this minor injury resulted in the loss of a great deal of time and money.

5.11 SECURITY MEASURES

Security policies and procedures can range from fairly simple and inexpensive measures to very comprehensive and expensive measures depending on the value of your business's products, raw materials, information, facilities, and equipment. At a minimum, security policies and measures should include restrictions on who has keys to your business's facilities and who is responsible for unlocking and locking the doors each day. Progressively stronger security policies and measures can include the following measures:

Installing a surveillance system to record the activities occurring in potential problem areas

Purchasing an alarm system that sounds whenever an emergency door or window that should not be opened is opened

Using internal security guards or an outside guard service

Restricting access to certain areas so only specifically authorized personnel enter those areas

Assigning two employees to work as a team for a check and balance to inspect all incoming and outgoing shipments

Providing security access codes for restricting employees to view or use certain computer screens and data

These security measures are just reminders of some that your business may want to implement.

NOTE

1. http://www.osha.gov/SLTC/ergonomics/

6

Selected Cost-Cutting Areas

6.1 RAW MATERIALS AND PURCHASED PARTS

Your procurement or sourcing staff must take the lead in the area of reducing the cost of purchased raw materials, products (e.g., for resale), and parts. Obtaining goods and services at favorable prices is part of the procurement staff's regular functions. However, when a business is conducting a cost-cutting program and the procurement staff is tasked with obtaining even better prices from suppliers, they are generally successful.

You can get cost-cutting results from the following actions:

Negotiating for better prices from current suppliers.

Negotiating for better prices from potential new suppliers.

Obtaining substitute products from current suppliers. A substitute product must adequately provide the same exact function, but at a lower cost.

Obtaining substitute products from potential new suppliers.

The bottom line is that you want to lower the unit costs of all the raw materials, parts, and products you purchase. This should not be just a goal that is part of the cost-cutting program; rather, it should become an ongoing goal year after year.

Your first efforts should focus on your high-volume purchased raw materials, products, and parts. Your next efforts should be with your high-cost purchased raw materials, products, and parts.

Many businesses now rely on international sourcing and importing goods from other countries to obtain overall lower costs. Several things other than the product cost must be reviewed when considering importing goods from other countries, including the lead times required, freight costs, any import duties, control factors, and, of course, quality.

No matter how small or large your business is, but especially with large businesses, you may want to get senior management or officers involved in negotiations with their counterpart senior management or officers from certain key high-volume and high-cost suppliers. This action should be taken only when the procurement staff believe they have done all they can possibly do to obtain lower prices. I have personally seen how effective it can be when a business's senior executive (usually the president) becomes involved in negotiating with a supplier's senior executive.

As previously mentioned in the book, negotiating with suppliers of goods and services is one of the most important things—if not *the* most important thing—you can do to cut costs. If you remember and apply only a few recommendations from this book, it must be included as one of them.

6.2 INSIDE VERSUS OUTSIDE SERVICES

Analyze service functions as you would analyze "buy versus make" decisions, and decide if you want to perform them in-house or have them performed by an outside service. You may decide that certain services should be performed partly or completely inside, or, conversely, that some services should be partially or completely performed by an outside business. When you decide to use one or more outside services, you must designate an appropriate employee to assume the responsibility of monitoring the relationships with each of the outside services.

Examples of service areas to consider include the following:

Janitorial functions. Some businesses choose to perform some of the daily functions in-house, including daily cleaning of restrooms and stocking of restroom supplies, but may decide to have an outside service perform major functions such as floor cleaning (e.g., waxing and carpet vacuuming) and window washing.

Security functions. Security functions may include guards stationed at your entrance and exit doors, and at other selected locations in your facilities, as well as manning monitoring cameras located at strategic locations to prevent pilferage or theft from employees and/or outsiders.

Printing. Printing requirements include brochures, price lists, product information inserts, and other documents. You may want to use in-house printing capability to produce certain less complicated documents that require black printing on white or colored paper, or that require quick turnaround. You may determine that hiring an outside printer is economically feasible when you need to print high-volume documents and more complicated documents involving color printing, artwork, or special paper.

Design of marketing and advertising materials. Desktop publishing software with graphics capabilities lends itself to performing some of these functions in-house. You may have inside marketing employees with skills who can design certain less complicated company publications such as price lists, but then choose to have an outside supplier design more complex and artistic publications such as brochures. As you can see, this function goes hand-in-hand with your printing requirements.

Landscaping and gardening, both inside and outside your facilities. You may want an outside gardener to maintain your facility grounds if they are large, and you may have an in-house gardener to care for the plants inside the facility. Of course, if you are in need of deep cost-cutting measures, you may simplify your gardening requirements and reduce the costs associated with them—for example, by making your gardening requirements as simple and low maintenance as possible, and by having fewer (or no) flowers and plants both outside and inside the facility.

Payroll processing. Payroll processing includes working with your employees to arrange for direct bank deposits of paychecks for those workers who desire that payment method, generating checks for employees who want them, calculating deductions, sending deducted tax funds to state and federal agencies, and preparing payroll reports for management.

Order entry and customer service. These functions include communications via telephone and/or the Internet. This area has caused some businesses problems when they outsourced order entry and customer service, especially to foreign countries. Due to excessive customer complaints, certain businesses either changed from employees in a foreign country to outside businesses in the United States, or else brought the entire functions back in-house. Be cautious when cutting costs in this area. You may have in-house order entry and customer service for your higher-priced and more complicated products, but outsource order entry and customer service for your simpler, less complicated, and less costly products. You can imagine how such a split system would create difficulties when a customer needs assistance with both types of products. Make certain your changes in this area make sense for your business.

Using common carrier truck lines or contract trucks and drivers rather than having your own fleet of trucks and drivers. This opportunity mainly applies to medium-size and large businesses. If your business needs to make many local area pickups for raw materials, supplies, or products, as well as deliveries of products to outside processors or customers on short notice, especially on the same day, you may choose to have your own truck(s) and driver(s) perform these functions. After analyzing your options regarding whether an in-house or outside service is best for you, you may determine it is less costly to use a freight carrier and/or a local area delivery service, or small package carrier to perform these pickup and delivery functions. You could assign someone in your accounting department to perform a simple feasibility analysis to determine which method is the best option.

Manufacturer's representatives versus your own sales force. Some businesses decide to use manufacturer's representatives exclusively to sell their products, while others use a combination of both their own sales force and manufacturer's representatives. One possible problem resulting from using a combination of manufacturers' representatives and your own sales force can be avoided by establishing very clear guidelines regarding who gets sales credit for specific overlapping geographic areas. You want to avoid costly duplicate credit for such sales and other kinds of disputes, which can be done through the wording on a contractual agreement with the manufacturer's representatives. One business chose to use a combination of manufacturer's representatives and its own sales force, which turned out to be disastrous. The business sold its products all over the continental United States. Its customers included large specialty retail dealers, small "Mom and Pop" stores, and pharmacies. Only the larger specialty retail dealers received discounts from the business, but the small customers could receive a small discount if they paid their invoices within 30 days. Obviously, the latter were considered "ideal" customers and were very profitable for the business. The manufacturer's representatives received a discount almost as great as the large specialty retail dealers. The company's expectation was that the business's own sales force would continue selling to the large specialty retail dealers and small "Mom and Pop" stores and pharmacies in the larger urban areas, and the manufacturer's representatives would sell in the more remote geographic areas to the small stores and pharmacies. Because the contractual agreements with the manufacturer's representatives were not worded properly, they started selling to the small "Mom and Pop" stores and pharmacies in the urban areas, in competition with the business's own sales representatives. Because they received a discount almost as great as the business's large specialty retail dealers, the manufacturer's representatives were able to "steal" away many of the "ideal" customers by offering them discounts that were greater than the discount they received for paying their invoices on time. Once they were used to receiving the larger discounts, they would never be satisfied with the small discount offered by the business. This was a contributing factor to the business eventually failing. Another thing to consider is that many manufacturer's representatives also sell for other businesses, so they do not use all their time selling on your behalf, and they may even work for some of your competitors.

Production of certain products that require hazardous material handling and cleanup. With these functions, such as painting and metal plating operations, it may make more sense to contract with an outside business.

Processing of mass mailings. It should be easy to determine the cost and difficulties associated with handling such mailings in-house versus having the function performed by an outside service.

Performing selected maintenance functions for equipment and facilities. Outside services are more likely to be retained to perform work on major equipment such as large machines, trucks, material handling equipment, and large facilities.

Whether it is scheduled or nonscheduled maintenance, an outside service is preferable or necessary when your in-house expertise is lacking.

Using contract software programmers and selected other IT functions versus having full-time regular programmers and other pertinent staff. It is especially valuable to consider using an outside service when the work will last for only a relatively short period of time, such as programming modifications to a new software system. Outsourcing such tasks avoids the possibility of hiring and later firing in-house programmers.

Recruiting employees using executive search consultants to narrow the list of candidates, or having your Human Resources Department staff do the recruiting. With the use of the Internet to assist with the recruitment of new employees, especially employees performing specialized functions, conducting the search in-house may be feasible. If the internal effort is unsuccessful, you can always retain outside recruiters.

Using outside consultants and contract employees for special projects. The reasons for using outside consultants have already been discussed in the book.

Using outside legal assistance versus having in-house counsel. Unless your business requires fairly routine ongoing legal assistance, it is usually more economical to use outside legal assistance on an as-needed basis.

Using a third-party logistics/distribution company (3PL), including those having their own warehouses and employees. Another option is retaining a 3PL to manage your employees in your own facilities.

Freight bill pre-audit/paying versus using your accounting staff to perform this function. A good freight bill pre-audit business can be very cost-effective for businesses with high volumes of freight bills. The cost to pay each freight bill through an outside service can be less than paying these bills in-house, and outside services are more likely to find and obtain credit for incorrect charges.

Using public warehousing versus your owned or leased facilities. This option might apply whether you have one main facility or you have decentralized facilities all around the country.

Production of some or all products. Some businesses may decide to produce certain easy-to-make products in-house and have complex products made outside, while other companies may do just the opposite. Of course, a key factor is the ability to maintain adequate quality levels.

Customs broker services. If and when you begin importing and/or exporting high volumes of products, you should initially use a customs broker. Later you could hire an experienced person, or have someone inside the business trained to perform this function.

Some service functions that have been performed internally for many years may have become very costly due to a maturing workforce, resulting in high employee wages. An outside service may be able to provide the service more cost-effectively. Conversely, if the service does not require a high skill level, hiring internal employees at low hourly wages may be more cost-effective than continuing to use an outside service.

As previously mentioned, competitive pressures and financial considerations have resulted in numerous American businesses contracting out their manufacturing functions to businesses outside the United States. Favorite manufacturing sites include Mexico and offshore, mainly Asian countries, due to their less expensive labor costs.

When the costs of performing certain services inside versus outside are similar, weigh other factors, such as the hassle, control issues, and quality when determining whether to outsource manufacturing or services. As with all analyses of whether to use an outside service or perform the same service in-house, you should first consider all the costs associated with each method, as well as other nonfinancial issues, both positive and negative (e.g., if you perform the function in-house, you have greater control; however, this effort may be more hassle than you believe it is worth).

6.3 TEMPORARY PLANT SHUTDOWNS

For years, many businesses have had a policy and practice of regularly scheduling annual temporary plant shutdowns. As mentioned earlier, this has been particularly true for businesses that have a lot of equipment requiring major annual preventive maintenance. It can also apply to businesses that have a large mature workforce of employees eligible for several weeks of vacation each year. The shutdown can take care of one or two weeks of vacation, which would make scheduling additional vacation time much easier without adversely impacting production requirements.

During periods of low demand for products resulting in excessive inventories, temporary plant shutdowns may make good sense for some businesses to help them reduce inventory. This was the case for some American auto manufacturers during the downturn of demand during the recession that began in 2008–2009.

6.4 RELOCATIONS, ACQUISITIONS, AND CONSOLIDATIONS

Under certain circumstances, including mergers, acquisitions, and when a business loses its lease, facility relocations or consolidations may be deemed cost-effective, provide better controls, improve customer service, and increase productivity. Almost certainly, whenever there is an acquisition or merger of two businesses, there are opportunities to streamline some departments and functions. As with many changes, a relocation or consolidation of facilities may be a fairly simple activity for some businesses; for other businesses that have a large number of facilities, it may be complex and challenging. In either case, if positive cost benefits can be determined, the effort will be worthwhile. Most businesses that grew by making acquisitions of other businesses within the same general business sector have determined that a consolidation of the various entities and facilities would be more cost-effective than keeping them separate.

Relocations may be deemed feasible if the result in less expensive facilities costs, fewer employees, or a lower-paid workforce. In addition, if relocation results in being closer to the majority of suppliers and/or customers, transportation costs will be decreased. Likewise, lead times to obtain raw materials and component parts, and the delivery time and cost to ship products to customers will be reduced.

Relocation Examples

I was involved in the following examples of relocations that included a physical move of facilities and outsourcing of the manufacturing of some products to offshore operations.

The first example involved a relocation of a business from Southern California to Missouri, with the expectations of lower hourly labor costs, lower facility costs, lower distribution costs, and decreased delivery times to customers, because most of the company's customers were located east of the Mississippi. I tell this story because it is a good example of both the positives and the negatives that can result from a business's relocation.

The business manufactured and distributed durable medical equipment products all over the United States. The products included hospital beds, home-care beds, wheelchairs, oxygen concentrators, walkers, and canes. All these products were manufactured and shipped from the company headquarters, which was located in Southern California. Finished goods were shipped directly to customers in the western United States, and replacement/service parts were sent to customers nationwide. Finished goods bound for the nonwestern United States were shipped to distribution centers (DCs) located in Texas, Illinois, New Jersey, and Georgia; the DCs, in turn, sent the products to customers in their respective geographic areas. The business was non-union, but it had a costly workforce of senior hourly workers because many had been with the business for more than 20 years.

As part of this relocation, the business decided to source chrome-plated component parts and most assembled wheelchairs from Indonesia. The chrome-plated products had become problematic due to environmental issues and rising costs to manufacture them or outsource them in Southern California. Approximately 72 percent of the business's revenue came from wheelchairs, and 87 percent of the cost of each wheelchair was attributable to the chrome-plated components. The other components were vinyl upholstery, vinyl-padded leg rests and armrests, wheels, rubber tires, and miscellaneous fasteners (e.g., screws, nuts, and bolts).

Specific anticipated annualized cost savings were to reduce labor costs by 34 percent, reduce facility costs by 60 percent, and reduce distribution costs by 27 percent, for a total of $2.6 million in savings per year. There was also a one-time $500,000 incentive paid to the business from the state of Missouri for the relocation there.

The relocation was not without problems, partly because of the move to Missouri and partly because of the manufacturing of chrome-plated products from Indonesia. Some of the lessons learned the hard way by this business may help your business avoid similar problems.

Inadequate quality control of chrome-plated products from Indonesia resulted in component parts not being properly identified or properly loaded in the 40-foot ocean containers in which they were shipped. The improper loading of component chrome-plated parts created scratched surfaces and led to scrapping of more than 20 percent of the contents of the first five containers. The chrome plating quality was excellent, but many of the component parts were out of tolerance, making it difficult or impossible to assemble the finished product. An acceptable compensation agreement was reached with the manufacturer due to the quality problems. These quality problems were eventually corrected, and the short-term shortage of chrome-plated parts did not result in many late customer order shipments.

Two employees were assigned to work in Indonesia for one year to ensure the quality problems were resolved. Arguably, this step should have been taken in the first place to prevent the problems from ever happening. One employee concentrated on the quality issues by developing procedures, conducted training, and then monitored implementation of the procedures to ensure they were followed and would continue to be followed. The other employee worked on procedures related to properly identifying component parts and loading and packing them in the ocean containers to prevent damage and facilitate unloading and moving the parts to their proper location in the Missouri facility.

Another unexpected relocation-related issue was that the buyer of the California facility demanded to occupy the facility sooner than was originally planned. This resulted in rushing to vacate the premises and some departments not making as orderly a move as possible. The business considered two options for the move. One called for the business to shut down completely for two weeks, with all the departments moving to Missouri at once. The other option, which was the one chosen, was to move in phases, relocating three departments at a time. Of course, some department moves went more smoothly than others, and key functions had some employees working in both the California and Missouri facilities for a while.

Because maintaining the ability to pick, pack, and ship replacement/service parts to customers without interruption was a high priority, it was decided to remove half of all the parts from the two-story flow racks from where customer parts orders were picked and place them on the floor in an available area. Picking locations from the flow racks, which were maintained in the business's system, were marked on the floor with large marking pens. Orders were picked from this area while the other half of the parts were shipped to Missouri along with the disassembled flow racks. Once the flow racks were assembled in Missouri and the parts placed in their picking locations, orders were processed from there, and the rest of the parts from California were shipped to Missouri.

Once the quality and flow of component parts and products from Indonesia were under control, certain products could be sold to customers at a lower cost. This resulted in the business gaining market share, and it realized a 4 percent overall profit increase. However, the business took longer than it anticipated to get the new workforce trained, which resulted in higher costs for workers brought temporarily from California to perform the training. The company also decided to permanently relocate more skilled employees from California than planned. The worst thing experienced by the business was a successful union campaign that resulted in higher labor costs and less employee flexibility and utilization. The combination of these issues translated into obtaining a 28 percent labor cost reduction instead of the 37 percent the business had expected.

Another relocation example involved a Southern California business that manufactured and distributed specialty footwear and clothing. It had recently acquired a new specialty footwear business, which had a product line that experienced peak sales during the last quarter of each year. The acquisition was seen as a way to have a smoother flow throughout the year of incoming product and outgoing sales. The acquisition also resulted in the business having four distribution and warehouse facilities in Southern California, which made it difficult to operate cost-effectively and efficiently. It also had distribution centers in Canada and the Netherlands, which are not part of this relocation/consolidation discussion.

The four Southern California distribution and warehouse facilities caused products to be moved from a leased warehouse and a public warehouse to the main distribution center for order processing and shipment to customers. Also, having the four facilities made physical inventories more difficult and inefficient. The business manufactured 25 percent of its products in Southern California; the other 75 percent was manufactured by contract manufacturers in Mexico, Costa Rica, Australia, New Zealand, and China.

The business had experienced rapid sales growth and a more complex supply chain resulting from its latest acquisition. The business's executives and managers had benefited from an increase in the stock price, but they believed that price should be even higher. The business had no real estate assets, because all facilities were leased. The investment community needed to see sustained profit performance from the business over a 12-month period before the stock price would grow substantially.

The business retained me as an outside consultant to perform an interim management role, tasked with planning and executing the consolidation of the four Southern California facilities and improving all aspects of inbound and outbound distribution, warehousing, inventory, and customer order processing. In addition, other key goals were to cut costs, increase productivity, and improve the percentage of on-time and accurate orders. Thanks to a thorough plan, the following results were achieved:

Completed the consolidation of the four Southern California warehouse and distribution facilities into one efficient distribution center on time and under budget.

Reduced the overall distribution operating expense by 23 percent. The business's stock price also began to rise. The continued steady increase of the stock price resulted in some very happy investors, executives, and managers.

Increased all measurable areas of warehouse and distribution performance to all-time high levels.

Discontinued manufacturing footwear in Southern California, thereby eliminating the expenses related to planning, shipping raw materials, storing raw materials, and manufacturing labor (this change was already planned by the business).

Arranged to send the majority of orders bound for Canada directly to that country, instead of first shipping them to Southern California to be quality inspected.

Reduced insurance-related costs for domestic and international small-package deliveries.

Educated and trained customer service and purchasing staff to make the most cost-effective choices for small-package deliveries and avoid using higher and more costly service levels than were needed.

Negotiated lower rates for all shipping requirements, including international inbound ocean containers, domestic and international small-package shipments, ocean container deliveries from the ocean port to the distribution center, and LTL (less than truckload) common carrier shipments.

Scheduled 40-foot ocean containers to be used instead of 20-foot containers, which are more cost-efficient.

Implemented procedural changes that reduced annual charge-backs from retail customers by 83 percent.

Increased inventory accuracy to 99.8 percent, without an automated system.

Obtained agreement from the internal and external auditors to eliminate three of four annual complete physical inventories because of the inventory accuracy.

Increased order accuracy to 99.6 percent.

Improved on-time shipments to 99.9 percent.

Convinced management to acquire a bar-code–based warehouse management system (WMS).

Other examples of relocations involve some aerospace businesses that do a majority of their work for the U.S. Department of Defense (DOD). They have relocated their company headquarters from Southern California to be near Washington, D.C., where their major customer is located.

As mentioned earlier, businesses with a very senior and experienced workforce may have excessive labor costs. Coupled with other compelling reasons to relocate, a business may achieve significant labor cost savings if it relocates and hires lower-paid employees.

When a physical consolidation is a result of an acquisition, you should determine whether any redundant functions exist that could be consolidated and enable a reduction in the workforce. Carefully review all functions by first looking at organizational charts of the businesses involved in an acquisition or consolidation to stimulate ideas for productivity-improvement and cost-cutting opportunities.

Businesses that plan to relocate some of their manufacturing facilities out of the country to cut costs must first do some thorough planning and evaluation of the potential advantages and disadvantages. Considerations for relocation or consolidation of facilities must include the following, among other things:

Maintaining the ability to ship product and/or provide service with minimal interruptions during the relocation or consolidation

Determining which, if any, employees will be encouraged to relocate if the move is beyond a reasonable commute for employees

Training of the new employees added to the business's workforce

Ensuring that adequate quality is maintained

The next few pages provide an example of an open-ended relocation or consolidation planning guide for a distribution center. You can use it as a starting point to expand and develop your own relocation and/or consolidation plan.

Open-Ended Relocation or Consolidation Planning Guide for a Distribution Facility

Sell, lease, or sublease the current facility or facilities.

Give notice to landlords or public warehouse owners regarding the business's plan to vacate the current facility or facilities.

Determine which equipment in the current facilities will be moved to the new facility.

If racking, conveyors, or other infrastructure will be required at the new facility, identify potential suppliers of new and used equipment.

Meet with suppliers of racking, conveyors, and other infrastructure to review requirements and obtain recommendations and bids.

Arrange for all utilities to be available, including electricity, natural gas, and water.

Arrange ahead of time to obtain telephone numbers at the new facility. If feasible, retain the business's current telephone numbers, which would make it easier for customers and suppliers to contact you.

If there is a current tenant in the new facility and you will buy some equipment from that party (e.g., racking, conveyor system), arrange for training of your appropriate staff regarding equipment prior to the tenant vacating the facility.

Determine which kind of security system(s) will be needed and contact potential suppliers to obtain recommendations and bids. If the current tenant will be leaving a security system, determine whether it will be adequate for your use.

If there is lighting in the building, determine whether it is adequate or needs to be augmented with additional lighting or have some existing lighting fixtures relocated.

Determine which kinds of repairs and painting will be required before moving in.

Determine whether a paging system will be required or whether cellular telephones for certain key staff would be adequate.

If time clocks will be used by certain employees, have the current ones relocated or purchase new ones.

Identify and sell excess equipment.

Arrange for the new facility to be completely clean prior to moving in.

Rekey all locks.

If landscaping is required for the new facility, meet with the current landscaper and potential landscapers to obtain bids, and then select the best one.

Arrange for a tour of the new facility for all key management and supervisory personnel and make specific plans for the layout of the facility. A detailed plan must be developed that specifies where everyone with an office job will be located, and which furniture will be located where.

As part of any warehouse layout plans, determine which type of storage location coding will be used (e.g., area, aisle, bay, level) and purchase identification labels with human-readable and bar codes included.

Determine which, if any, equipment, furniture, or other items will not be required after the move, and identify potential buyers of the equipment; then sell the items and schedule for them to be picked up.

Determine whether existing material handling equipment will be adequate, or if other equipment will be required (e.g., due to a larger facility, higher racking, or some other factor).

Determine whether electrical outlets at the new facility will be adequate. If not, arrange for installing additional outlets, including specialized types of outlets (e.g., if you need battery chargers for electric-powered material handling equipment).

Determine which computer lines will be needed and arrange for them to be installed.

Decide whether the relocation or consolidation will be done in phases or all at once.

Arrange for as little disruption of customer shipments as possible. If possible, the relocation and/or consolidation should be undertaken during a "slow" period. Consideration should be made to move part of the inventory of finished goods and replacement parts to the new location and leave the balance for fulfilling customer orders, or possibly to move product lines one at a time.

Order telephones with local access and toll-free access to be placed in the employee lunch/break room(s).

Estimate the number of truckloads required to move products, furniture, and equipment from existing facilities to the new facility.

Determine whether the freight carriers would spot trailers to facilitate the loading process.

Develop a list of service companies to assist at the new location(s), including plumbers, electricians, and equipment repair and maintenance (e.g., conveyors).

Select a freight carrier for the move of products, furniture, and equipment, and schedule shipments.

Notify all customers of the planned move and indicate when they should begin to use the new address for returns.

Make sure the new address is included in your agreements with freight carriers to ensure that you continue receiving your proper discount.

Change business cards, stationery, bills of lading, websites, and other points of contact to reflect the new address.

Notify utility companies of the last day of service at the old facilities and the first day of service at the new facility.

Submit a change of address request with the U.S. Postal Service.

Determine the detailed security requirements, including the locations of cameras, security guard service hours, access codes for doors, and so on.

Establish schedule dates for relocating specific areas (e.g., office, receiving).

Arrange for vending machines to be installed at the new facility.

Obtain quotes for and select a janitorial service for the new facility.

Arrange for a lunch (catering) truck to be at the facility for scheduled break and lunch periods. If the employees are not happy with the food, select another lunch truck.

Arrange for fire extinguishers to be installed at the new facility, and move the existing ones if feasible.

If an acquisition is involved, identify excess workforce who could be reassigned or reduced from the business.

Obtain a city business license.

Retain your current business to supply first aid kits, eye-wash stations, and other safety measures if you are geographically close enough to justify using the same supplier, or select a new supplier.

Begin moving according to the plan.

6.5 SELL EXCESS EQUIPMENT

If you have excess equipment you do not believe you will need in the future owing to a relocation and/or consolidation, sell it. This is an excellent one-time revenue-generating action to take that hits the bottom line of the P&L immediately. If you do have things you want to sell, you may want to try something I did for a business years ago that worked well for everyone involved.

As part of the relocation/consolidation project at my client's business, excess warehouse equipment and office equipment were identified at three of its distribution centers. I arranged for experts in assessing the salable price of the equipment to visit those locations and estimate the range of value for each piece of equipment, including trucks, pickup trucks, pallet jacks, forklift trucks, battery chargers, racking, floor scales, conveyors, PCs, copiers, printers, desks, chairs, bookshelves, and file cabinets. After determining the total estimated value for all the equipment, I executed formal agreements with the managers of the distribution centers, which called for paying them 50 percent of all revenue exceeding 90 percent of the high-end range of the total estimated value of the equipment. The managers did a great job for the business and themselves and sold the equipment for 29 percent, 32 percent, and 36 percent more than the total estimated value of the equipment at the distribution facilities. Obviously, it was a win-win situation for all concerned.

6.6 PAPER USAGE REDUCTION

Reduce the volume of computer-generated reports printed by the Information Technology (IT) Department. The IT staff should perform a review of printed computer-generated reports to determine where they can accomplish the following goals:

Eliminate printing some reports.

Decrease the frequency with which some reports are generated.

Generate some printed reports only on a demand basis instead of on a routine scheduled basis.

Reduce the quantity of some printed reports that are distributed (who needs them?).

Consolidate/combine some printed reports.

Generate more exception reports, which results in less data and fewer printed pages. An example of an exception report would be a list of inventory items whose quantities exceed 4 months of estimated usage, instead of a report that includes all inventory items regardless of their estimated usage.

Encourage more online data retrieval and report viewing, with a goal of reducing the printing of computer-generated reports. This step would have to be done as part of an education and training effort by your business.

Each department should also analyze all of its printed input and output reports with a view toward reducing paper usage. (Paper reduction also adds to the going green philosophy and saves some trees from being cut down.) An old trick is to discontinue distributing selected reports you suspect are not necessary to see if anyone complains.

At a former client, the business's president had all the routinely generated reports printed out one month, but did not distribute the reports that he and other officers subjectively thought were not needed or were not being used. Some were daily reports, some were weekly reports, and some were monthly reports. Only one inquiry was made by a department regarding what happened to its reports.

The daily, weekly, and monthly reports the president and officers believed were not needed or were not being used for that month were stacked in a conference room in two 6-foot-high piles and one 4-foot-high pile. As the old saying goes, "A picture is worth a thousand words"—and what a picture this made. All the managers of departments for which the reports were printed were requested to have a meeting in the conference room. There were many red and enlightened faces when the managers saw the stacks of reports. Everyone except the IT staff was shocked by the visual illustration of the excess.

The president started the meeting by saying, "A picture is worth a thousand words," and then he proceeded to explain the experiment. He informed everyone that the data contained in the unused reports would be generated in the future for departments only if they request the reports and deemed them to be needed. After all was said and done, the reports that were identified as required and asked for by users each month amounted to a pile that was only 3 feet high, instead of 16 feet high for the previously generated reports.

Train appropriate individuals how to use the report generation feature of your business's software system to design and produce ad hoc reports when needed. Another option is to teach appropriate individuals how to download certain data from the mainframe system and generate PC spreadsheet reports.

Use checklists for keeping a record of documents you distribute to individuals instead of making and keeping copies of each document, if the documents are generic. An example of how this practice was implemented comes to mind: A now thriving private university was experiencing financial difficulties that contributed to a real threat of losing its accreditation. The university's very future was at stake, and my team and I had to explore opportunities for cost cutting and improving productivity. The university's president was very paternalistic and hated to accept the fact that many employees might lose their jobs as productivity-improvement measures were put into place. He did agree that such a step was necessary, but needed strong proof to justify each termination. In addition, he insisted that every effort be made to reassign the employees affected to other positions at the university, which was accomplished in most instances.

Many creative and great ideas were implemented to reduce costs and staff. However, one simple idea proposed by one of the consultants on my team impressed the president more than any other, and he highlighted the idea numerous times when he spoke of our work and how it helped save the university. It was not a big cost-saving idea, but it was the president's favorite one. The idea was to have a check sheet to record when all standard documents were mailed to prospective students, instead of making and filing photocopies of each document before they were mailed out. The check sheet had an entry for the prospective student's name, a list of all the standard documents sent out, and a column for entering the date when each document was sent out. Of course, nowadays, the checklist could be in a computer file for each student, so no paper would be used for a checklist—that helps save another tree.

Conduct training for employees regarding communicating more efficiently, including how to communicate clearly, concisely, and without too much verbiage, whether via memorandum, telephone, or email.

Although most businesses that have employees with desk jobs provide them with PCs and communicate to them via email, many businesses still choose to distribute hard-copy memoranda to all concerned. Because not all employees use PCs, many businesses maintain bulletin boards in key locations with posted memoranda and announcements that are required reading. I have seen various titles for these bulletin boards, including "Need to Know News," "New News," "Read and Heed Information," and "Required Reading."

Encourage employees to generate short (one page, if possible) memoranda whether for hard copies, a fax, or emails. Use the two-sided feature of copier machines whenever it is appropriate to save a piece of paper. Train employees how to transmit facsimiles directly from their PCs, instead of making a photocopy and then putting it through the fax machine.

Design and use a cover sheet for facsimile transmissions. Sometimes the cover sheet can contain all the data for an entire message, thereby eliminating the need for additional pages being transmitted. Another method to use, instead of a cover page for facsimile transmissions, is a rubber stamp containing "from," "to," "subject," and "date" fields that can be stamped onto the first page of the documents you are transmitting. This saves time and paper by not creating a cover page. Also, when it is possible, transmit a fax without a cover page or rubber stamp. This approach is appropriate when you know the fax machine to which you are transmitting is used by only one person, your recipient.

A terrific cost-cutting idea has resulted in some manufacturers of greeting cards producing a greater number of cards in much smaller sizes. Due to the volumes of cards involved, the costs of raw materials (including paper and ink), storage space, shipping costs for inbound and outbound freight, and other factors were significantly reduced. This example may stimulate your imagination so that you come up with some other terrific cost-cutting ideas. As previously mentioned, the *Los Angeles Times* newspaper reduced the size of its paper to reduce costs, and numerous other newspapers have done the same thing.

If you must generate numerous printed documents, consider recycling the paper after the documents have served their purpose. Determine the feasibility of recycling paper by analyzing what you spend for trash removal and what percentage of your trash paper and/or corrugate is potentially recyclable. Even if you receive a small amount of money for recycled paper and corrugate, this effort is probably more cost-effective than paying for these items to be removed as trash.

Determine the feasibility of using the cartons in which you receive products and supplies as shipping cartons to ship out some of your product orders. Generally, the cartons should be void of the supplier name and contents. This topic is also briefly covered in the "Product Packaging" section of this book.

If you generate enough corrugate trash from discarded cartons used by suppliers to ship products or supplies to you, this is also a potential area for recycling. Some businesses can even justify the purchase and use of a baler for corrugate if there is adequate volume. You need to discuss your various options with paper recycling businesses. Obtain and compare proposals from the various businesses and determine the best method for managing your recycling effort.

Do not forget to shred documents containing sensitive information prior to recycling them.

6.7 RECYCLING

There may be potential areas to recycle other than paper, depending on which products your business produces. Following are some examples:

A boot and shoe manufacturer used to throw away scraps of leather that were too small to use for making boots or shoes. Then it reached an agreement to sell those scraps to another business. The second business made belts and key chains from those scrap pieces, so it was a profitable recycling venture for both parties involved.

A lumber sawmill operation sold wood chips and sawdust to another business that packaged the sawdust for pet bedding and stuffed the wood chips in canvas to make dog pillows. Previously the business paid to have the wood chips and sawdust hauled away.

Apparently Henry Ford used to pay a man to haul away slag, which was a waste by-product scum that formed on molten metal when it was used to make metal parts for Ford cars. The man was very clever and found a use and market for the slag—he sold it to businesses that used the slag as an aggregate in producing asphalt to pave roads.

A business that produced Styrofoam egg cartons, meat trays, and avocado trays (mentioned earlier in this book) cut costs by recycling the unused excess Styrofoam to mix with new plastic raw materials to make more Styrofoam.

If your business generates enough scrap copper or other metal, sell it. If you are in the jewelry-making business, you would probably prefer to recycle the scrap gold, platinum, and silver for your own business's use.

6.8 FREIGHT PRACTICES

I will discuss freight practices in more depth than other topics because it is an area where I have helped save many clients that do a lot of shipping millions of dollars in annualized savings. It is a great area in which to cut costs, because the savings you realize hit the bottom line on the P&L immediately.

An obvious way to cut shipping-related costs is by obtaining lower rates for the shipping services you utilize. Remember to negotiate, negotiate, and negotiate. Consider freight as a cost center or another commodity you purchase, and obtain competitive bids for all your inbound and outbound freight services.

Another way to look for ways to cut freight-related costs is to review and possibly revise your current freight-related practices and policies. Perhaps your business is small and ships only domestically (within the United States), and has small products sold in small quantities that require you to use only one type of shipping service, such as a small-package carrier. Alternatively, your business may be large and ship internationally, and have a variety of products of different weights, sizes, and order quantities that require you to use all types of shipping services.

Domestic freight categories include letter packages; small ground packages; small air packages; air freight (heavier and larger shipments); less than truckload (LTL) intrastate shipments (shipments made from and to destinations within the state); LTL interstate shipments (shipments made from within the state to destinations outside the state, and vice versa); partial truckload (PTL) shipments, in which least one fourth of the trailer will be used to ship to one location; full truckload (FTL) carrier shipments preferably to the same location, or possibly two or three locations in the same geographic area (if you need maximum space, request a 53-foot trailer instead of a 48-foot trailer; you can put four more pallets in a 53-foot trailer than a 48-foot trailer if the pallets are stackable); and rail shipments via piggyback or stack train. In piggybacks, truck trailers including the chassis and wheels are put on a rail car. Stack trains are containers without the truck chassis and wheels that are put on a rail car stacked two high, so a rail car normally contains four stack train containers. Because more stack train containers can be put on a rail car than piggyback trailers, their cost is lower.

International freight categories include letter packages; small air packages; FTL shipments (e.g., between the United States and Canada and/or Mexico); LTL shipments (e.g., between the United States and Canada and/or Mexico); less than ocean container (LCL) or loose freight; air-freight; ocean containers (typically 40 feet or 20 feet, although some other sizes are used); flat racks (for ocean shipment items that cannot be placed in containers); and customs broker fees (not a shipping method, but rather a cost you will incur).

Inbound Shipments

Determine if each supplier's LTL carrier discount is better than your company's discount. If the suppliers have better discounts, will they pass them on to you? If your LTL carrier's discount is better than your suppliers' discounts, instruct the supplier to send shipments collect via your preferred carrier, which enables you to obtain the better discount. "Collect" does not mean the carrier collects for the shipment when it is delivered; rather, you are sent an invoice if you have an account set up with the carrier.

It is necessary for you to monitor your suppliers' shipments to ensure they are using the method you designate. You can stipulate in your Routing Guide (the guidelines for suppliers regarding freight methods and freight carriers to use for their shipments to you) that your suppliers must use your preferred carriers or incur a penalty. Some retail businesses work hard at penalizing their wholesale suppliers if they do not follow their routing instructions exactly.

If some of your suppliers send a high volume of small packages to you (e.g., at least 50 cartons per week), discuss the potential benefits of a consignee-billing program for inbound-collect shipments with your small-package carrier. This program may provide you a better discount than what the supplier passes on to you.

Coordinate with your procurement staff to have them obtain supplier product pricing with freight included (FOB your location) and without freight included (FOB the supplier's location). With some evaluation of what your freight costs are compared to the freight costs of your suppliers, you can make the best choice of which method to choose. Many suppliers price their goods so they can ship their raw materials and/or product freight prepaid (no freight cost to their customer) if they are geographically close to them.

For domestic full truckload shipments to locations where you do not already have good negotiated prices, request one-time "spot" price quotes from two or three carriers or freight brokers that service the routing you need. Then select a carrier based on the lowest price quoted and the service level you need.

If you import products via ocean containers and have sufficient volume to justify it, instruct your suppliers or your offshore factories to ship using 40-foot, 40-foot-high cube, 45-foot, or 48-foot containers whenever possible, and avoid using 20-foot containers. The reason for this is that 40-foot and larger containers are much more cost-effective. For example, a 20-foot container will cost 75 percent of what a 40-foot container costs, but has only 50 percent the capacity of the 40-foot container. This obviously translates into lower product unit cost, which means you can obtain more profit and/or be more flexible with pricing and discounts for your customers.

Outbound Shipments

When negotiating with LTL carriers, be aware that the discount they offer is not all you need to consider, because the basis from which the discount is applied can vary between carriers depending on their tariff. You must determine what the costs would be for your business by comparing the LTL carriers' costs for example shipments to various typical destinations to where you ship your products. Then you can compare costs on an "apples to apples" basis between various LTL carriers to decide which carriers are best for you. Another way to compare prices is to have all the LTL carriers submit discount quotes using the same independent third-party tariff.

Other LTL carrier negotiation considerations can include the following:

Obtain rate class exceptions, especially if you ship some light, bulky products, which cost more than shipping small heavy products.

Have the carrier provide a Freight All Kinds (FAK) agreement to rate most or all of your shipments under one freight class that is lower than normal for most or all of your products. A lower freight class translates into lower shipping costs.

Negotiate to eliminate certain assessorial charges that impact your shipments. This approach can save money, depending which types you frequently incur.

Be certain you know the National Motor Freight Classification (NMFC) codes for all your products, so you can list them on your bills of lading correctly for LTL shipments and avoid overcharges or adjustments. Your LTL freight carrier can provide this information to you.

If you ship over-the-road full truckloads of products across the country, compare the service and cost for that option to piggyback and stack train rail service. Determine whether piggyback and stack train carriers service the areas where you ship your goods, and whether the service (total delivery time) is acceptable. If this approach is feasible, the rail costs can be as much as 30 percent lower than the FTL rates.

Select your small-package carrier by using a similar method as applied to the LTL carriers. You should obtain competitive quotes, being certain you obtain "apples and apples" quotes for comparison purposes. Identify high-volume shipment examples, based on data including the "ship from" locations (e.g., ZIP code) and the "ship to" destinations (e.g., ZIP code), weight, quantity of cartons, dimensions of the shipment cartons, shipment value, and service level required. When the prospective freight carriers respond to your request for quotes, it will be easy to determine which one you want to negotiate with and select as your preferred carrier for the small-package business.

If you pay the shipping costs for your shipments and add shipping costs to your invoices to customers when billing them for the products you ship to them (pre-pay and add shipments), you have an additional revenue-generating opportunity. If you obtain freight discounts from any or all your freight carriers, you do not have to pass these discounts on to your customers. Depending on competitive pressures, you may choose to pass on none, or some of the discount to your customers. This practice, which is called off-bill discounting, is a perfectly legal practice. If you ship to the U.S. government, however, the customer will expect to receive items freight free or at the lowest freight rate, so you cannot implement an off-bill discount in this case.

If you do pass on all the discounts to the customers, make certain your sales force and customer service staff leverage this information when dealing with the customers. You may gain a significant competitive edge over your competitors if you can show customers that your products have a lower net cost when shipping costs are considered.

Another revenue-generating method is to add a handling charge to your freight charge, especially for small-package shipments. I recommend that you do not include the handling charge as a separate line item on your invoice. Instead, include it with the freight charges. You may choose to title the line item on the invoice that includes the freight and handling charge as "Shipping and Handling."

As you might suspect and understand, some businesses make more profit on shipping charges than on the low-price products they sell.

Insurance Options for Small-Package Shipments

Evaluate the feasibility of self-insuring small packages, or determine if you can obtain better insurance rates from a third-party insurer. If you choose not to self-insure your small-package shipments, there are businesses that provide third-party insurance on such shipments that costs less than what the small-package carriers charge. Small-package carriers automatically insure each carton you ship for up to $100 at no cost to you; however, it can be a hassle to apply for and receive payments. To determine whether self-insuring is a good idea, you must first look at your history of loss and damage claims. If the total cost of insurance is greater than your loss and damage claim history, you should consider self-insurance.

Another option is to declare value and pay insurance for only shipments over a certain dollar amount. If your products are packaged well and are not prone to damage, you may have very few damage claims. Also, if the value of each individual carton you ship is small, the $100 free insurance you automatically receive from the small-package carriers at no charge may be adequate.

Internal Shipping Policies and Controls

You can do an excellent job of negotiating for low freight rates; however, within your business, people may cost you more money than is necessary due to lack of policies or no control over existing policies. The usual areas where internal staff may be costing you more money for freight than is necessary include the Customer Service, Sales, Marketing, and Procurement Departments. Customer Service or Sales staff, for example, may provide free freight, reduced freight, or a higher class of service than is necessary or authorized at no extra cost to customers. This may make customers happy, but it costs your business unnecessarily.

One of my clients had a policy of sending all its small-package shipments within the continental United States free of charge to customers using second-day air service via a major small-package carrier. The client, like many other businesses, may have established a policy to send all small-package shipments via second-day air service to provide good customer service. It may be a good policy to get the customers their products in two days, but second-day air service may not be needed for many of your customers that are geographically near you.

Obtain service maps from your small-package carrier(s) to determine the areas where regular ground service would normally get your products to the customers within two days. Once you have this information, ensure that all shipments to those areas are sent via ground service. This could be accomplished in a number of ways. One way would be by providing education, training, and a procedure for the employees making shipping decisions to follow. Another way would be to enter the shipping instructions for each customer in the customer database. The best way would be to program the shipping system to apply proper shipping methods based on the destination ZIP codes. The ZIP codes where ground shipments would normally be delivered in one or two days would be coded for shipment via ground service, and all other ZIP codes would be coded for second-day air service. Making the policy change to send packages via ground service instead of second-day air when the customers are within the geographic area that will receive ground shipments in one or two days saved the previously mentioned business a lot of money.

You need to educate and train the people who are responsible for determining freight methods to be cost-conscious and responsible regarding freight. After you have established internal shipping policies, you must monitor them to ensure the applicable employees are following your policies so your freight costs are controlled.

One excellent education and training tool is a bar chart that indicates what it costs to send the same item to the same destination using various small-package classes of service. Same-day delivery of a small package, where it is available, is the most expensive shipping method, and next-day air morning delivery is more expensive than next-day air regular (afternoon) delivery. Second-day delivery is far less expensive than next-day delivery, and there is a third-day delivery service that is less expensive than second-day delivery. Ground shipments are less expensive than any other shipment method. You get the idea—so make sure you provide this education and training. Every time you remind your employees that unnecessary costs can contribute to your business not having enough money to give your employees a bonus or a pay increase, it gets their attention.

Review your small-package delivery bills for "adjustment" charges. These "adjustment" charges may occur when you used an incomplete or inaccurate address, or charged a lower rate than you should have. The "adjustment" charges for charging too low a rate generally occur when the shipping staff does not know how to properly determine dimensional weight charges for oversize packages and when they do not know that the address is a residential address rather than a business address, because residential deliveries cost more. React to what you find and follow up to ensure the proper addresses are put in your customer master files. Make certain your Shipping Department employees are trained regarding determining and charging for dimensional weight for oversize packages. Your small-package carrier will provide this training and some reference tools at no cost to you.

Employees must be taught to send products based on when customers really need the shipment to be at their location—not too late, but not too early in certain cases. Normally, you want to ship as soon as possible in the most cost-effective way. Nevertheless, there are certain businesses—especially some large aerospace and retail businesses—that specify shipping windows that you must adhere to or incur a penalty of some kind.

Establish approval levels and guidelines for when Customer Service can ship products to customers free of freight charges, or at a higher class of service but while paying for a lower class of service rate. I have seen instances where some customer service representatives for a business wanted to provide their personal favorite customers with free or reduced freight charges. This practice can be unnecessarily costly and is exactly why education, training, and controls are needed.

I performed consulting assignments for a business that introduced a creative policy that rewarded sales representatives for not discounting freight for their shipments to customers. The business's products were large, which resulted in high LTL shipping costs. The salespeople were paid a commission for the products sold and for the freight charged to customers if the freight was not discounted, or discounted no more than 20 percent of normal rates. If the salespeople discounted the freight by more than 20 percent of normal rates, their commission for the products sold was discounted by the dollar amount of the freight discount given in excess of 20 percent of normal rates. This was a big deal for salespeople, and it resulted in greater cost savings to the business. If you choose to try something like this program, have your IT staff help you administer it.

Maintain accurate and up-to-date mailing lists of current and prospective customers. If you send sales and marketing information to current and prospective customers, and you receive numerous items back due to incorrect addresses, you are throwing away money. Think of the time, materials, and postage costs involved. If the addresses on your mailing lists are not updated based on returned items, you will continue to waste the effort and money until you do correct the addresses. Establish a system in which an employee is designated to review all returned mail to determine why the customer address was incorrect. If the address was entered into the system database incorrectly, the customer moved, or the customer went out of business, either the correct address must be identified and used, or the customer removed from the system database (i.e., if it went out of business).

Learn if and when it may be cost-effective to ship using the U.S. Postal Service (USPS) instead of a small-package carrier, and vice versa. Understand the various USPS classes of service and their related costs to select the best methods to meet your shipping requirements.

6.9 PRODUCT PACKAGING

There are many considerations regarding packaging your products that can possibly save money. As mentioned previously, proper packaging is necessary to avoid damage to your products when they are shipped, and you can also determine whether it is feasible to utilize the cartons in which you receive products and supplies for packing your products for shipments to customers. You can provide your suppliers with specific carton specifications so the cartons can be reused for packing and shipping your customer orders.

If you ship a lot of small, heavy products, evaluate whether the USPS priority mail flat-rate boxes, which enable you to ship anything up to 70 pounds that fits in the box, would be beneficial for many of your shipments. The flat-rate cartons are provided free as part of the flat-rate charge. Also, FedEx provides some free cartons for priority (air) shipments that may be beneficial for your business.

Some businesses need to pack certain products in wooden cartons that must be nailed shut and banded to ensure the products are secure. These crates are typically used for exceptionally large and heavy products such as machinery.

Carton size and the number of cartons used to pack and ship a customer order have an impact on small-package carrier shipping costs. Understand what your small-package carrier considers oversize and overweight packages. By avoiding the use of oversize or overweight packages, you can save your business and/or the customer money.

Establish policies, procedures, education, and training for appropriate employees regarding the proper type and amount of filler material to use, and how to tape, staple, and/or band shipping cartons to ensure you are not wasting time or materials and your products are secure when they are shipped. Remember the business that used 24 or more strips of 2-inch-wide clear tape to close its shipping cartons until we convinced them to use 3-inch-wide clear tape and only two to a maximum of six strips of tape per carton—it is a great example of improving productivity and cutting costs.

One business used six large metal staples to close the cartons of product at the end of its assembly line. More than 35 percent of the cartons later had to be opened to include a small option part prior to shipment, with the carton then being closed with an additional six staples. After analyzing the models of product that usually had an option part added prior to shipping, new stapling guidelines were developed. The guidelines included using three staples at the end of the assembly line for the models of products unlikely to be reopened prior to shipping, but only two staples for the models of products likely to be reopened to add an option part prior to shipping. If a carton with three staples was opened to add an option part, the business also used three staples to close it. If the carton with two staples was not opened, it added only one more staple to close it. Due to the high volume of products produced, this packaging-related improvement resulted in a significant cost savings.

An international business that produced and distributed various types and sizes of medical devices and supplies undertook a packaging-related cost-reduction project. Part of the project was to make as many of the product packages smaller due to certain hospitals complaining that the business's packaging was too large and required more storage space, which was at a premium for those hospitals.

An industry requirement for medical device manufacturers includes having information sheets placed inside each package with the addresses of company locations and a description of icons printed on labels placed on the packages (e.g., expiration date, no latex). A second insert included with each product was an "Information for Use" booklet; printed by an outside company, it contained instructions for using the product in approximately 15 languages. The booklets were stapled together and ranged in size from approximately 3 inches × 4 inches to 5 inches × 6 inches. Their cost ranged from $1.76 to $2.87 depending on the size and number of pages. To reduce costs, we recommended eliminating the booklets and using one piece of paper with printing on one or both sides as needed and folded like a map. The instruction sheets would be made by the business on its own copy equipment, and the cost of each instruction sheet would range from 4 cents for an 8½ inch × 11 inch sheet with printing on one side to 11 cents for an 11 inch × 14 inch sheet with printing on both sides. This equaled a 96 to 98 percent cost reduction per insert.

Another recommendation was to print the bulk of the "Instructions for Use" documents and company locations in English, French, and Spanish, and a smaller quantity with all the languages. When a product was shipped to a country other than the United States, Canada, Central and South America (except Brazil), France, and the United Kingdom, the insert with all the required languages would be put in with the product.

6.10 COMMUNICATIONS (MAIL, FACSIMILE, TELEPHONE, AND EMAIL)

Establish, publish, and enforce telephone, email, and Internet usage policies at your business.

Limit inbound and outbound personal telephone calls. As you know, they reduce productivity, as well as possibly increase your telephone usage charges, depending on the telephone agreements you have with your telephone carrier. Most employees now have and use cellular telephones. These devices may not cost the company directly, but they can cost the company indirectly through lost work time if you do not limit their use to emergencies, break times, and lunch times.

Restrict certain telephone units in your facilities to enable internal or local calls only. A good application for these telephones would be in break rooms.

Consider providing telephone credit cards or cellular telephones for employees who are required to make frequent business calls away from the business's facilities, such as for sales and service employees. Evaluate various telephone companies' calling plans, cellular telephones, long-distance carriers, and calling cards, and then select the best ones to fit your business's requirements. Audit telephone bills and follow up with applicable employees regarding apparent misuse and questionable calls, including education, training, and disciplinary action if necessary.

There are good and bad sides to everything. Certain telephone plans allow unlimited local and long-distance calling for a set monthly fee. A problem with most of these plans is that you are not provided with a list and details of the calls made and received from each extension (e.g., time of day, originating number, and call duration), which prevents you from checking for misuse and unnecessary calls. I recall an instance where employees working for a department manager complained that the manager was on personal telephone calls an excessive amount of time. It was discovered that the manager had more than 4 hours of calls each day to the same telephone number, which was discovered to be a friend of the manager. The manager was confronted with this information and afforded the opportunity to discontinue this practice. The manager responded positively, and when this practice was discontinued and the manager paid proper attention to his operation, the manager's department was noticeably improved.

If you have a voice mail system, train employees to always leave a complete message to avoid "telephone tag" and unnecessary high volume of return calls. Of course, discretion must be used regarding which information is included in the messages.

Although emails are theoretically free, the unproductive time factor for using telephones also applies to them, if there are excessive personal messages sent and received. Likewise, there have been numerous alarming studies performed regarding the amount of time spent (wasted) by employees using the Internet for non-work-related purposes.

While performing performance evaluation and lost-time studies at one business, a consultant working with me observed two employees in one department who were always playing video solitaire or other games on their PCs when they were observed. This was one of those situations where it was the employees' fault, but it was also their supervisor's fault for letting it happen. These employees needed enough work assigned to them to keep productive, and they needed supervision to ensure there was no more game playing while on the job. One of the employees did not learn to stop, or was addicted to the video solitaire game, and it cost him his job.

Although you want to avoid a "Big Brother is watching you" atmosphere at work, you must put in some controls to monitor and help prevent non-work-related use of the Internet. Many organizations instruct their IT Department to implement controls to monitor for misuse and report it to management for appropriate follow-up action.

6.11 TRAVEL AND ENTERTAINMENT

Travel and entertainment (T&E) is a "hot button" issue with many businesses. If your business requires numerous employees to travel as part of their work, you need to establish fair travel and entertainment policies.

Make a list of travel and entertainment items that will and will not be approved for payment. Examples of items that will not reimbursed might include, but not be limited to, the following: in-room adult movies when at a hotel; laundry service for overnight stays of two days or less; and more than one personal telephone call per day charged to the hotel bill. If you do not establish policies limiting what employees can charge for and how much they can charge, you are just asking for possible problems.

Design an easy to complete T&E report form with separate sections for the various types of expenses: airfare; car rental and associated fuel costs; gas mileage (when an employee uses his or her own personal vehicle); parking; hotels; meals; taxis; telephone; laundry; gratuities; entertainment; and other (explain). Number each section of the report (for reference purposes when someone audits the reports). Require receipts to be turned in with T&E reports for all expenses over a certain dollar amount.

Remind air travelers to plan ahead to take advantage of lower fares whenever possible. Develop clear rules regarding the class of service that is acceptable for air travel and rental cars. Set maximum allowable dollar limits for meals; set maximum allowable dollar limits for hotels. If your business has special rates with certain hotels and/or car rental agencies, require their use by your employees.

Provide guidelines regarding which employees can entertain current and potential customers, clients, business partners, and other parties. In this context, provide guidelines regarding who can be entertained and which types of entertainment and dollar limits are acceptable.

Require approval of T&E reports from the immediate supervisor of the originator. Assign an objective and detail-oriented individual in the Accounting Department to audit T&E reports. Stress the importance of conscientiously auditing T&E reports—do not "rubber-stamp" them. Once you identify a questionable item on a T&E report and bring it to an employee's attention, it will probably preclude future potential T&E problems of this nature.

Develop T&E auditing guidelines. Design a T&E report audit worksheet to use to document cases in which errors or failure to follow your business's accepted policy guidelines is found. This worksheet should contain the following sections: name of originator (individual being audited); date of report; original report total dollar amount; adjustment amounts and reasons (e.g., addition error, no receipt, applicable policy violation); and revised report total dollar amount, which will be the amount reimbursed.

Send copies of adjusted T&E reports and corresponding audit worksheets to the originator and his or her superior. If there are apparent purposeful misrepresentations (fraud), notify the head of the Human Resources Department and the appropriate executive responsible for the department where the employee works. They will decide which disciplinary action is appropriate to prevent the situation from happening again.

6.12 SCRAP AND REWORK

If you believe your scrap and rework costs are too high, you are probably right. You should maintain reports that indicate scrap and rework costs. These reports must contain an adequate level of detail to help identify the source of the scrap or rework. The source could be a manufacturing department, work area, specific work center (cell), employee, or product that may possibly be the cause of repeated scrap or rework.

Assign a group to address any scrap or rework issues. This group should include individuals from the appropriate manufacturing departments and the Quality Control Department. The resolution of problems could include additional training of certain employees who create rework or scrap, replacement or repair of some equipment or tool, a change in the way a product is designed, or a change in the manufacturing process and/or router for products that are frequently being scrapped or reworked. A router is a card or paper that accompanies a manufactured part as it physically moves through the various steps of production, and it describes what is to be done at each step. In most paperless manufacturing systems, there are electronic routers.

The Quality Control Department can help identify better quality control points for a specific part and report on actions taken to reduce scrap and rework costs for that part and all parts in general. Remember, the earlier in the workflow you discover and correct a problem that could result in rework or scrap, the better it is.

6.13 HIRE SOME MENTALLY CHALLENGED WORKERS

I have found from my personal experience that, under certain circumstances, hiring some mentally challenged (some people prefer the term "mentally handicapped") employees is cost-effective; it also does a lot of good for less fortunate and deserving people. I am not suggesting that you hire mentally challenged employees as part of your business's regular workforce. Instead, I suggest that you determine whether there are agencies or organizations in your area such as the Association for Retarded Citizens (ARC), which is a national organization, that strive to put mentally challenged individuals in work situations with local businesses.

What I did when I met with local ARC representatives was to ensure that there was an "easy" job function that would be good for mentally challenged individuals. At one business, the job function was assembling boxes; at another business, it was affixing price tags or labels onto products.

ARC assured me that they would provide adequate full-time on-site supervision for the workers. At one business, they provided six workers and two ARC on-site supervisors; at the other business, they provided 10 workers and two ARC on-site supervisors.

Both businesses received more production for less pay than if they had used regular employees. At the business with six workers assembling boxes, the production output was 4 times greater than what it would have been with two regular full-time employees, and the cost per hour was far less, especially when you considered that the regular company employees also received fringe benefits. At the business where the workers affixed price tags or labels, the productivity and cost savings were even greater because the two supervisors said they were bored, so they performed work while they supervised, and they were excellent workers. It was another example of a fortunate win-win situation.

6.14 OVERTIME

Overtime (OT) may possibly be needed for peak workload periods, leaves of absence, vacations, absenteeism, and special projects. I say "may possibly be needed," so only approve overtime if you feel absolutely certain it is needed. Use overtime to prevent the need to add permanent or temporary staff when it is deemed to be an overall more cost-effective thing to do. Also, always require prior management approval for working OT.

If a department or area with frequent overtime does not appear over-worked, eliminate the OT and observe whether problems arise or whether the area can function adequately without the OT. Too much overtime can cause employee dissatisfaction, as well as lead to possible quality and safety problems, due to employees' being tired and careless. You do not want nonexempt employees (employees who get paid for overtime) to like and depend on overtime pay, because they may attempt to create the need for it. I have known this to be the case all too often.

If the business is a one- or two-shift operation at maximum capacity that is unable to keep up with the production demands, try to avoid adding another shift by using overtime and adding a staggered or small-size shift for the capacity-limiting work centers or equipment.

7

Quality-Related Issues

7.1 QUALITY AND SERVICE "AS THEY SHOULD BE"

I want to make it clear that I do not advocate under any circumstance a sacrifice of acceptable quality levels when taking cost-cutting or productivity-improvement actions. We all know that a lack of quality or service can be costly and result in the following undesirable outcomes:

Scrap, which results when poor-quality parts are discovered that cannot be reworked.

Rework, which results when poor-quality parts are discovered and can be revised to an acceptable quality.

Warranty replacements and repairs, which result when a customer receives unacceptable-quality products that require repair or replacement during the warranty period.

Shipping costs to have warranty replacements/repairs sent back from the customer.

Shipping costs to deliver warranty replacements/repairs to the customer.

Customer quality-related complaints of various types. You certainly do not want or need these problems.

Poor quality/service reputation. You certainly do not want or need this problem, either.

Loss of potential future sales. This is obviously something you want to avoid, and you can do so by providing quality products to your customers.

Too much quality or service can also be costly and result in the following issues:

Extra raw materials that exceed specifications and/or customer needs or expectations.

Excessive labor, such as providing an aesthetic finish to a component part of a product that is not visible when the product is completely assembled.

Buying custom or special parts to be assembled into a product when less expensive "off the shelf" commodity stock parts would suffice.

Unnecessary service that is not needed or expected to be competitive, such as free shipping, or no extra charge for next-day delivery of a product.

An example of excess quality is the business previously mentioned that made Styrofoam cartons for a major American fast-food chain. Samples of the cartons were inspected after each major production run, and if too much of the raw materials were used, it was too late to do anything about it. Putting an inspection point in for testing the thickness and weight of the rolls of Styrofoam sheets as they were being produced, but before they were used to make the products, resulted in a significant cost reduction. Adjustments could then be made to the thickness and weight of the Styrofoam sheets as soon as possible after discovering they were out of tolerance. This practice ensured that the Styrofoam sheets and products produced using them had "quality as it should be"—not too little and not too much (i.e., not less or more than was needed).

Remember that high quantity equals high opportunity. If you produce a high quantity of product with excess and unnecessary quality, it results in a loss of money.

A quality manager I knew had some very creative ideas on how to get management involved with certain quality-related issues. This quality manager convinced top management to require all managers, regardless of the departments where they worked, to spend one hour per week randomly inspecting some finished goods when they were ready either for packing and shipment or to be put into inventory. This resulted in numerous improvement ideas that were implemented and that reduced or eliminated many quality problems.

One recommendation was to change the way the quality problems with finished goods were identified and fixed. Of course, this case arose when the problems could be fixed without scrapping the product. Originally, whenever a quality inspector found a quality problem, the product was immediately given to a repair person to fix the problem. After that specific quality problem was fixed, the product was then taken back to be inspected again. If another quality problem was found, the product was given to a repair person to fix that second problem. After that problem was fixed, the product was taken back to be inspected again. A product sometimes had as many as five or six quality problems that had to be identified and repaired, one problem at a time. In addition, when quality problems were discovered, they were not listed and totaled up.

One of the method changes recommended and adopted was to have the entire product inspected to identify all possible quality problems upfront, so they could all be repaired at one time, instead of having the product go back and forth from a quality inspector to a repair person as many as five or six times. Another method change was to total up the quantity of each type of quality problem that had been identified each week and present it in the form of a report. The high-volume quality problems were researched to determine their sources; actions were then taken to eliminate the root causes of the problems. This practice reduced the number of quality problems affecting finished goods.

As an aside, the quality manager always used the word "opportunity" instead of "problem." We had some heated discussions regarding this terminology, because I agreed that the word "opportunity" fit in many or most instances, but not all instances. I believe some things are best described as "problems."

A manager who had recently attended a problem-solving training course made another good recommendation. What the problem-solving training course taught the manager was to always try to find the root cause of a problem. The manager believed that most of the quality problems could be identified and fixed in the process flow exactly where the problem component part was made or attached onto the finished product. The manager acknowledged that the business's piecework incentive system resulted in a greater quantity of component parts and products being made, which was its purpose. However, the incentive system also resulted in more poor-quality parts being produced because workers were only interested in the incentive pay they would receive based on the quantity of parts they produced.

The changes recommended and adopted in this case were to revise the piecework incentive system to include qualitative as well as quantitative measurements, and to require inspections at each step in the production process to identify and correct quality problems immediately. The production workers, including those on the incentive system, were required to inspect and approve or reject the parts they made for quality before they were moved to the next production step.

Also, most of the quality inspectors were moved from the area where finished goods were inspected back to the various departments in the production flow, and the production workers who caused the quality problems were required to correct the problems. The results from these recommendations included an increase in the number of quality parts produced and the number of quality inspectors was decreased. The piecework incentive system was revised and made to be more equitable for the employees and the business, which reduced costly quality problems. The workers who produced high quantities of quality parts were rewarded

Look for, recognize, and eliminate unnecessary excess quality and service when you observe it. Improve or change product design and specifications, bills of material, and routing instructions where appropriate.

One business eliminated unnecessary quality and cost when it stopped using high-cost preprinted color labels on which it also printed more information for some of its products. The business changed to use a less expensive method of printing on blank white labels and saved money.

Restaurants, especially restaurant chains, help control costs with portion control procedures for menu items. For example, at one chain, spaghetti was a popular menu item, which called for a 3-ounce ladle of sauce for each portion. When a quality audit was performed at the various restaurants in the chain, it revealed that most of the food preparers were serving more sauce than the 3-ounce portion called for. Some food preparers were using a 4-ounce ladle, instead of a 3-ounce ladle; some were using two servings from a 2-ounce ladle; and many who were using the proper 3-ounce ladle were adding more than the one ladle full of sauce. The food preparers were educated and trained regarding using the 3-ounce ladle, and the servers were told that they could request more sauce for a customer if they asked for it.

Another example of poor portion control at this restaurant chain was the amount of tuna salad used for sandwiches. The food preparers should have used one ice-cream-type scoop of tuna salad per sandwich; however, many were adding more than what was called for.

The lack of portion control added up to unnecessary excess cost—this was an example of "large quantity equals large opportunity." Due to the high volume of spaghetti dinners and tuna salad sandwiches being served, there was a noticeable increase of profit at several restaurants in the chain after portion-control education and training were performed following the audit findings.

Remember that the gross cost of raw materials, purchased parts, equipment, and supplies is not the only factor to consider; rather, it is the net cost/benefit balance that counts. For example, if you have many rejects or quality problems with parts from the lowest-cost supplier, the net cost will likely actually be higher after considering all factors involved in the situation. Also, if you are not including the shipping costs when you look at the product or raw material costs, start looking at the total cost: your net cost with a supplier geographically closer to your location is likely to be lower than with a supplier located far away. Supplier quality, service, warranty, terms, and delivery times are other key considerations in addition to cost.

7.2 UNDERSTAND YOUR QUALITY-RELATED COSTS

Identify and determine the various costs associated with quality in your business, such as the following:

Prevention costs: quality assurance and quality engineering. This includes manufacturing specifications, product design, qualifying suppliers and providing them with inspection requirements and receiving criteria, education and training of your quality inspectors for goods when they are received, and package design (to prevent shipping damage).

Identification costs: quality control. This includes the quality inspectors, test equipment, and provision of inspection guidelines to machine operators, along with responsibility to help identify quality problems before more value (labor or materials) is added to the product.

Internal costs: problems with your products identified and corrected in your facility before they are shipped to customers. This includes scrap, rework, reinspection, and sorting out poor-quality parts.

External costs: problems with your products identified by customers after the goods have been shipped from your facility. This includes warranty returns, replacement parts or repairs, free freight to ship defective products back from the customers, free freight for replacements and repairs, unhappy customers, damaged reputation, and lost potential sales.

Table 7.1   ABC Company's Quality Costs Analysis

Quality Costs	Thousands of dollars			
Category	Scenario 1	Scenario 2	Scenario 3	Scenario 4
Prevention	200	400	500	600
Identification	300	300	400	500
Internal	1,000	800	650	400
External*	3,500	2,000	1,250	750
Total	$5,000	$3,500	$2,800	$1,250

*Plus intangible costs, such as loss of credibility and loss of future potential business.

Determine your business's optimal distribution of quality cost types. Remember—the highest priority is to minimize external quality costs, because they are the most costly quality problems found by your customers after the products are shipped to them. Placing more emphasis on prevention will decrease other quality-related costs. If you place more emphasis on prevention and identification, both your internal and external costs should decrease. If you place more emphasis on prevention, identification, and internal costs, your external costs should decrease. If you work hard at it, you should reduce your total overall quality-related costs.

Review the example chart in Table 7.1 depicting ABC Company's quality costs analysis. The table includes four theoretical scenarios of a business's quality costs, as the company tries to reduce its overall quality costs, but especially its external quality costs. Scenario 1 depicts the current situation. Scenario 2 shows how the increased cost for prevention results in lower internal costs and external costs. Scenarios 3 and 4 illustrate that the increased costs for prevention and identification translate into a greater reduction of internal and external costs. As the scenarios indicate, the more costs and efforts you allocate upfront, the less external costs you should experience. Ideally, your external costs should be reduced even more than depicted in Scenario 4.

7.3 DO THINGS RIGHT IN THE FIRST PLACE

Doing things right in the first place is more "motherhood and apple pie" advice, but it is very important for you to emphasize this point to your employees. If you do not do things right the first time, it costs you in many ways. This applies both at work and away from work. Following are some examples of costs and problems that may occur if you do not do things right in the first place:

Unnecessary extra effort is needed to correct whatever it was that was not done right in the first place.

If you have to redo something, it delays or prevents other things from being done in a timely manner.

Scrapping and reworking parts that were made wrong are both unnecessarily costly.

A shipment may be delayed due to parts shortages caused by ordering the wrong quantity of raw materials or component parts.

A major report or important letter may need to be redistributed due to an error, such as indicating a quantity of 1,000 instead of 10,000, or vice versa.

Resending a product to a customer may be necessary if the wrong product was sent the first time.

It hurts your credibility if a customer discovers you did not do something right in the first place.

When your credibility is hurt, it could possibly result in lost future sales.

Bar-code equipment significantly increases the ability to capture data in your system quickly and accurately. It is a good example of doing things right the first time when you compare the results to hand-prepared paperwork and manual data entry, even by highly skilled data-entry employees.

I fondly remember when I introduced bar-coding technology to one particular business. It was a day when I was in the factory and the business's president walked by. I was working with an excellent data-entry clerk who was opposed to using the bar-code wand reader provided to her, and I was trying to change her mind. Her main job function was to enter inventory transactions into the system. This included entering quantities when products were put into the warehouse and entering quantities when products were taken out of the warehouse and moved to an assembly area or the Parts Shipping Department.

I requested the president to stop and see a demonstration of the use of the new bar-code reader wand. I requested the employee to make a stack of 30 inventory transaction input documents that had bar codes indicating the part number and quantity printed on them, as well as a tab-down function code to move from one entry to the next one required in the automated warehouse system. We had also provided the clerk with a menu of other bar-code function codes, quantities, and so on. I requested that the president note the time it would take for the clerk to enter the 30 inventory transactions by manually keying them by hand and then by using the bar-code reader wand. I asked that the clerk first manually key the data into the system, which was her preferred method. Two transactions she tried to enter were initially rejected because she entered invalid part numbers, so she had to reenter them. When she finished, I requested that she reverse each transaction using the same method of data entry by hand. Then I requested the clerk to use the bar-code wand to enter the same 30 inventory transactions, and then reverse the transactions using the same method.

The results were enlightening to both the clerk and the president. It took 20 percent less time to perform the inventory transactions using the bar-code wand than the data entry by hand. Also, there were no transactions rejected. Everyone agreed that, as long as the bar codes on the paperwork were correct, there was only one chance in a million of an error using the bar-code wand. The clerk was like a convert to a religion, and the president asked where and when I would introduce the use of bar codes and bar-code wand readers next. This was a great example of an ROI project that improved productivity—and of doing things right in the first place.

A client in the business of selling rehabilitation pain-relieving devices did a poor job of ensuring the proper processing of initial claims to insurance companies for reimbursement. The errors resulted in more than 35 percent of initial claims being rejected, which required rework to redo and resubmit the corrected claims. The poor processing also delayed the business from getting reimbursed from the insurance companies.

We recommended that the business divide the claims processers into groups, based on the insurance companies for which they processed claims. In addition, the business trained designated employees to be experts regarding the requirements of the insurance companies in their group. These experts reviewed the claims their group prepared for completeness and accuracy before sending them to the insurance companies for reimbursement. Although a claim form may not have been prepared properly in the first place, the incomplete or inaccurate paperwork was corrected before it was sent to the appropriate insurance company. This resulted in a productivity improvement because there were very few rejected claims that had to be corrected and resubmitted, and it improved cash flow by speeding up the time by which the insurance companies paid claims.

I am fairly sure you can think of examples of where not doing things right in the first place has already been or could be costly to your business. Prevent unnecessary costs by educating, training, and continually stressing the importance of doing things right the first time to all your employees.

7.4 INVENTORY CONTROL AND ACCURACY

If the data in your inventory system are inaccurate, either on the low side or high side, it can cause several problems:

Difficulties for materials requirement planning (MRP) planners regarding which manufactured parts should be produced, as well as when and which quantities to make . . .

Difficulties for buyers regarding which purchased parts should be ordered, as well as when and which quantities should be bought . . .

Difficulties for master production schedule (MPS) planners regarding which finished units should be produced, as well as when and which quantities should be made . . .

Difficulties for the distribution requirements planning (DRP) planners regarding which finished goods (salable parts and units) should be available in the warehouse(s), as well as when and which quantities are needed . . .

Underbuying or overbuying of raw materials and purchased parts . . .

Expedite charges from suppliers for rush orders to fill shortages of purchased items, as well as added freight costs, such as sending items via air instead of truck . . .

A lack of space due to overbuying or overproducing parts . . .

Production parts shortages due to thinking more quantity is on hand than is actually the case . . .

Unnecessary cash outlays for excess inventory, as well as carrying costs when buying unnecessary parts or raw materials . . .

Expedited and extra effort necessary to make up for shortages . . .

Employees working on the wrong priorities due to planners and schedulers having wrong information . . .

Poor execution of the production plan . . .

Employees wasting time researching inventory errors . . .

Potentially excessive overtime . . .

Incorrect calculation of inventory value . . .

Bad decisions regarding coordinated changes, when you phase out an existing part and phase in a new one . . .

Excess parts that may become obsolete, require rework, or be scrapped

Poor customer service (e.g., late orders) . . .

Lost sales and reduced profits if your lack of available products leads the customer to buy from one of your competitors . . .

A good inventory system is important, but it does not guarantee inventory accuracy. Good people, education, training, and discipline are needed, along with a good system to ensure high inventory accuracy. A medium-size or large business may have an automated warehouse management system (WMS). The system may be paperless, or it may use paper transactions. A small business, in contrast, might use a manual perpetual inventory system. The manual perpetual inventory system requires updating a card for each SKU (stock-keeping unit) when inventory for that SKU is received, when inventory is moved within the warehouse, when inventory is removed due to being shipped as part of a customer order, or when a part is taken from inventory to be used as a component to make a finished goods product.

Some examples illustrate how good people can be as important as a good system to maintain inventory accuracy:

Careful counting of parts during physical inventories and cycle counts.

Accurate data entry. You can count the parts correctly and fill out the required paperwork correctly, but if you enter the data into the system incorrectly, the inventory quantity will be incorrect.

Processing paperwork and/or transactions in a timely manner, and not losing paperwork.

Adhering to the proper priorities.

Putting parts away in the correct location and entering the proper location, part names or numbers, and quantities in the inventory system. This is the most important thing to do, because if the information is incorrect upfront, it will cause problems and inaccuracies until the issue is discovered and corrected when a physical inventory is performed, a cycle count is made for that location or part, or research is done when that part is not found or is found in the wrong location.

Picking from the proper location.

Being sure the part being picked or received matches the paperwork.

Informing managers of inventory-related problems as soon as practical.

Determining the cause of errors and taking quick corrective action.

As mentioned previously, bar-code equipment facilitates performing inventory transactions quickly and helps maintain inventory accuracy.

One of my clients performed quarterly inventories that resulted in a complete shutdown of its operation for three to four days. By using bar coding and improving its receiving, picking, and cycle-counting policies and procedures, the business obtained approval from its outside auditors to perform only one annual physical inventory. Later, the outside auditors for the business approved it to not perform any physical inventories as long as its cycle counts proved that inventory accuracy was being maintained at an acceptably high level.

Some instructors help their students remember the importance of inventory accuracy by encouraging them to think of the warehouse as a bank, and the inventory as money in the bank. If you have a checking or savings account, you would want your bank to process every transaction accurately, and on a timely basis. Use this analogy when educating and training your applicable employees regarding the importance of inventory accuracy.

The following example of an inventory control and accuracy interview guide can be used to gain an understanding of your business's current inventory practices and to identify potential areas for improving inventory control and accuracy.

Inventory Control and Accuracy Interview Guide

1. What is your inventory accuracy ($book to $physical), based on the last physical inventory?

2. How is your inventory accuracy calculated? How often do you calculate it?

3. What is your annual inventory turnover (annual sales dollars divided by current inventory value in dollars)?

4. How many SKUs do you have in your warehouse? A SKU is a unique inventory item (e.g., a red long-sleeved cowboy shirt, size large, is a SKU; a red long-sleeved cowboy shirt, size medium, is a different SKU).

5. Are stocking locations fixed, random, or a combination of both?

6. Do you have a manual inventory control system, an automated inventory system, or an inventory module of an ERP (Enterprise Resources Planning) system?

7. When items are received, how are the stocking locations assigned or selected?

8. What are the stocking location codes, and are they clearly marked?

9. How do you train new and temporary employees regarding receiving, putting away, picking, and consolidating inventory?

10. Which duties that impact inventory do you assign to temporary employees?

11. If you use pick tickets or handheld devices, are items listed in stocking sequence to facilitate picking?

12. Do standards exist, such as for orders picked per hour or items per hour?

13. Do you maintain individual and/or group performance reports? Obtain copies.

14. Is there an order inspection function after picking and before packing?

15. Do you maintain statistics regarding errors found by employee and type of error (e.g., over, short, incorrect)?

16. What are the major types of errors?

17. What is the procedure to correct the order prior to shipment when an error is found?

18. Is your material handling equipment adequate (types and quantity)?

19. Are there security concerns or possible pilferage?

20. What is the procedure for when an order picker finds a shortage or a wrong item in a storage location?

21. When is inventory relieved? When the order is picked, shipped, or invoiced?

22. Which reports are used to document customer complaints and credits for short, over, and wrong shipments?

23. Is your cycle-count procedure by product, by location, or both?

24. Do you perform any other auditing of receiving, stocking, or locations?

25. What do you believe are your major obstacles to maintaining inventory accuracy?

26. Which problems result from inventory inaccuracy?

27. Which procedures, reports, or system tools do you have to control inventory levels to prevent excess inventory?

28. Which procedures do you have to identify slow-turning inventory and obsolete inventory? Depending on the business, "obsolete inventory" could be defined as inventory that will never be used or sold, inventory that has lost value due to a new product replacing it, or something else.

29. Which recommendations do you have to improve inventory control and/or accuracy?

8

Human Resources Involvement

8.1 RETAIN GOOD EMPLOYEES

Hiring, developing, and retaining good employees are very important things that a Human Resources (HR) Department can help to accomplish for the business. Excessive turnover is costly due to hiring expense, possible relocation expense, and the training/learning curve before many employees make positive contributions for their new employer.

Screen potential employees very carefully, and always check their references. Some employers and executive recruiters do not always take this basic action, and they may be very sorry later for not doing so. Develop and use appropriate tests for applicants to ensure they have the basic skills and potential to succeed. I knew of a company that relied heavily on a test over the telephone for applicants who would be performing customer service functions using the telephone.

Watch new employees carefully during their probation/evaluation period. Help them develop good work habits through education and training. Counsel poor performers and determine whether they should be retained or terminated before their probationary period is over.

Conduct yearly or (preferably) twice-yearly formal reviews to provide feedback regarding how each employee is performing. Do not wait for the formal reviews to recognize and reward good performers, however, or to counsel and retrain poor performers. Whenever possible, provide a career path for employees with the potential to grow and be continually valuable to your business.

Perform periodic compensation reviews to determine whether your wages and benefits are competitive to reduce the possibility of employees quitting to take better-paying, similar jobs elsewhere. When turnover of employees does occur, make the most of it by trying to hire better replacements from within the business or new employees with good skills, positive attitudes, and new ideas.

8.2 JUSTIFY ALL REPLACEMENTS AND NEW HIRES

Establish a stringent review process prior to adding a new position or replacing existing positions due to attrition. Determine whether the functions performed by an employee who is leaving the business can be redistributed among the other existing staff in that department. If they can absorb those duties, the business can avoid the need to fill the position with another employee. Assess the possibility of using cost-effective, limited overtime to complete the tasks of the employee who is leaving rather than hiring a replacement. Consider whether a part-time employee could handle the work performed by an employee who is transferring to another department or leaving the business.

Require executive-level and the head of HR approval prior to hiring any new employee. Top management should be satisfied that all options were considered before approving a new hire or replacement.

8.3 OFFER OR REQUIRE A SHORTENED WORK WEEK OR WORK HOURS

If you have a downturn in business—and especially if you believe it will not be permanent—consider having a shortened work week and/or shortened work hours for some or all employees. Of course, this means less pay for hourly employees, and possibly for some nonexempt employees (e.g., salaried employees who are eligible for overtime pay). A highly visible example of this practice occurred in the state of California. This state instituted furlough days for many state employees to help deal with its budget deficit.

Understandably, most employees do not like the idea of a pay cut for any reason; however, it is a way to keep your workforce intact during difficult times for your business. Help employees realize that when an action such as a shortened work week or work hours is taken, it may mean the business will not find it necessary to implement more drastic measures. Most employees would prefer a pay cut and fewer work hours over being terminated.

8.4 EARLY RETIREMENT

If the business experiences a downturn, especially if you believe the decline will be a long-term trend, or if it has a budget deficit, consider offering early retirement to employees under certain circumstances. This is a fairly common practice. Have your Finance Department analyze "What if?" scenarios to determine the long-term financial impact of such a measure. Be aware that some businesses will not be in a financial position to offer early retirement to many, or any employees.

Work with the HR Department and Finance Department to develop eligibility requirements for early retirement. Such requirements for early retirement typically consist of a combination of the employee's age and years with the company.

8.5 EFFECTIVE USE OF TEMPORARY AND PART-TIME EMPLOYEES

Identify predictable peak work periods when temporary and/or part-time employees could help, rather than adding regular full-time staff. As the old saying goes, "Don't build the church for Easter Sunday." Some examples of predictable peak work periods include the following:

Yearly peaks such as during audits, tax preparation, physical inventory, sales promotions, seasonal high sales volume periods, and conventions

Monthly peaks such as a month-end push to ship orders, closing the financial books, preparing monthly reports, and mailing statements

Weekly peaks such as the receipt of a routinely scheduled large supplier shipment, payroll processing, Monday mail delivery, and weekly reports

Daily peaks when the mail arrives and when the small package carrier shipments arrive

Most banks, grocery stores, restaurants, retail stores, and schools/universities, and many manufacturing and distribution businesses, have obvious predictable peak and valley work-volume periods. The use of temporary or part-time employees is appropriate for handling peak work-volume periods for some of these businesses. For example, a bank in an area with a large population of retirees will be busy when Social Security checks are received. A bank near a business with a large workforce will be busy on the business's payday. Grocery stores have a daily predictable peak after normal work hours for most local businesses, as well as on the day of week when many grocery stores offer a senior discount.

Temporary and part-time employees enable a business to maintain a key core workforce during work volume fluctuations, and help avoid hiring and firing cycles. The functions assigned to temporary employees must be carefully determined.

Consider hiring temporary workers for permanent job openings where feasible. This could apply to selected direct and indirect production workers, as well as certain clerical positions. If applicable, let temporary employees know there is a regular position to be filled if they perform satisfactorily.

Observe and evaluate a temporary employee's performance carefully, just as you would during an initial probationary period for a regular (permanent) employee. If poor work habits, absenteeism, tardiness or attitude problems persist with a temporary employee, replace that person as soon as possible. In most cases of problem behavior by a temporary employee, if you believe it would be difficult to change the person's problem behavior, you may not want to try counseling the worker to give him or her every chance to succeed prior to terminating the individual. This is a subjective decision, but terminating a potential problem employee while he or she is a temporary employee is easier and less costly than terminating a regular (full-time) employee.

8.6 BARGAIN WITH THE BARGAINING UNITS

Just as you should bargain and negotiate with all your suppliers, so you can and should bargain and negotiate with any unions with members working for your business, especially when your business is experiencing a downturn in sales, cash flow problems, and/or pressure from competitors regarding pricing. These negotiations will not necessarily be in anticipation of a scheduled expiration of a bargaining agreement, but instead can be a part of the cost-cutting and productivity-improvement program.

You should include the employees who normally handle union negotiations such as a department within HR. Also, if top management is not normally involved in union negotiations, they possibly should be in this case. The union representatives need to understand the motivation for the cost-cutting and productivity-improvement program. If the business is facing a dire situation due to a downturn in business, the possibility of layoffs, plant shutdowns, and even going out of business if concessions are not given should be discussed. What you want from union negotiations could be wage concessions, the ability for your union employees to be more flexible regarding functions they can perform, changes in benefits provided to union members, or something else.

You should recognize that union negotiations will probably be contentious, but they are necessary if you have a serious need for cost cutting.

8.7 PREPARE FOR AND MANAGE CHANGE

If your productivity-improvement or cost-cutting efforts result in major changes in your business, you must prepare for and manage those changes. Examples of major changes can include a reduction in force (RIF), tighter supervision, implementation of a new computer system, introduction of automated equipment, use of robotics, and moving to a smaller facility. To prepare for the change, you must educate everyone involved regarding why the changes are necessary, how the changes will affect them, and what will be done to prepare for the changes. Training will be especially necessary when work assignments are changed, a new system is implemented, or automated equipment is to be used.

This is an area, like many of the other topics covered in the book, where there are good books and consultants who can assist you deal with what otherwise would be the side effects of difficult changes.

8.8 EMPLOYEE BENEFITS

Perform periodic reviews to determine whether your business's employee benefits are competitive compared with those of other employers that would be recruiting your potential and current employees. The trend for most businesses is to provide fewer benefits and/or to pay for less of the cost for benefits. Nevertheless, it may be better to be in the higher range of employee benefit offerings to prevent employee dissatisfaction and turnover.

8.9 POLICY REGARDING SUPPLIER GRATUITIES

Establish and communicate a clear policy to all employees making or influencing buying decisions that they cannot accept any gratuities from suppliers for their personal use. This policy should ensure impartiality and reduce the possibility of making bad buying decisions.

I have seen many examples in the past where suppliers of goods and services got the business because they provided gratuities to the buyers or influencers, even though their pricing, services, or products were inferior. Do not let this happen with your business.

8.10 AVOID RECRUITING FEES

When you need additions or replacements to your management team, technical staff, or other areas needing experienced employees, allow your HR Department to perform the recruiting before resorting to executive search firms. Nevertheless, some businesses prefer to use an executive recruiter they have used successfully in the past. A good executive recruiter will follow your specifications and thoroughly check out the candidates prior to proposing that you interview them.

The use of the Internet to assist with employee recruiting was previously mentioned in this book. Post the position with appropriate sites on the Internet. The Internet sites may be specific for certain types of positions, such as accounting, information technology, logistics, various categories of engineers, sales, and marketing. Using the Internet has proved to be a real money-saving way to identify potential new employees.

The key elements to recruiting new employees include the following:

Understand and be able to communicate why the position is available. If it is due to turnover resulting from inadequate compensation, determine what the fair compensation range is for the position.

Develop a thorough and accurate position description.

Identify the minimum education and prior work experience requirements for the position.

Fill the position from inside the business if possible, because you know the employees understand the business and organization. Also, it is good for morale when employees see that someone is hired from within.

Decide whether you are willing to pay a hiring bonus.

Decide whether you are willing to pay for relocation expenses.

List the position in appropriate newspapers and publications.

Require salary history, as well as work and personal references, from all candidates.

Verify candidates' education and check references.

Interview your top candidates and select the best fit for your business.

Conclude all steps in the process expeditiously, because in a tight labor market, the good candidates may select another employer before you make them an offer.

8.11 REDUCTIONS IN FORCE

The news headlines during the turbulent financial times of 2008–2009 reported that numerous businesses, including many famous names, were laying workers off. Numerous medium-size and small businesses all around the country also deemed it necessary to reduce their workforces during this economic downturn.

I always prefer working on projects for clients that are seeing increasingly higher demands for their products, so improving productivity is what they need. However, sometimes a reduction in force is required for a business when it believes all other options have been explored. Whether it is termed "downsizing" or "rightsizing," reducing the workforce in a business is one of the most obvious cost-reduction measures to take. A RIF should be done without sacrifice to necessary quality and service levels.

Making arbitrary percentage budget cuts across all departments in a business is usually not a good approach. This topic was covered briefly earlier in the book, and the message from the earlier discussion is worth repeating. Across-the-board cuts may hurt some lean and efficient areas, but may not be enough in other loosely managed, overstaffed, and inefficient areas.

The results of productivity analyses in each department can be used to help make RIF decisions. In addition to performing productivity analyses in each department, instruct all managers to do the following in their department:

Rank all employees, from top to bottom, based on each individual's overall importance and potential future contribution to the business's success.

Rank every position, from top to bottom, based on each position's overall importance and contribution to meeting the business's objectives.

Use performance evaluations and ranking data to make RIF decisions if possible. Reduce staff from the bottom of the lists up, based on the aforementioned ranking data, unless the HR Department determines that you cannot do it that way. For example, if the HR Department says seniority must be considered as the primary factor in determining who is reduced from the payroll, you must work from the person with the lowest seniority up. Unfortunately, this may result in your business losing some of its better performers.

Consider offering to pay benefits for selected employees if they take a temporary leave of absence, if you think their jobs will become needed again in the near future.

Coordinate with the HR Department each step of the way. The HR staff will know how to help determine which employees can be terminated or laid off, based on established policies and/or labor union agreements.

8.12 CONDUCT EXIT INTERVIEWS

It is a good idea to conduct exit interviews with all employees who leave your business, regardless of the reason they are leaving. If you do not conduct exit interviews, I encourage you to do so. As part of the agenda when you conduct an exit interview, ask the person if he or she can recommend how your business could improve productivity and cut costs. You never know what departing employees might say, and it could be something very helpful.

9

Measure Results and Reward Positive Efforts

9.1 DECIDE WHAT TO TRACK

You cannot track the results of your cost-cutting and productivity-improvement efforts unless you know what you want to track. Even if you did not monitor and report on certain measurable data prior to the cost-cutting and productivity-improvement program, you must try to create a baseline for comparison purposes from historical data in your systems. If you believe this is not feasible, develop and use baseline data as you begin your program. The measurements must be understandable and meaningful for evaluation purposes, or they are not worthwhile to track.

9.2 TRACK AS MUCH AS POSSIBLE PROGRAMMATICALLY

Work with your IT Department to determine the most efficient method(s) to track and report how the various areas in your business are performing. Downloading certain data from the main system into PC spreadsheet formats may be a good method for some businesses. If you determine you want to maintain a measurement for each department, determine the appropriate output measurement and the corresponding input measurement for each department.

For the various production departments, you may decide on units produced per day for the output measurement and hours worked per day in the department as the input measurement. IT personnel should be able to obtain the units produced by a department from a section of the manufacturing system and the hours worked for the corresponding departments from the manufacturing, HR, or payroll system. In a small business that lacks an automated system, you will have to do this calculation manually, or else use a PC spreadsheet.

For the Shipping Department, you may decide to use units shipped per day and/or total dollar value of shipments per day for the output measurement and hours worked in the department as the input measurement. IT personnel should be able to obtain the shipped units from the billing (invoicing) system data and the hours worked for the Shipping Department from the HR or payroll system. With these data, the IT Department should produce a performance report indicating units shipped per hour by dividing the units shipped by the hours worked. Following is an example of how to manually calculate the performance increase for a small company with three employees in its Packing/Shipping Department:

> The Packing/Shipping Department had been shipping an average of 1,357 units per week using 120 work hours. Its performance was 11.3 units per hour (1,357 ÷ 120).

> Due to some new products the business started selling, its sales volume increased, as did its average shipping volume. The Packing/Shipping Department's new shipping average was 1,704 units per week using the same 120 work hours per week, so its performance was 14.2 units per hour (1,704 ÷ 120).

> The performance increase was 26 percent, based on 14.2 units per hour −11.3 units per hour = 3.2 units per hour; 3.2 units per hour ÷ 11.3 units per hour = 26 percent increase.

> There were no new methods used or new equipment used to increase the Packing/Shipping Department employees' productivity. The improvement was simply due to having more work volume to process, and their capacity was still higher than their revised productivity level.

If you have established standard hours for the various jobs performed in each department, use the standard hours earned as the output measurement and the hours worked in the department as the input measurement.

9.3 SET FAIR STANDARDS OF PERFORMANCE

You cannot measure productivity or how well you are doing without some standards of performance. These standards must be fair. If the standards of performance are too tight, they will create employee dissatisfaction, resentment, and poor morale. If they are too loose, they can result in hidden poor productivity, employees may lose respect for management, and workers will not have the necessary incentive to be productive and do a good job.

I was on an assignment in Europe for a major heavy construction equipment manufacturer that was concerned about one plant that reported high employee, department, and plant performance; however, the plant was only marginally profitable. The plant management was very proud of their daily reports, which showed individual employee, department, and plant-wide performance. Performance overall was 127 percent of the standard, with some departments' level of achievement being as high as 138 percent of the standard.

There were more than 900 union employees in this plant, and we found from performing observations that very few employees were at their workstations at all times. We observed that most employees started the day at their workstations, but many spent as much as half their time wandering around visiting in other departments or in the huge employee break room at the facility. Some employees were often found sleeping. It turned out that the performance reported was so high because most of the standards were set far too low, and employees could meet or exceed their established standard without much effort.

Eventually, working within the management/union agreement guidelines, we were able to slowly but surely raise the standards, increase productivity, and reduce the employee workforce. This was accomplished mainly through improved supervisory controls that required the employees to report their production output on an hourly basis to their supervisors. The daily production output standards were broken into hourly increments, against which the supervisors could measure performance and identify problems.

If employees did not meet the hourly standard, the supervisor would determine the reasons why. The employees were given the benefit of the doubt and were asked if they missed the standard because of equipment problems or a lack of available work at their workstation. As expected, the problem was always simply due to poor performance—some employees were not at their workstations for up to half the day.

The requirements of the management controls we implemented called for the employees to be at their workstations each hour to report their production output to their supervisors. Therefore, they spent less time visiting other employees or in the break room, and production output increased dramatically for most employees. The plant became very profitable as a result of establishing fair standards and improving supervisory control.

The following example of setting standards, while a little lengthy, provides a worthwhile lesson. When I was a neophyte consultant, I learned how important it was to establish a meaningful unit of measure for the standards set and used to schedule work and monitor performance. Although I was a green consultant, I was deemed trustworthy enough to work on a project alone with virtually no oversight, except for telephone updates I made to my boss every other day and in-person visits from my boss every two weeks. For the first two weeks on this solo project, my work schedule included determining all the functions performed at this major business's printing facility as well as establishing work standards for each function.

On my first day, while I was interviewing a manager to help develop my list of functions performed at the facility, a rail car arrived filled with various huge rolls of paper supplies. The manager suggested I might want to observe the unloading process. I excused myself from the manager (no complaint there), and felt fortunate that I was able to observe from beginning to end all the individual activities involved in unloading the rail car and storing the supplies in their proper locations.

With my watch turned to the inside of my wrist so I could time the activities and my note pad in hand, I observed the person assigned to unload the rail car get the special lift truck he would use to unload the rail car. Instead of having forks like a standard lift truck, this vehicle was configured with rounded grippers specially made for lifting and moving the huge rolls of paper.

The start of the process to unload the rail car included going to the charging station where the electric-powered lift truck was being charged, checking that it had adequate charge, and driving it to the rail dock. Instead of setting a standard for those three tasks, my first activity was "Take the lift truck to the dock." The unit of measure was "occurrence" and the standard was 5.5 minutes. It actually took the worker 7 minutes; however, 1.5 minutes was spent talking sports news with a coworker, so I did not include that time.

The employee broke the seal on the rail car's door lock with a bolt cutter, unlatched the door, and slid it open. Again, I thought I was smart to name the activity "Open the rail car door," instead of setting a standard for the three component tasks involved. The unit of measure was "occurrence" and the standard time was 3.5 minutes.

Next, the employee climbed into the rail car and began removing the dunnage, which is packing materials to keep the rolls of paper from shifting in transit. He threw it on the ground, then picked it all up and took it to the dumpster. The activity was to remove and discard dunnage, the unit of measure was "occurrence," and the standard was 14 minutes. During this time, the worker uttered some loud profanities when he encountered some black widow spiders.

The employee extended a steel bridge from the dock to the rail car for the lift truck to drive on. Therefore, my next activity was "Extend dock-bridge," the unit of measure was "occurrence," and the standard was 2 minutes.

Finally, the employee began unloading the rolls of paper. There were three rows of 12 rolls stacked 2 high, for a total of 72 rolls. Of this total, 24 rolls were white card stock, 24 rolls were white continuous-form paper, 6 rolls were carbon paper, 6 rolls were yellow continuous-form paper, 6 rolls were light blue continuous-form paper, and 6 rolls were pink continuous-form paper. Of course, I set standards for unloading and storing rolls of white card stock, unloading and storing rolls of white continuous-form paper, unloading and storing rolls of carbon paper, unloading and storing rolls of blue continuous-form paper, and unloading and storing rolls of pink continuous-form paper. The unit of measure for each activity was "roll," and the standard was 5 minutes.

The next activity was "Complete paperwork," which entailed indicating all the products received compared to the manifest and turning the paperwork into the accounting clerk. The unit of measure was "paperwork," and the standard was 1.5 minutes.

The last activity was "Return lift truck to the charging area" with a unit of measure of "occurrence" and a standard of 2 minutes.

And now I will get to the point of the story. When I had my first telephone update with my boss, I told him proudly that I had documented and set standards for 27 activities including the activities associated with unloading the rail car. He asked me to list them, and when I was done, he said that I had probably documented and set standards for only 5 activities. When I asked him what he meant, he told me I should find out if the rail cars with rolls of paper always contained 36 rolls (it turned out that it did). If so, I should combine all the activities involved in unloading the rail car into one activity titled "Unload the rail car," use "rail car" as the unit of measure, and set the standard at 3.5 hours. That took my list of activities for which I set standards down to the 5 activities, like my boss had told me.

My boss then told me how these standards would be used to help plan and control work performed at the facility. He explained how much simpler it would be to assign an employee to "Unload the rail car" and know the total activity should take 3.5 hours. This is a good example of learning the "KISS" ("Keep it simple, stupid") principle.

Performing observations will help you understand how to develop standards for each activity performed in a department as well as evaluate performance for individual employees. One of the worst scenarios a business can have is to have inconsistent standards of performance for jobs that perform functions requiring the same level of skill and difficulty. This situation can arise within a department or between different departments where employees perform totally different jobs but require the same or less skill level and work effort. If and when employees learn that other employees are paid more for performing jobs requiring the same or less skill and work effort, it can cause big problems if not addressed. Inequity is understandably very upsetting to those employees who have to meet higher standards for the same or less pay than other employees. If some employees are held to a higher standard than others (especially if the standard is unfair), it creates friction and causes morale problems. If employees complain about such inequities, address them immediately and revise standards as necessary to restore management's credibility and employee morale.

Businesses that have piecework standards as part of their incentive system need to be careful to prevent overpaying employees based on the products they produce. Employees who are paid for piecework as part of an incentive system in addition to their base pay have been known to fool the industrial engineers or standard setters by looking like they are more productive than they really are. This results in loose standards and employees being overpaid for the work they produce.

Also, be careful when employees are paid a "day rate" as part of the incentive system. A "day rate" is what employees are paid when no incentive standard is available for a new product. It is based on the average pay an employee receives when he or she is working on an incentive system. Employees have been known to "squirrel away" some products they make while being paid the day rate and bring them out to be counted and receive credit when the incentive standard for that product is established.

Here is a final word of caution regarding the need to expedite the process of setting incentive standards for new products to avoid paying a "day rate" any longer than is absolutely necessary. I saw employees at the boot and shoe manufacturing business previously mentioned in the book get paid a day rate while they waited for an incentive standard to be established for a new product. They were producing exactly the same shoes for which there was a piece-rate standard; the only difference was that the color was brown instead of black. Until there was an incentive standard for the brown shoe, the workers received the day rate. This was due to a weakness in the management/employee incentive system agreement that called for industrial engineers to perform time and motion studies to establish new incentive standards for any product that had not been previously produced. We were able to work with the client and employees to fix the weakness in the management/employee incentive system agreement so that, when a model of shoe or boot was made in a new color, it would have the same incentive standard, instead of requiring that a new standard be established by industrial engineers.

9.4 MAINTAIN, MONITOR, ANALYZE, AND USE STATISTICS

Maintaining certain statistics can help you identify areas where costs are under control or where cost cutting could be achieved. Whatever statistics you maintain, they should be generated preferably daily, or weekly, but at least monthly. They should compare the current week's or month's data to historical data, including the data for previous weeks or months for that fiscal year, as well as the same week or month for the previous fiscal year. Cumulative year-to-date statistics should also be maintained.

Some examples of meaningful statistics include the following:

Productivity performance (the most important item) by individual and department

Quantified cost-cutting program results

Breakdown of the detail of causes and the related costs of quality rejects that resulted in scrap or rework

Product return volumes, reasons, and percentages of returns by reason

List of products that are being returned

Names of individuals who make costly errors

Planned versus actual sales

Manufacturing efficiency

Sales by sales territory

Sales by customer

Sales by product category

Purchase price variances

Accounts receivable average days outstanding

Equipment down time

Absenteeism by individual, department, and overall

Employee turnover by individual, department, and overall

Inventory turnaround (this helps you reduce inventory levels)

Overtime

Remember—whenever you use sales dollars for any comparisons or evaluations, if you reduce or increase sales prices, you must adjust your comparisons up or down accordingly.

Graphs and charts are good tools, because comparisons are easier to make and trends (good or bad) are more obvious. Displaying and distributing certain statistics can be a motivator. It is a particularly effective tactic to create some competition related to productivity among different departments, manufacturing managers, shifts, sales regions, distribution centers, and manufacturing plants. If you have monthly group incentives based on sales dollars, it is a good idea to display your progress each day. Continually measure your performance against existing standards or benchmarks. Audit and revise standards as needed due to the introduction of improved methods or processes.

9.5 EVALUATE COST-CUTTING RESULTS

Be prepared to evaluate the results of your cost-cutting efforts, put them into a report, and present them to management on a regular basis, starting with any initial positive results. Determining the exact financial benefits of your cost-cutting efforts depends on the availability of a good reporting system to measure improvements made because of your program. Thus you must make a comparison of certain measurements prior to and after your cost-cutting program begins.

The evaluation reports will be of great interest to top management and management responsible for the areas where the cost-cutting program is being implemented successfully. Top management should see reports regarding cost-cutting results of individual departments or operating units, as well as a report indicating overall cost-cutting results. Some managers may also want to see more detail information. Of course, the top-management reports will normally be in more of a summary format, whereas the reports for individual departments or operating units will have more detail. In fact, some reports for managers of departments should include performance by individual employees.

Remember the old saying, "Liars can figure and figures can lie." Make certain your evaluation methods are sound and accurate. Many items may appear to be good examples of cost cutting on their own when other pertinent factors are not considered. However, when they are evaluated along with other factors, the results may not actually represent a cost savings. At the boot and shoe manufacturer mentioned previously, productivity increases were over-emphasized; however, this priority resulted in generation of more scrap in the area where the pieces of leather were cut to make the shoes and boots. The loss of leather (yield) outweighed the productivity improvements. The evaluation method for workers in the area that cut leather to make shoes and boots was revised to include qualitative factors as well as quantitative factors, and the scrap problem was resolved.

Following are some cost-cutting evaluation category examples:

Employee head-count reduction. This is meaningful only if other significant factors are also considered. For example, if production output has declined, the reduction in employee head count may or may not really be a cost savings, depending on how much the production output has declined. It is a cost savings only if the ratio of head count to production has improved to a greater degree than it was previously. For example, if the head count was 6 and workers produced 100 units per day, the production for a head count of 5 would have to be at least 84 units per day or more to realize a true savings. This is based on 100 divided by 6 for a ratio of 16.7 units per head count, compared to 84 units divided by 5 for a ratio of 16.8 units per head count.

Expense dollar reduction, which could be aggregate, by department, or by an expense category. Again, you must be cautious when determining whether there are really cost savings. The fact that expenses have been reduced is good; however, if income dollars have decreased at a greater rate than expenses, the expense reductions may not actually be a cost reduction.

Decreased payroll and fringe benefit costs, including part-time and temporary employees.

Sales per employee.

Scrap and rework as a percentage of production.

Overtime savings.

Reduced number of facilities and/or cost of facilities.

Inventory turnaround (the best measure is inventory dollar value).

Ratio changes of managers to employees and/or supervisors to employees.

Ratio of indirect workers to direct workers.

Revenue generated from the sale or rent of excess facilities. Of course, the sale of excess facilities is a one-time cost savings or revenue generator, whereas the rent of excess facilities is an ongoing revenue generator.

Income from the sale of excess equipment, furniture, and supplies, which is another one-time revenue generator.

Freight recovered, which is the income you receive when you receive more money from your customers for freight than you have to pay due to off-bill discounting.

Increased units produced per hour worked. For example, you can show the results of your performance/productivity improvement efforts by determining the difference in the hours worked each week compared to the hours that would have been worked if you continued performing at the old rate, then multiplying the hours times the current average hourly pay, including fringe benefit dollars, which indicates your cost savings.

Following are the elements of a sample report to calculate savings:

1. The units produced per hour prior to implementation of the cost-cutting and productivity-improvement program. In this example, we will use 10 units produced per hour.

2. Units produced per hour for the current weekly evaluation period. In this example, we will use 12 units produced per hour.

3. Total units produced for the current weekly evaluation period. In this example, we will use 70,000 units produced for the first week.

4. Current average hourly pay rate, including fringe benefits. In this example, we will use $20 per hour.

5. What the cost to produce the total units produced in this weekly evaluation period would have been if operating at the old units produced per hour rate (#3 ÷ #1 × #4), which is 70,000 ÷ 10 × $20, for a total of $140,000.

6. Actual cost to produce the total units produced this weekly evaluation period (#3 ÷ #2 × #4), which is 70,000 ÷ 12 × $20, for a total of $116,667.

7. Cost difference (+ or −), which equals the savings (#5 − #6), which is $140,000 − $116,667, for savings of $23,333.

8. Cumulative savings, which is the cost difference for the first week (#7) plus each subsequent week (#7 + #8, from the previous

week), except for the first week, when the cumulative savings is the same as the first week. When you begin a report for a new quarter, use the last entry for column 8 on the previous quarterly report.

There is a section at the bottom of the report for pertinent comments. When preparing the report, enter the week-ending date and comments, if you believe they are worthwhile to include in the report, to explain exceptionally high or low cost savings.

Refer to Table 9.1 for an example of a weekly cost-cutting and productivity-improvement savings report that incorporates the above-mentioned elements. The report includes 13 weeks, so one report can be prepared each quarter.

9.6 FOLLOW-UP AND ACCOUNTABILITY

As with any management program, follow-up and accountability are absolutely essential elements to make the cost-cutting and productivity-improvement effort successful. Regardless of which approaches you choose to use, the follow-up must be immediate and consistent throughout the life of the program for it to be successful.

Of course, you cannot have follow-up and accountability unless you have something on which to follow up and provide accountability. The assignments made to departments and individuals during the course of the program from beginning to end provide the basis for these assessments. The overall program leader and all other managers and supervisors assigned to manage certain aspects of the effort must provide the follow-up and accountability for their areas of responsibility to ensure actions are initiated and followed through to completion.

9.7 GIVE CREDIT WHERE CREDIT IS DUE

Most employees thrive on praise, and a cost-cutting and productivity-improvement program provides the opportunity for recognition beyond the employees' normal areas of responsibility. Of course, this is in addition to any financial rewards individuals may receive as part of the program, which I have found is their major motivator. Such recognition also makes management aware of some employees with potential whom they might have previously overlooked or not otherwise noticed.

Table 9.1 Weekly Cost-Cutting and Productivity-Improvement Savings Report

Department: Shipping

	1	2	3	4	5	6	7	8
Saturday Week-Ending Date	Old Units per Hour Rate	Units per Hour This Week	Volume Produced This Week	Average Hourly Pay	Total $ This Week at Old Rate (3 ÷1 × 4)	Total Dollars This Week (3 ÷ 2 × 4)	Cost Savings (5 − 6)	Cumulative Savings (7 + 8)
7/7/2012	10	12	70,000	$20	$140,000	$116,667		
7/14/2012	10	12	75,000	$20	$150,000	$125,000	$25,000	$48,333

Comments: *Enter the Saturday week-ending date and comments you believe are pertinent, such as "4-day work week due to holiday," "High work volume due to sales promotion," or "Worked Saturday to ship as many orders as possible at month end."*

9.8 PERFORMANCE REVIEW PROCESS

If your business's performance review process includes less frequent than quarterly reviews, revise it as it relates to the cost-cutting and productivity-improvement program, so the reviews are monthly for the duration of the program. Once affected workers see benefits from their roles in the cost-cutting program, it will usually lead to more participation by them and other employees.

10

Concluding Comments

10.1 RECAP OF KEY POINTS

Please read this recap of key points before you use the Cost-Cutting and Productivity-Improvement Program Planning Worksheet to help plan your program. The key messages are listed in the same order they appear in the text:

Think about what your business would do if it realized big savings, or even modest savings, from a successful cost-cutting and productivity-improvement program. This might be the impetus you need to initiate a program at your business.

At some time, cost cutting and improving productivity become important or absolutely essential to most businesses.

Cost-cutting savings begin to hit the bottom line immediately.

As part of the initial cost-cutting and productivity-improvement program planning, you should establish objectives, including a range of how much money you want to save and what you plan to do with the savings.

Often, a business will use a variety of approaches to address different cost-cutting opportunities. Based on my experience, utilizing multiple approaches provides the best results.

You can call it what you like, but whether it is a team, a task force, or a committee you form, it can be one of the most effective approaches to planning and managing a cost-cutting program.

Consider using inside or outside consultants to help plan, organize, implement, and manage portions of, or your entire, cost-cutting program.

Many businesses choose to try goal setting before considering any other method of cost cutting.

Assigning cost-cutting goals to all levels of management or selected managers can obtain positive results. If there are no goals, generally no actions will be taken.

Instructing all departments to make arbitrary percentage cuts in budget or employee head count can be effective; however, it has drawbacks that must be considered.

Working with your suppliers of goods and services and your customers as partners can make your business run more efficiently and help you cut, contain, and avoid costs.

Discuss your cost-cutting goals with your suppliers and customers, and create mutually beneficial strategies to achieve them.

Results from Kaizen can include increased productivity, increased capacity, reduced setup times, reduced lead times, reduced inventory, and less floor space required.

Look at two or three years of budget expense history, because it is a very good way to identify possible cost-cutting and productivity-improvement opportunities.

To perform proper analysis, you must include an adequate level of budget detail.

Look at two to three years of payment history to your top 25–50 suppliers, based on the dollars you spent on them, to identify opportunities to cut costs.

Negotiating for better prices, quality, and service with your suppliers is one of the most important things you can do.

Conducting personal survey interviews with all appropriate employees and major suppliers to solicit cost-cutting and productivity-improvement ideas is generally far more effective than implementing a suggestion program.

Be aware of the advantages and wary of the disadvantages of employee suggestion programs.

There are certain sources to help identify areas for possible cost cutting that are free and without obligation.

Encourage departments other than purchasing to ask existing and potential suppliers how their goods and services could help cut costs and improve productivity.

Line managers and supervisors should understand their area's needs better than anyone else, and they can best evaluate alternatives that the suppliers may recommend.

One effective method for dealing with potential new suppliers, especially if they sell commodity-type items, is to send them a list of the items you currently purchase on a regular basis and ask them for "apples and apples" quotes. It becomes easy to determine who is worth seeing based on their quotes. If nothing else, this information can be used to determine whether you are getting good pricing from your current suppliers or whether prices could be reduced.

The objective of and approach to value engineering are to look with creative new eyes at ways to manufacture your products differently so they can be made more cost-effectively.

It is best to start with your high-volume or high-cost products.

You can choose from a variety of methods to determine individual and group productivity, which will help identify whether the business is staffed properly. Of course, overstaffing is unnecessarily costly, and understaffing can mean you may not achieve your production goals efficiently or in a timely manner.

Conducting observations of all the job functions (tasks or activities) being performed by the applicable employees helps identify how long each task should take and enables you to set standards of performance you can use to plan work and measure performance.

The observations can also help determine whether the tasks are truly necessary. If they are necessary, potentially better methods may be obvious to an objective outside observer who does not work in the area.

Observations may also identify wasted or unproductive time and the reasons for it, which you can work on to eliminate.

It is essential that top management lead the cost-cutting program by example, down through all levels of the organization.

Kick the cost-cutting program off with business-wide meetings and announcements so that all employees understand the program.

The first thing employees will want to know when they hear about the cost-cutting and productivity-improvement program is "How will it affect me?" and "What's in it for me?"

Employees need to know why the program will be a good thing for them individually and for the business as a whole.

You must provide education and training on the cost-cutting and productivity-improvement program. The education part includes communicating why the program is needed and what a successful program could mean to your business. The training part includes the specifics of how to proceed with various steps of the program.

There are certain areas where you should be cautious regarding cost cutting:

If the cost cutting could result in sacrificing acceptable quality levels.

If the cost cutting could result in unacceptable service levels.

If the cost cutting could jeopardize safety.

If the cost cutting could result in possible security risks.

If the cost cutting could damage employee morale.

Do not cut costs in Research and Development, except in dire situations, and then only for the short term.

An employee at a business conducting a cost-cutting program made an excellent cost-saving recommendation and was asked why she had not made the recommendation before. She responded, "Because nobody ever asked me to make recommendations before."

A lot of cost cutting can be accomplished without any upfront expenditure. If cash flow is tight, these are the types of cost-cutting measures to look for first. You can use some of the money you save in this way for other cost-cutting improvements that do require upfront expenditures.

Certain investments of time, effort, and/or money will provide a worthwhile return on the investment (ROI).

Many people believe that obtaining competitive bids and negotiating for better prices for goods and services are the most effective ways to cut costs.

It has always been my philosophy and policy to give the incumbent suppliers a chance to retain the business.

Consider using as much up-to-date technology as you can, including the Internet, to simplify tasks and save time and money.

If different policies and procedures exist at multiple locations, compare and analyze them. If there are not compelling reasons to justify the differences, select the best ones and standardize them for all locations to follow. It might be a good idea to implement a combination of the best policies and procedures used by many locations.

Cost-cutting and productivity-improvement opportunities may "drop into your lap" if you are constantly alert and open to them.

As you progress and grow professionally with added experience, you will trust your instincts more and pursue—instead of ignore—potential opportunities.

Small material savings on each unit produced add up when high volume is involved. Likewise, small labor savings on each unit produced add up when high volume is involved.

Do not spend effort on activities that are not worthwhile, because it is a waste of time and money that could be spent on productive activities.

Productivity is a measure of the output of production compared to the input of resources used to produce that output.

Do managers and supervisors have the proper spans of control, based on how complex the work performed by their subordinates is, as well as the physical area covered?

Can some managers and supervisors assume greater responsibility, or do you need additional supervisors to improve control, quality, and productivity?

Are employees adequately cross-trained to ensure flexibility and prevent some staff from being overworked, while others are less productive or idle when the work mix changes?

Follow this credo: "Do as much as you can, as fast as you can, as long as you do it safely and accurately."

As performance is measured, feedback could be in the form of praise, counseling, education, training, demotions, promotions, reassignments, or terminations.

The major areas where I have frequently seen unproductive time are at the beginning of a work shift, at break times, at lunch time, and at the end of a work shift. Without proper controls, the start-up is slow, breaks and lunch periods are extended, and many people stop working too early before time to quit.

Mismatched capacities in an assembly line or workflow process can result in lost time when one step in the process takes more time than the next step(s), and the bottleneck causes some employees to be idle, waiting for something to work on.

Maintaining an adequate ongoing backlog of available work at each workstation is an essential element to avoid unproductive time. If there is nothing to work on, employees cannot do any work.

As the old wise saying goes, "A chain is as strong as its weakest link."

It is especially easy to identify the weak link on an assembly line type of operation.

When a product or process involves numerous separate steps in a flow sequence, you can easily determine which step takes the longest time by performing observations, performing time and motion studies, or maintaining workflow logs at each step.

The earlier a constraint or bottleneck is found in the process or flow, the more unproductive time will occur downstream in the process.

A constraint or bottleneck may be a piece of equipment that does not produce fast enough; a slow, poor-performing employee; or an imbalance in workloads that results in one operation being slower than the others.

When I asked why a task I observed seemed inefficient the way it was performed, and the answer was "Because it has always been done that way," there was almost always an easier and more cost-effective way to accomplish the task.

Put yourself in your employees' shoes to imagine how a little something unexpected, such as occasional free doughnuts at the morning break or cookies at the afternoon break, would make you feel.

The best thing a manager or supervisor can do is give a literal or figurative pat on the back when an employee or department does a good job.

Allow adequate time for your business's budget process, including initial preparation, review, revisions as needed, and approving the final budget. "Haste makes waste" really applies when preparing budgets is concerned.

Every manager must ask the question, "Is it a nicety or a necessity?" whenever someone in the organization wants to spend money or effort on something new.

Generally try to avoid product-liability problems that could lead to legal costs and damage your business's image by designing and producing safe products.

Develop a preventive maintenance (PM) plan for all your key equipment (expensive and/or vital for production) and for your facilities.

Negotiate for long-term free or low-cost service and maintenance when purchasing new equipment or computer systems, because that is when you have the most negotiating strength for these items.

Sometimes an unnecessarily costly practice originates from overreacting to a specific situation or problem in the past.

I do not advocate, under any circumstance, a sacrifice in acceptable quality levels when taking cost-cutting or productivity-improvement actions.

If you do not have one, implement an illness and injury prevention program to ensure your business is working safely and in compliance with OSHA requirements.

Expand your definition of safety to include the one I developed years ago: "You do not get hurt, your coworkers do not get hurt, the products do not get hurt, the equipment does not get hurt, and the facility does not get hurt."

Security policies and procedures can range from fairly simple and inexpensive measures to very comprehensive and expensive measures depending on the value of your business's products, raw materials, information, facilities, and equipment.

Obtaining goods and services at favorable prices is part of the procurement staff's regular functions. However, when you are conducting a cost-cutting program and these personnel are tasked with obtaining even better prices from suppliers, they are generally successful.

The bottom line is that you want to lower the unit costs of all the raw materials and parts you purchase. This should not be just a goal included as part of the cost-cutting program, but should become an ongoing goal year after year.

Your first efforts should focus on your high-usage-volume raw materials and purchase parts, followed by your higher-cost raw materials and purchase parts.

Several factors other than cost must be reviewed when considering importing goods from other countries, including the lead times required, freight costs, any import duties, and quality.

Analyze service functions as you would analyze "buy versus make" decisions, and decide whether you want to perform them in-house or have them performed by an outside service.

You may decide that certain services should be performed partly or completely inside the business, or partly or completely by an outside service.

For years, many businesses have had a policy and practice of regularly scheduling annual temporary plant shutdowns. This has been particularly true for businesses that have a lot of equipment requiring major annual preventive maintenance and businesses that have a large mature workforce of employees eligible for several weeks of vacation each year.

If you have excess equipment you do not believe you will need in the future, sell it. This is an excellent one-time revenue-generating action that hits the bottom line of the P&L immediately.

Each department should analyze all of its printed input and output reports with a view toward reducing paper usage.

An old trick is to discontinue distributing selected reports you suspect are not necessary to see if anyone complains.

Your business may be able to recycle items other than paper, depending on which products the business produces.

An obvious way to cut shipping-related costs is by obtaining lower rates for the shipping services you utilize. Remember to negotiate, negotiate, negotiate.

Another way to look for ways to cut freight-related costs is to review and possibly revise your current freight-related practices and policies.

Many considerations regarding packaging your products can be exploited to possibly save money.

Use only the minimum amount of staples or tape necessary to keep your cartons secure when they are shipped.

Establish, publish, and enforce telephone, email, and Internet usage policies at your business.

Travel and entertainment (T&E) is a "hot button" issue with many businesses.

If your business requires numerous employees to travel as part of their work, you need to establish fair travel and entertainment policies.

Make a list of travel and entertainment items that will and will not be approved for payment.

You should obtain and maintain reports that indicate scrap and rework costs. These reports must contain an adequate level of detail to help identify sources of repeated scrap or rework. A source could be a work area, specific work center, employee, or product.

The Quality Control Department can help identify better quality control points and report on actions taken to reduce scrap and rework costs. The earlier in the workflow you discover a problem that will result in rework or scrap, the better the outcome will be.

Under certain circumstances, hiring some mentally challenged (also known as "mentally handicapped") employees is cost-effective and does a lot of good for less fortunate and deserving people.

Overtime (OT) may possibly be needed for peak workload periods, leaves of absence, vacations, absenteeism, and special projects. Nevertheless, you should approve overtime only if you feel certain it is needed.

Use overtime to avoid adding permanent or temporary staff when it is deemed to be a more cost-effective approach overall.

Always require prior management approval for working overtime.

Too much overtime can cause employee dissatisfaction as well as lead to possible quality and safety problems, due to employees' being tired and careless.

You do not want nonexempt employees (employees who get paid for overtime) to like and depend on overtime pay, because they may attempt to create the need for it.

We all know that a lack of quality or service can be costly, but too much quality or service can also be costly.

Look for, recognize, and eliminate unnecessary excess quality and service when you observe it.

Identify and determine the costs associated with quality in your business, and determine your business's optimal distribution of quality cost types.

The highest priority is to minimize external quality costs, because they are quality problems found by your customers after the products are shipped to them.

Doing things right in the first place is more "motherhood and apple pie" advice, but it is very important to emphasize.

If you do not do things right the first time, the failure costs you in many ways.

If the business's physical and/or book inventory is inaccurate, either on the low side or the high side, it can cause various problems.

A good inventory system does not guarantee inventory accuracy. Instead, good people, education, training, and discipline are needed, along with a good system, to ensure high inventory accuracy.

Hiring, developing, and retaining good employees are very important things an HR Department can help to accomplish. Excessive turnover is costly due to hiring expense, possible relocation expense, and the training/learning curve before many employees make positive contributions for their new employer.

Establish a stringent review process prior to adding a new position or replacing existing positions due to attrition.

Determine whether duties can be redistributed among the existing staff so they can absorb the work functions of the employee who is leaving before you seek to fill the position.

Assess the possibility of using cost-effective overtime to complete the tasks of the employee who is leaving rather than hiring a replacement.

Consider whether a part-time employee could perform the work of an employee who is transferring to another department or leaving the business.

Require executive-level and the HR manager approval prior to hiring any new employee. These managers should be satisfied that all options were considered before approving a new hire or replacement.

If you experience a downturn in business, especially if you believe the trend will not be permanent, consider having a shortened work week or shortened work hours for some or all employees. Of course, this means less pay for hourly employees, and possibly for nonhourly employees.

If you experience a downturn in business, especially if you believe it will be a long-term decline, or if you have a budget deficit, consider offering early retirement to employees under certain circumstances.

Identify predictable peak work periods when temporary and/or part-time employees could help, rather than adding regular full-time staff. As the old saying goes, "Don't build the church for Easter Sunday."

Just as you should bargain and negotiate with all your suppliers, so you can and should bargain and negotiate with any unions with union members working for your business, especially when your business is experiencing a downturn in sales, cash flow problems, or pressure from competitors regarding pricing.

If your productivity-improvement or cost-cutting efforts result in major changes in your business, you must prepare for and manage those changes.

Examples of major changes can include a reduction in the workforce, tighter supervision, implementation of a new computer system, introduction of automated equipment, and use of robotics.

To prepare for the changes, you must educate everyone involved regarding why the changes are necessary, how the changes will affect them, and what will be done to prepare for the changes.

Perform periodic reviews to determine whether your business's employee benefits are competitive with those of other employers who might be recruiting your potential and current employees.

Establish and communicate a clear policy to all employees making or influencing buying decisions that they cannot accept any gratuities from suppliers for their personal use.

When you need additions or replacements to your management team, technical staff, or other areas needing experienced employees, allow your HR Department to perform the recruiting before resorting to executive search firms.

When clients have increasingly higher demands for their products, improving productivity is often what they need. However, sometimes reductions in force are required when there is a significant downturn in demand for a business's products and/or services.

When you conduct an exit interview with a departing employee, ask the person if he or she can recommend how your business could improve productivity and cut costs.

You cannot track the results of your cost-cutting and productivity-improvement efforts unless you know what you want to track, and you must understand and document a baseline of historical data with which to compare the results.

Work with your IT Department to determine the most efficient method(s) to track and report how the various areas in your business are performing.

You cannot measure productivity or determine how well you are doing without some standards of performance.

The standards of performance must be fair. If the standards are too tight, they will create employee dissatisfaction, resentment, and poor morale. If they are too loose, they can result in hidden poor productivity, employees may lose respect for management, and workers will not have the necessary incentive to be productive and do a good job.

Maintaining certain statistics can help you identify areas where costs are under control or where cost cutting could be achieved.

Be prepared to evaluate the results of your cost-cutting efforts, put them into a report, and present them to management on a regular basis, starting with any initial positive results.

As with any management program, follow-up and accountability are essential elements to make the cost-cutting and productivity-improvement effort successful.

Most employees thrive on praise, and a cost-cutting and productivity-improvement program provides the opportunity for recognition beyond the employees' normal areas of responsibility.

If your business's performance review process includes less frequent than quarterly reviews, revise it as it relates to the cost-cutting and productivity-improvement program, so the reviews are monthly for the duration of the program.

10.2 PLAN YOUR WORK AND WORK YOUR PLAN

Apply the saying "Plan your work and work your plan" to your cost-cutting and productivity-improvement program. Use topics discussed in the book and incorporate them into your plan of what you want to do at your business. Table 10.1 provides a Cost-Cutting and Productivity-Improvement Planning Worksheet.

10.3 CONTROL THE WHOLE BY CONTROLLING THE PARTS

Control the details of the project with specific assignments to appropriate individuals or groups of individuals. Design a form to make assignments or just use a memorandum. Make sure you include a number for each assignment, assignment date, description of the assignment, name(s) of the individual(s) responsible for the assignment (if a group is assigned, one person must be assigned overall responsibility), the planned completion date, and the actual completion date.

Maintain an assignments list to monitor and control the program's progress. The list should include the basic information contained in each assignment, such as the assignment reference number, assignment date, brief description of the assignment, name(s) of the individual(s)

Table 10.1   Cost-Cutting and Productivity-Improvement Program Planning Worksheet

---

Best Approach or Approaches to Use (Check all that apply):

Goals for Managers with Budget Responsibility (e.g., reduce budget and/or head count by a certain percentage) _____

Employee Suggestion Program _____

Establish Committees and/or Teams_____

Describe the Program's Committees and/or Team's Organizational Structure (top to bottom):

_____

_____

Frequency of Progress Meetings

Describe: _____

Group Incentive Program _____

Use Consultants _____

Combination of Approaches _____

Describe: _____

Areas to Include in the Program:

Entire Company _____

Selected Divisions, Departments, or Other Units _____

Describe: _____

Methods to Identify Opportunities:

Analyze Budget Expenses _____

(continued)

Table 10.1   (continued)

Review Top Suppliers _____

Observe Functions Performed in Selected Areas _____

Describe Which Areas: _____

Conduct Employee and Supplier Interview Surveys _____

Conduct Kaizen Events _____

Describe Areas for Selected Kaizen Events: _____

General Areas (e.g., product costs, operations costs, administrative costs)

Describe: _____

Specific Expense Categories (e.g., travel and entertainment, freight, scrap and rework, cost of quality, overtime)

Describe: _____

Areas Not to Include (e.g., safety, security, quality, sales, service, research and development)

Describe: _____

ROI Areas to Save Money by Spending Money (e.g., automation, programming, new equipment, robotics, CAD, new system)

Describe: _____

Recognition and Rewards Options (what's in it for the employees)

(*continued*)

Table 10.1   (continued)

Describe: _____

_____

How Will the Business Benefit from the Cost Cutting and Productivity Improvements?

Describe what will be done with the cost savings?

_____

responsible for the assignment (if a group is assigned, the name of the person with overall responsibility), the planned completion date, the actual completion date, and a column for comments regarding progress and concerns or possible problems.

10.4 CONCLUDING THOUGHTS AND KEY COST-CUTTING QUESTIONS

Get in the habit of asking yourself and your staff the following questions throughout the course of your cost-cutting and productivity-improvement program:

Am I running my organization (areas of responsibility) as I would if I owned the business?

Are we continuously and objectively looking at all aspects of our operation with new eyes to seek out cost-cutting and productivity-improvement opportunities?

Is this expense item or activity a necessity or a nicety?

What are all the possible negative ramifications of eliminating this expense item or activity?

If the expense item or activity is a necessity, can we obtain the item less expensively or perform the activity more cost-effectively?

Which cost-cutting recommendations were made and/or implemented this week? If the answer to this question is none, you need to ask one more question: Have we been trying hard enough, or can we be congratulated for having completed a successful cost-cutting effort?

Have I periodically reread the table of contents of this book and used it as a reminder of where additional cost-cutting and productivity-improvement opportunities or ideas might be found?

What is the best way to make the most of the cost-cutting savings we generated by investing the savings wisely to improve our business and make it more successful?

Does everyone do as much as they can, as fast as they can, as long as they do it safely and accurately? If everyone in your business follows this credo, you will have a productive organization.

The final chapter offers some examples of successful cost-cutting and productivity-improvement projects, highlighting the results achieved from these efforts.

11

Examples of Successful Cost-Cutting and Productivity-Improvement Efforts

11.1 BRIEF DESCRIPTIONS OF SUCCESSFUL COST-CUTTING AND PRODUCTIVITY-IMPROVEMENT PROJECTS PERFORMED AND WRITTEN BY VARIOUS MANAGERS AND CONSULTANTS

The examples provided in this chapter are intended to give you some ideas of what you might be able to accomplish at your business to cut costs and increase productivity. The examples are written by the contributors and appear alphabetically by contributor. Some are more descriptive than others in terms of what the business did to obtain the cost savings and productivity improvements. The results may inspire you to undertake a cost-cutting and productivity-improvement program at your own business.

The following example was provided by Evan Ackerman.

Project business:	Business-to-business (B2B) portal for a music/entertainment company.
Project description:	In 2001, the Internet was gaining popularity for B2B functions. The music company had several teams (approximately 50 people) that replied to marketing material requests from business partners. These requests included electronic assets (album covers, artist photos, full-length tracks, and audio clips) in different formats and sizes that could be published in magazines (*Rolling Stone* and *Billboard*), in newspapers (articles and

advertisements), and on Internet sites (bestbuy.com, itunes.com, and amazon.com). Replying to these requests took significant time and effort. The goal of the project was to provide a fast self-service option for marketing professionals and business partners to download the files and information needed.

Project details: I started the first day of the project by meeting with the project team that was struggling with the approval of the requirements document, which was holding up the design and the development efforts. After reviewing the requirements document with the team and the business constituents, I devised a new plan of attack, project schedule, and process to finalize the requirements and end the stalemate. By the end of the second week, the requirements had been rewritten to the specifications of the business users, design templates had been started, and the developers had a prototype of the final application. After four months, the project was completed on time and on budget. The internal business units were excited by the feedback from the 2,500-plus users. The site had more than 10,000 assets available for download, and each could be rendered in various sizes, formats, and levels of quality. The number of users doubled within a year, and the site is still in use today. The people who spent hours each day responding to these marketing requests were able to move to different areas in the company and focus on artist development and other marketing efforts.

Project benefits: It was estimated that this project generated more than $750,000 in hard cost savings each year.

The following examples were provided by John Bryan.

Project business: Polyester processing.

Project description: The project had the stated objective of improving the productivity and profitability of a large polyester processing plant. The primary area of focus within the plant transformed polyester pellets into polyester fiber. Examples of the eventual use of this fiber include filling for disposable diapers and polyester fabrics and yarns. The overall process involved heating the pellets into a liquid, then extruding the liquid into various deniers (thicknesses) of polyester filaments. Next, the filaments were cooled and twisted together, with as many as 39 other filaments, to form a length of yarn. This yarn was then joined with a number of comparable lengths of yarn to be later heated and crimped and, if for fabric or disposable diapers, finally chopped into small pieces.

The Extrusion area converted polymer pellets into polyester filaments through a combination of heat and pressure. During the course of the project, it became evident that the keys to productivity and profitability of the Extrusion area were the amount of time during which the extruders were out of production, individually and in aggregate; the temperature in the extruders; and the proportion of time during which the extruder melt temperature varied from the specified temperature. The plant reprocessed more than 90 percent of its post-extrusion processing waste, which amounted to more than 10 percent of the total extrusion volume. Examination of the use of process controls revealed that extrusion temperature could be used to predict the need for extruder maintenance.

Project results: Implementation of extrude-predictive maintenance showed the following results in less than six months:

- Scrap and rework were reduced to less than 1 percent, which effectively increased productivity and saleable material by more than 10 percent.
- Extrusion department attainment versus plan improved from 91 percent to 97 percent.

- Extrusion department unscheduled down time dropped from 6.5 percent to 2 percent.

- Processing line operating time dropped by more than 200 hours per week despite an increase in average weekly production from 3.8 million pounds to 4.5 million pounds (mostly through reduction in scrap and rework) in an operating unit that had historically experienced more demand than it could meet.

- Labor cost was reduced by more than $1 million on an annualized basis.

- The increase in effective capacity was valued at approximately $700,000 per week in revenue, with no increase in raw materials and the previously mentioned reduction in labor.

Project business: County Department of Health Services.
Project description: The Department of Health Services primarily provided health care to indigent county residents. The scope of this program included the accounts payable, data processing, claims processing, income recovery, long-term care, and utilization review functions of the department.
Project results: In the Accounts Payable area, work assignments were shifted to balance the workload and to allow parallel processing of incoming claims. Accounts Payable added a second shift to reduce backlogs and to avoid capital expense associated with the purchase of computer terminals, and automated a link between two previously separate computer systems to eliminate the need for manual rekeying of data. Causes for rejecting claims were documented. Once documented, formal action could then be taken to eliminate that cause and its corresponding rework. In addition to reducing the backlog of claims to be paid, the implemented changes reduced the cycle time of the bill-paying

process by more than 80 percent and increased Accounts Payable productivity by more than 50 percent, an improvement valued at more than $1.1 million annually.

Project business:	Major hotel chain.
Project description:	Hotel reservations call center for one of the world's leading hospitality companies. The company employed more than 2,500 reservations agents in multiple call centers answering more than 20 million calls annually. The hotel chain sought a strategic transformation, which would raise levels of selling effectiveness while protecting the client's world-class status with respect to service and cost, leading to three specific objectives: (1) improve the conversion of inbound calls into room reservations; (2) reduce performance variability among reservations agents; and (3) redesign resource-planning processes and associate productivity measures.

Goal alignment coupled with new goals focused call center agent and management attention on revenue generation and productivity. New-agent profiles defined best practices and observable behaviors of successful agents and became the benchmark for coaching suboptimal performers and recruiting new agents. Supervisors shifted their attention to lower performers, and top performers received incentives for helping their lower-performing associates. New performance appraisals and new individual, team, and brand performance measurement and management systems were aligned with the new performance expectations. Supervisors and managers attended to variances in performance rather than average performance for individuals and teams. A new self-funded, contingency-based agent incentive program rewarded individual, team, and center sales effectiveness and productivity and was supported by a new closed-loop continuous improvement process.

Project results: • Increased front-line "managing" capacity by 45 percent through job redesign

• Reduced new hire turnover by more than 50 percent

• Agent productivity improvements valued at $1.2 million annually

• Call conversion performance reduced costs by more than $1.6 million and yielded more than $10 million in incremental annual revenue

The following examples were provided by Carlos Conejo.

Project business: Rice Mill

Project description: The client was a rice mill in Northern California. Approximately 200 employees processed about 50,000 pounds of rice per shift, two shifts per day. When I arrived, there was lots of conflict. People were keying one another's cars, punching holes in the tires, and vandalizing company property. Yes, these were adults!

I had a feeling something was amiss, because the company failed the Carlos Conejo test for employee job satisfaction. When I take an initial tour at a client company, there are two places I always go to gauge the level of employee satisfaction. One is the break room; the other, the men's room. Both are critical barometers for me as indicators of the type of culture that I am getting into. It is not scientific, but I am usually right (at least 80 percent of the time). I guess it's the old 80/20 rule at play.

If there is no break room or the production floor doubles as a break room ("Hey, pull out the folding table . . . "), this tells me that management really does not care, and in most cases an adversarial relationship exists between the employees and management. Oftentimes, this spurs on union talk and union organizing efforts. There is an increase of worker's compensation cases and dubious "accidents" occur. Again, I have no scientific proof, for those literal individuals reading this description, but I am right 80 percent of the time.

On the flip side, I have seen beautiful break rooms that look like a nice cafeteria, and the really "top-end" companies even subsidize employee meals. I have worked at and contracted at a couple of these companies, and it sure was nice to get a really nice lunch for less than $5! What a deal! These companies are usually pretty large employers, but not always.

Now, you don't have to go "high end" to satisfy employees. Another company provided a really nice break room for its employees. It had a battery of microwaves so that people would not have to wait during their breaks, it flew every flag that represented each employee's nation of origin on the production floor, and the employee lockers were large, made out of white oak, and had no locks on them. Yes, that is right—no locks. You see, employee morale and trust were so high that locks were not needed and people respected this. Indeed, this was a good place to work.

As mentioned earlier, the other place I go to is the men's room. The litmus test there is graffiti in the stalls and boogers on the walls (sometimes worse). To me, these things show disdain, frustration and anger, and obviously lack of respect. They tell me that management is out of touch, or there is a strong personality in management who tries to control matters usually by force and not through scientifically proven methods such as Lean or Six Sigma. One CEO was so egotistical that he pulled the whole "plug" during the training. We had 14 projects just starting out and his ego was more important than the growth of his company.

"We do not have time for this nonsense. We've got to get back to work," was the clear message that was sent.

Project results: No results. Pity—the company had such great potential.

_____

_____

Project business: Thermo forming/food packaging

Project description: I contracted out with a more enlightened management team who understood the value of employee motivation, empowerment, and involvement. This project included executive management: The vice president of operations and the plant manager were both present, and then engineering, tooling, and the front-line mechanics who did the work on machinery setups.

Working together, this group went out to the production floor and studied the current situation. In Japanese, this is called Genshi Genbutsu, or "go see." The production floor is called Gemba, but literally it means "where the action is." You see, things don't get resolved in the conference room alone; one needs to go and study, get dirty, get under and inside the machines (safely), ask questions, and find out how to leverage and best utilize others' skills and talents to improve the process.

The bottom line for this group was that together, with my guidance and their expertise, we took the machine setup from 6 hours, using three mechanics, to 1 hour and 15 minutes, with only two mechanics. With three mechanics, they expect to do the change-over in 30–45 minutes. This not only reduces costs, but also makes this company more flexible and agile. It reduces the down time significantly and increases production capacity. When a press is standing idle, it is a problem for everyone because no one is making money.

I am proud and honored to be called "Sensei," which is the Japanese term for "teacher." The word literally means "guide," or one who has previously gone through the experience.

For employees to gain more experience, management needs to make sure to get as involved as possible in participating, mentoring, and empowering the workforce through experiential learning experiences that increase skills, communication, efficiency, productivity, and quality, with the ultimate goal of better serving the critical needs of the customer.

Most importantly, I recommend that you select a process that is reliable, such as Lean or Six Sigma. When you follow the right process, you get the right results. Part of this process is creating a new culture at your organization—not just a culture as an initiative, but as a "way of life," a new "way of doing business."

Project business:	Optics and eyewear manufacturer.
Project description:	We trained the company's staff, and they earned Six Sigma Greenbelt Certification.
Project results:	The project generated $5 million in new improvements and a 25 percent increase in quality.

Project business:	Magnetics and electronics manufacturer.
Project description:	We started with leadership classes, including the owner. We conducted office Kaizen and production floor Kaizen to improve the work flow.
Project results:	The client increased sales from $390,000 per month to more than $1.2 million per month. The office Kaizen event looked at the sales order processing procedure, which was taking 5 days to complete. With a team of six employees and utilizing Lean concepts, value stream mapping, Five S, spaghetti diagrams, and literally moving three offices to improve the work flow, we were able to reduce the procedure to 4 hours.

The *APICS Dictionary* describes Five S as follows: "Five terms beginning with 'S' used to create a workplace suitable for lean production. (1) Sort means to separate needed items from unneeded ones and remove the latter. (2) Simplify means to neatly arrange items for use. (3) Scrub means to clean up the work area. (4) Standardize means to sort, simplify, and scrub daily. (5) Sustain, which means to always follow the first four Ss. The Five Ss are sometimes referred to by the Japanese equivalents: seiri, seiton, seiso, seiketsu, and shitsuke."

Project business: Cellular repeater manufacturer.
Project description: We conducted Lean training and established a sequence of events, cycle times, and cellular manufacturing. During the implementation, the engineering department was motivated to eliminate blueprints on the production floor and go to electronic documentation via computer screens.
Project results: The client projects increased production flow by 80 percent. Electronic documentation eliminated the need for paper, and the latest blueprints were always on the production floor.

Following are overviews of successful cost-cutting projects provided by Peter A. Crosby regarding projects performed by CGR Management Consultants.

Project business: Paper products distributor.
Project description: The $1 billion distributor of paper and related products asked us to assist in developing a strategy to guide future distribution decisions in its largest marketing region. The objective of the project was to determine the optimal mix of master and branch warehousing given current and projected sales volumes plus customer service

requirements. Detailed data developed during the study included the following (for existing and potential facilities):

- Landed cost for 13 product groups
- Costs (fixed and variable) and capacity limits for:
  - Master warehouses
  - Branch warehouses
  - Will-call/customer pickup sites
- Transportation costs for:
  - Master-to-branch warehouse routes
  - Branch warehouse-to-customer delivery routes
- Inventory carrying costs
- Product group demand (over a five-year horizon)

These data were input into a mathematical programming-based supply-chain model that generated optimal network configurations for current and future operating scenarios.

Project results: The optimal network configurations indicated the relative cost-effectiveness of alternative mixes of master and branch warehouses, provided cost trade-offs for various levels of customer service, and produced annual savings potential of more than $1.2 million.

Project business: Distribution and marketing.
Project description: We were retained by a $300 million food cooperative to analyze the distribution and marketing functions for all operating groups. In addition, the business wanted to better understand its market position relative to the competition.

Our analysis revealed a number of improvement opportunities in operations, warehousing, and transportation:

- Order-processing procedures and invoicing policies could be strengthened and selective staff reductions made without impairing customer service levels.
- Scheduled deliveries from forward warehouses should be explored to verify the predicted savings potential; selective warehouse relocations should also be pursued.
- Selective upgrading to more favorable freight rates for plant-to-warehouse shipments should be negotiated.

We worked closely with Distribution Department staff members throughout the engagement. Consideration was given to plant-direct shipments as well as shipments through forward warehouses. An analysis of customer service/order-processing activities was also undertaken to identify opportunities for improving department effectiveness as well as service-level performance. Customer interviews were conducted and customer service comparisons made with representative companies in the same industry.

In addition, the need for a more integrated distribution management and reporting system was identified. Similarly, a realignment of the existing organization structure was suggested that would blend line control with functional responsibilities.

The customer survey pinpointed specific elements of the customer service mix that were most important, and suggested selective areas where service-level reductions could be instituted without loss of revenues. We also developed a competitive profile highlighting areas for increased marketing attention and prioritized actions to sustain and improve the business's current service position.

Project results: The study results identified short-term cost-reduction/profit-improvement actions amounting to nearly $1 million annually as well as a number of longer-term opportunities.

Project business: Food products company—development of a logistics strategy.

Project description: We were asked by a large food company to develop a logistics strategy for one of its frozen food lines. This company was experiencing nationwide competitive pressure from other suppliers, which were providing superior customer service and distribution services in the form of lower laid-down costs at the customer's warehouse. Because distribution costs accounted for more than 30 percent of the landed product price, logistics strategy was an important dimension in overall product marketing strategy.

We conducted a series of interviews, data analysis, on-site reviews, competitive interviews, and customer surveys. On the basis of this diagnostic review of the company's policies and practices, we developed a strategy geared toward strengthening:

- The customer service function in operations, thereby relieving the sales force of this function
- Carrier negotiation activities with irregular route common carriers, contract carriers, and rail carriers
- Order fill rate
- In-plant materials management
- Freight accounting practices
- Forecasting, order entry, inventory management, and production planning
- Inter-departmental communication

Project results: The company received benefits from the study by reducing "lost" freight charges, increasing order fill rates, and justifying a customer service function positioned at the division level rather than the sales level. Other benefits were obtained by lowering customer freight costs through negotiating equipment supply and reduced freight-rate rail contracts. The corresponding increase in sales volume was estimated to be in the millions of dollars.

Project business: Grocery products company.

Project description: Consolidation center feasibility study. We were retained by a $120 million grocery products manufacturer to determine the feasibility of consolidating East Coast customer shipments from three operating divisions. A related reason for the study was to establish a viable base from which to generate incremental revenues by penetrating additional grocery product markets.

Operating data were developed, including the following elements:

- Customer shipment volumes and costs
- Inventory levels and carrying costs
- Warehousing costs (handling, order consolidation and storage)

Candidate consolidation center locations were identified and current plant-to-customer annual costs compared to alternative scenarios encompassing consolidated shipments.

Project results: As a result of the analysis, a single consolidation center was determined to be attractive, in that warehousing and transportation costs were minimized and additional inventory impacts manageable. The project also prescribed a more cost-effective mix of common carrier and private fleet vehicles, and established guidelines for an improved inventory-management system and warehouse operations.

Project business: Frozen food manufacturer.

Project description: Consolidation of customer service activities. We were asked by a $300 million frozen food producer to develop organization and staffing guidelines for combining the order-processing operations of two subsidiaries. While warehousing and transportation activities had already been combined, the customer service functions were still independent.

Historical order volume and staffing data were analyzed from a statistical perspective to develop staffing-versus-order volume relationships. Work sampling studies were also performed to confirm workforce utilization levels. In addition, interviews were conducted to assess the impact of consolidation on related organizational activities.

During this project, we analyzed current and projected activities of two related customer service organizations. The evaluation considered variations in customer service requirements due to the following factors:

- Customer type (e.g., retail, food service, military)
- Customer location (e.g., East, Midwest)
- Shipment mode (e.g., CL, TL, LTL, pooled)
- Order type (e.g., TWX [teletypewriter exchange], mail, telephone)
- Volume changes (e.g., seasonality, monthly/ weekly peaks)

Project results: The study provided the client with guidelines for consolidation of customer service activity, procedures for determining order-processing department staffing as a function of forecast sales levels, and yielded approximately $100,000 in annual direct labor savings through selective staff relocations and reassignments.

Project business: Nationwide restaurant chain.

Project description: Corporate consolidation of distribution activities. A major restaurant and specialty convenience store chain asked us to conduct a diagnostic study of its two major divisions' captive restaurant fulfillment operations. The objective of the study was to quantify the benefits to the corporation of combining distribution operations, including the following elements:

- Order fulfillment from restaurants
- Order-fulfillment center facilities
- Equipment and rolling stock
- Labor (human resources)
- Management
- Information systems and e-commerce systems
- Customer delivery routes
- Supplier purchasing

We first developed a profile of each division's operations. By describing each operation in geographic and delivery characteristic terms, we captured the essence of the major functions performed by the divisions. We then hypothesized a consolidated scenario, estimated the same measures of performance, and compared the present and the consolidated operations from financial and operational standpoints. The company then took advantage of the following opportunities:

- Consolidation of warehousing
- Department of Transportation "TOTO" authority

- Intercorporate hauling provisions
- Trip leasing to a third party
- Other major provisions of the Motor Carrier Act of 1980

Project results: As a result of the study, more than $2 million per year of savings was realized in the form of reduced freight, warehousing, inventory, and order-fulfillment and processing costs. Phase II implementation involved closing specific warehouses, outsourcing selected "in-house" food-processing activities, reorganizing management and labor positions, and changing accounting practices.

Project business: Municipal school district.

Project description: Vehicle fleet strategic and operational planning. A large school district that operated a fleet of more than 2,500 vehicles asked us to prepare a strategic and operational plan after reviewing its current activities. The following areas were included in the review:

- Organization and staffing for more than 3,000 employees, managers, and professionals
- Equipment purchasing, replacement, and maintenance
- Vehicle route planning and control
- Use of computers in district-wide transportation operations
- Cost reduction for a $170 million annual budget

We identified and tested the concept of a decentralized operations and planning organization. Computerized route planning software was identified that would generate more cost-effective routes than existing manual methods. We also evaluated computer-aided dispatching concepts and systems.

Project results: The study identified capital cost reductions that would lower annual outlays by as much as 50 percent; a plan was also developed to achieve $50 million savings in annual expenditures.

Project business: Integrated petroleum company.

Project description: Private truck fleet strategy. A major oil company asked us to review its local delivery truck fleet operations and management with the objective of developing a distribution strategy. The company had recently designed and installed a refined product marketing model that was used to evaluate the following issues:

- Exchange agreements
- Choice of carriers
- Terminal location
- Terminal size

We visited the major terminals in a region where 25 terminals were located. During our visits, we gathered fleet operations profile data that were used to evaluate the current operations. We also conducted a survey of other fleet operators to assess the competitive practices used in the industry.

Project results: Our analysis resulted in a strategy of scheduling overtime, replacing vehicles earlier, and using a driver control system based on computerized devices. More than $1 million in annual operating expenses was saved by this client from reduced driver and maintenance costs.

Project business: Dairy products company.

Project description: Private fleet operations assessment. A major producer of dairy products retained us to evaluate the operational effectiveness of its private fleet. Included in our assessment were the following issues:

- Equipment and driver deployment
- Equipment type (e.g., tractor, trailer)
- Equipment and driver utilization
- Transport and local delivery routes
- Vendor pickup potential
- Opportunities for outside carriage
- Operating policies and procedures
- Alternative fleet management organizations

Project results: As a result of our analyses, transport fleet operations were centralized, an improved mix of private and outside carriage was established, increased utilization was achieved, excessive equipment and drivers were identified, and more formal operating procedures were instituted. Annual labor cost savings of more than $300,000 was also achieved.

Project business: Consumer products company.

Project description: We were asked to develop a 10-year supply chain strategy for a division of a $600 million consumer products manufacturer. The objective of the study was to determine the optimal mix of raw material sources, production facilities, and warehouses given current and projected sales volumes, plus future capital expenditure requirements. Detailed data developed during the study included the following items (for existing and potential facilities):

- Raw material costs and supply limits
- Alternative product formulations
- Production costs (fixed and variable) and capacity constraints

- Interplant transportation costs
- Warehousing costs
- Freight-to-trade delivery costs
- Worldwide product demand (over a 10-year horizon)

These data were input into a mathematical model tailored to the specifics of the situation. Optimal networks generated were subsequently analyzed using a net present value approach to verify that capital investments required over the 10-year period were justified.

Project results: The optimal procurement/production/distribution networks selected produced annual savings of as much as $20 million and defined a capital investment decision strategy to be pursued over a 10-year horizon.

Project business: Communications equipment manufacturer.
Project description: Restructuring channels of distribution. As a part of an overall strategy-development assignment, we developed a plan and approach to restructuring the company's channels of distribution. The company originally had more than 10 strategic business unit segments in areas as diverse as audiovisual equipment, antennas, and medical electronics. A direct sales force was employed to market some product lines; broker groups were used for others. In many cases, the brokers and company salespeople competed with one another; in other territories, brokers competed with the company's direct contract selling through a national accounts program.

We calculated the costs of selling and distributing under a variety of scenarios and channel structures, and estimated the sales volume by using a direct sales force versus broker network. A one-step versus two-step distribution process through distributors and dealers was also evaluated by examining the pricing and discount structure of the product lines. In addition, from this information we identified the overlapping territories and product lines of brokers and company sales representatives.

Project results: We recommended an improved structure of distribution channels for the client that reduced selling expenses by more than 10 percent when this program was implemented. The number of brokers, distributors, and dealers was also reduced, thereby increasing surviving broker, distributor, and dealer commissions. Most overlapping product lines and territories were eliminated, as was major account competition between brokers and the company's sales representatives. The distributor sales and marketing departments were streamlined and a market research group was established.

Project business: Food processing company.
Project description: Manufacturing/distribution strategy. A $150 million food products firm asked us to analyze the company's current distribution network and identify alternative production and distribution strategies to support future growth.

Detailed data developed during the study included the following items (for existing and potential facilities):

- Manufacturing costs for five product groups
- Warehousing costs (fixed and variable) and capacity limits
- Transportation costs:
  - Plant to warehouse
  - Plant to customer
  - Warehouse to customer

- Inventory carrying costs
- Product group demand (over a five-year horizon)
  These data were input into a mathematical model that generated optimal production/distribution network configurations for current and future operating scenarios.

Project results: The study findings realigned customer shipment patterns, which produced immediate savings of nearly $200,000; defined alternative production strategies offering annual savings potential of as much as $1 million; and identified increased market penetration potential attainable through expansion of the existing field warehousing network.

Project business: Consumer products company.

Project description: Production and distribution strategy. We were asked to develop alternative distribution strategies for a $350 million manufacturer and marketer of consumer products. Primary issues to be addressed included the following:

- Customer service maintenance/improvement
- Manufacturing alternatives (inhouse versus contract)
- Master warehousing (in addition to regional distribution centers)
- Customer delivery alternatives (e.g., UPS)

Detailed data developed during the study included the following items (for existing and potential facilities):

- Manufacturing costs for 11 product groups
- Warehouse costs (fixed and variable) and capacity limits
- Transportation costs

        – Plant-to-distribution center

        – Distribution center-to-customer

- Inventory carrying costs
- Product group demand (over a five-year horizon)

These data were input into a mathematical model that generated optimal plant/warehousing network configurations for current and future operating scenarios. The study findings resulted in a reallocation of contract and internal manufacturing, realignment of future warehouse locations, specification of a fixed customer service level for all products, and development of a more effective customer shipping policy.

Project results: Total production and distribution costs were reduced by more than 20 percent while maintaining current customer service levels, and annual operating savings of $4 million was identified.

Project business: Electrical products manufacturer.

Project description: Sales forecasting and production scheduling system. A $200 million manufacturer of electrical products asked us to develop an improved system for scheduling production based on sales forecasts. Current forecasting utilizing industry indicators had not been sufficiently accurate to guide the production scheduling process, causing both inventory out-of-stock and surplus situations.

We examined existing forecasting and scheduling procedures for three major product groups and established optimal techniques to be used. For forecasting, a variant of exponential smoothing was applied to monthly shipment forecasts; production levels were then established to achieve customer service and inventory level targets at plant and field warehouse locations.

Project results: The revised system improved forecasting accuracy as much as 50 percent, identified safety stock reductions of $150,000 annually, and established guidelines for raw materials purchasing.

Project business: Medical electronics manufacturer.

Project description: Reduction of manufacturing costs. A well-known, fast-growth, high-technology manufacturer of external and implantable devices was facing debt restructuring and planning a public common stock offering. For the business to create the most favorable image among the financial community and to improve cash flow, we were asked to help develop a better method of controlling manufacturing costs as well as to identify areas for immediate overhead expense reduction.

We conducted interviews with the key managers of the company and collected detailed manufacturing data regarding product volume, cost, and personnel head count. We also analyzed current methods for calculating standard costs. On the basis of our review, we recommended the following plan of action:

- Installation of a new product design, release scheduling, and project control system
- Design and installation of a detailed sales-forecasting system to balance the finished goods inventory, safety stocks, and smooth production scheduling
- Design and installation of a multiple-product, volume-sensitive manufacturing cost-planning and control system

Project results: Manufacturing cost reduction was achieved through minimizing additional quality assurance personnel hiring, thereby saving more than $500,000 annually.

Project business: Industrial plastic fittings manufacturer.

Project description: Consolidation of operations. We were requested by a subsidiary of an $800 million manufacturing company to establish a plan for consolidating the machining and assembly operations of three separate production facilities. The objective of the study was to maximize utilization of existing equipment and human resources.

Our focus included establishing operating methods, engineered standards, production shift manning levels, and facility layouts, which maximized productivity while minimizing cost. Predetermined standards were used as well as time and motion analyses. Total production costs for all manufactured items were developed and equipment specified to satisfy current and projected production volumes.

Project results: Improvements to material flow and inventory levels were achieved, as well as annual operational improvement opportunities of more than $50,000.

Project business: Construction company.

Project description: Profitability analysis. We were requested to conduct an analysis of operational profitability for a privately held construction firm. The purpose of the study was to determine the immediate and long-term viability of the company.

Our evaluation focused on immediate cost savings and debt-reduction opportunities as well as addressed the organizational and operational resources necessary to support future business. Industry associations and selected competitors were also contacted to verify business trends in both the private and public sectors.

Findings identified operational improvements in transportation, maintenance, and administrative activities through a more effective organizational alignment. On the basis of industry forecasts predicting zero or negative growth, a portion of the company's capital equipment was determined to be excessive and was subsequently sold.

Project results: Immediate annual savings identified exceeded $500,000, with ongoing savings of more than $100,000 per year.

Project business: Steel products distributor.

Project description: A major distributor of steel pipe and related products asked us to develop recommendations for improving the operations in three of the company's warehouse locations. In our evaluation, we reviewed the following elements:

- Paperwork and paper flow
- Accounting activities
- Traffic activities
- Office automation alternatives
- Staff capabilities

Study findings pointed to the following opportunities:

- Administrative workload reductions through paperwork forms redesign, revision of existing reporting systems, and reallocation of accounting and traffic responsibilities
- Reduction in clerical efforts through automation of word processing, accounting, and inventory management
- Increased management and staff productivity through implementation of a formal goal-setting and performance measurement system

Project results: Overall operational effectiveness was strengthened, and administrative support costs were reduced. Projected annual direct labor savings exceeded $250,000.

Project business: Soft drink manufacturer.

Project description: Purchasing appraisal. A $200 million beverage producer requested an analysis of the company's purchasing activities to identify areas for profitability improvement.

Purchased materials, which represented more than two-thirds of the total cost of goods, included the following items:

- Aluminum cans
- Steel cans
- Glass bottles
- Metallic foil containers
- Labels
- Packaging materials

The costs of these materials were examined as well as current purchasing policies, practices, and procedures. Interviews were also conducted with marketing, distribution, and field operating personnel plus selected suppliers to identify areas for cost reduction and purchasing economies.

Project results: As a result of our appraisal, immediate savings opportunities of more than $4 million were realized, a series of longer-term actions prescribed, and annual operating cost reductions of nearly 10 percent identified. In addition, guidelines were developed for stronger centralized purchasing and improved reporting systems.

Project business: Wine and spirits wholesaler.
Project description: Consolidation and layout of distribution centers. One of the largest wine and spirits wholesalers in California was operating five regional distribution centers in a major metropolitan area. We were asked to evaluate the feasibility of facility consolidation, locate a consolidated site, lay out the new building, select equipment vendors, and determine the staffing of the new center with warehousemen and drivers.

One of the major tasks of the assignment was to develop warehouse labor time standards for receiving, put away, picking, and truck loading. We simulated alternative layouts, material handling methods, and equipment configurations and selected the alternative with the lowest risk and highest return on investment.

Project results: Labor staffing was reduced by more than 50 percent with the consolidation, and order selection rates were doubled using sortation and merge materials handling equipment. Return on investment for the overall project was greater than 20 percent.

Project business: Dairy products processor.
Project description: Distribution strategy and cost reduction. One of the largest dairies in the United States asked us to participate in its turnaround efforts prior to the company sale to a competitor. The scope of our work was to reduce costs wherever possible, using improved distribution strategies and computer systems. We were involved in a series of projects that focused on the following areas:

• Plant and distribution terminal location
• Frozen product inventory management
• Computerized vehicle routing and control
• Driver schedules and compensation

- Fleet replacement justification
- Automotive fleet lease versus ownership evaluation
- Line haul fleet justification
- Multiple-product backhaul
- Reorganization of the distribution function

Project results: Savings were achieved totaling more than $500,000 per year. The after-tax return on investment with a new truck fleet was confirmed at 12 percent.

Project business: Protective coatings manufacturer.

Project description: Logistics network analysis. We were asked by a $40 million manufacturer and distributor of industrial protective coatings to review its finished goods distribution network. Two plants, five leased facilities, and three public warehouses were currently servicing customers nationwide, and alternative service methods were to be examined.

Operating data were developed, including the following items:

- Customer sales volumes (dollars and units)
- Transportation costs:
  - Interfacility transfers
  - Customer shipments
- Warehousing costs
  - Customer service/order processing
  - Occupancy (e.g., lease, depreciation, insurance, taxes, utilities, security)
  - Communications
- Inventory levels and associated carrying costs

Alternative networks analyzed included the following:

- All distribution from a single plant
- Distribution from both plants
- Plants plus leased facilities
- Plants plus public warehouses

Project results: As a result of the analysis, the two-plant network was determined to be the most cost-effective alternative, in that warehousing and inventory expenditure reductions more than offset increases in transportation expense. Annual savings were projected to be $1.3 million, or approximately one-fourth of the total distribution cost. Another alternative was to combine the two-plant operation with the use of public warehousing. This approach would minimize the impacts on customer service by maintaining a presence in the market and still provide annual savings of approximately $700,000.

Project business: Soft drink beverage producer and distributor.

Project description: Facility location analysis. A large producer and distributor of soft drinks asked us to assist in realigning the company's current distribution network. Three plants were supplying 13 branch locations that delivered 70 million cases annually to 45,000 customers. Each branch had its own sales force, warehouse, and delivery capabilities serving a defined geographic area.

The purpose of the project was to determine the least-cost facility network, including specifying the number, size, location, and type of each facility. Issues to be considered included the following:

- Combined versus separate sales and distribution territories

- Trade-offs between cost, service, and market penetration for numerous small facilities with fewer delivery vehicles compared to larger facilities with larger fleets
- Use of a shuttle and depot system as an alternative to the branch system
- Impact of market shifts over a 10-year period

The following approach was adopted:

- Historical data were assembled into groupings (geographic, product, average order size).
- Market forecasts for three years were obtained considering regional/local population estimates and consumption trends.
- Facility data were developed considering productivity by shipment mode, indirect costs, and proceeds from closure.
- Fleet data were established considering costs and loading/unloading rates, plus stem and cluster mileage and times.
- A software package was selected and customized to address the quantitative aspects of the analysis.

Project results: Operating practices were modified in such a way as to produce annual savings exceeding 20 percent.

Project business: Grocery products manufacturer.
Project description: Logistics reengineering and inventory reduction. A $400 million canned goods manufacturer and distributor to supermarket chains asked us to rationalize its warehouse network and to establish an inventory reduction program. The first phase of work was to identify the benefits to be realized by reengineering the logistics processes for shipping goods to customers and replenishing the company's 10 public warehouses from its four processing plants. The plants were located in the United States and overseas.

A series of steps was taken during a diagnostic review of this business:

- Broker and buyer surveys were conducted that focused on customer service requirements.
- Representative samples of inventory items, daily replenishments, and daily customer orders were collected.
- An annual shipment profile was developed.
- Cost and product characteristics were estimated.

Two logistics decision support tools were used in our analyses, including a PC-based facility location optimizer and an inventory transaction simulator.

Project results: The results of our analysis indicated that savings in inventory carrying costs of $1 million to $2.6 million were attainable through cutting slow-moving items and reducing safety stocks. An additional $3 million of savings in freight, warehousing, and inventory carrying costs was identified through reengineering warehousing assignments to customers and by reducing the number of warehouse locations.

Project business: Health products company.
Project description: Supply chain strategy and reengineering. A nutritional food processor's line had become very popular with gym clubs, health and fitness stores, vitamin outlets, and New Age natural foods markets. When this company grew beyond the small outlet market and penetrated the supermarket, drug chain, and mass merchandisers market, its original supply chain was outgrown. To capitalize on opportunities for logistics and product cost reduction, improvements in customer service, and manufacturing, this client retained us to conduct a supply-chain turnaround assignment.

The turnaround was focused on three vital areas of the supply chain:

- Strategy
- Structure
- Processes

The supply-chain strategy focused on the "make or buy" decisions in outsourcing manufacturing, distribution, and other supply-chain functions. The supply-chain structure focused on the location, number, and size of plant and warehouse facilities. The process reengineering effort was directed at the following areas:

- Demand forecasting
- Production planning
- Purchasing ingredients and packaging
- Managing raw materials and finished goods inventories
- The logistics processes of the order-to-delivery chain, inventory deployment, traffic, transportation, warehousing, and customer service

Project results: We identified $750,000 in operating cost savings from the realignment of warehouse territories and the shifting of finished goods packaging from the plants to the distribution centers. This flexible supply-chain system, driven by more accurate forecasts and supported with variable service-level safety stocks, was the cornerstone of the company's efforts to maintain profitability and positive cash flow.

Project business: Computer hardware distributor.

Project description: Interim management of purchasing function and inventory reduction. A $500 million computer hardware distributor was struggling due to having made seven acquisitions in the prior year and not having completed the integration of these new organizations. One of the functional areas in disarray was purchasing. The Purchasing Department staff was scattered in three locations, with overlapping vendor responsibilities and lack of clarity for functional objectives, overall direction, reporting relationships, and accountability. As a result, despite high inventory levels, stock-outs (shortages) were excessive, resulting in poor fill rates to customers.

We were asked to assume responsibility for the purchasing function on an interim basis, reorganize the function, reduce costs, develop improved processes and procedures, and improve both inventory turnover and customer fill rates. Actions taken included the following:

- Consolidated all buying into one location with improved clarity about roles, responsibilities, and reporting relationships
- Rationalized buying responsibility so that no more than one buyer bought a supplier's line
- Reorganized by product categories (e.g., only one buyer would handle all printers)
- Developed and implemented better tools and processes to make buying decisions for both replenishment purchases and "deal" or "opportunity" buys
- Pruned the least important suppliers in each product category
- Eliminated "brokerage" purchases and sales and their related losses, write-offs, and "dead" inventory

Project results: The Purchasing staff was consolidated into one location and head count reduced by 20 percent; inventory turnover increased from 10 to 13.

Project business: Computer software distributor.

Project description: Warehouse stocking strategy. A $3 billion software distributor had eight warehouses spread across the United States, but never seemed to have the right item in the right place at the right time. All eight warehouses attempted to carry all 15,000 stock-keeping units (SKUs), resulting in too much inventory in some locations and too little inventory in others. Fast-moving items always seemed to be in stock in the wrong place, resulting in poor customer service and excessive expenses for expedited freight.

We worked with the vice president of operations and built a model that allowed us to look at the trade-offs among the following issues:

- Warehouse capacities
- SKUs stocked
- Inventory investment: safety and cycle stocks
- "Splits" (when an order for a SKU is not filled from the nearest warehouse)
- Freight expenses (including premium freight for "splits")

After the model was developed and benchmarked against actual demand history, we used it to evaluate alternative scenarios for stocking different types of SKUs in various warehouses. We paid particular attention to individual warehouse capacities, as this was already a major problem at several warehouses. As a result of examining these scenarios, we developed the following stocking strategy:

- Slow movers, customer-specific items, troublesome consumer products, and very expensive SKUs are now carried in only one warehouse.
- Fast movers and/or big dollar generators are carried in all eight warehouses.

- All other SKUs are carried in two "master" warehouses.

Project results: When the stocking strategy was implemented, significant improvements were realized: premium or emergency freight was cut by more than two-thirds; fill rates (both before and after "splits") increased by 10 percent; and inventory turns were improved by 15 percent.

Project business: Drugstore chain.

Project description: Development of optimal sourcing and distribution strategy. A $3 billion retail drugstore chain allowed individual store managers to decide which items to stock and how to acquire them. While this policy enabled store managers to match their stores' product assortment to local markets, it created significant problems:

- Economies of scale in purchasing were almost impossible to achieve.
- Direct store delivery (DSD; the primary distribution method) was being cut back by suppliers due to rising costs, which resulted in fewer options for the stores.
- Delivery minimums were being increased dramatically, requiring the stores to order and carry more inventory.
- Rack-jobbers had raised their markups on merchandise to the point that this option had become uneconomical for many product categories.
- Other drugstore chains were increasingly using captive warehousing and distribution alternatives, resulting in lower "landed-on-the-shelf" costs.

We were asked to identify the optimal sourcing and distribution strategy for each of the business's nonpharmaceutical product categories. Specific alternatives to be considered included various wholesalers and rack-jobbers, DSD, and various forms of chain-controlled self-warehousing and distribution.

The actions we pursued included the following measures:

- Extensive interviews with store managers and suppliers
- Documentation for each key product category
  - Current volume (e.g., dollars, cube, pounds, shipments, minimums)
  - Current pricing, including markups and volume discounts
  - Key attributes (e.g., delivery frequency, minimum shipment, inventory levels)
  - Capabilities and costs for each distribution alternative

We developed a financial model that enabled "what-if" analysis of various combinations of product category, sourcing and distribution alternatives. As a result:

- A third-party logistics provider (3PL) was selected for warehousing and delivery.
- Centralized purchasing was developed for selected product categories.
- Specific wholesalers, rack-jobbers, and DSD were used for selected categories.

Project results: "Landed-on-the-shelf" cost reductions yielded more than $6 million of savings in cost of goods sold (COGS).

Project business: Consumer products company.
Project description: The client was a consumer products company making photographic film, and the project was to

improve its distribution center (DC) operations. Characteristics of the DC included:

- 500,000 square foot master DC serving a network of six branch warehouses
- Processing annual sales volume of $3 billion
- Handling and storage for eight product groups consisting of 18,000 SKUs

We developed more than 50 recommendations that would benefit the client. Specific initiatives were identified that provided the greatest and most immediate return on investment:

- Reengineering of distribution by:
  - Implementing work standards and performance metrics
  - Improving supervisory skills and job flexibility
  - Maximizing material flow and equipment utilization
- Centralization of transportation, focusing on:
  - Carrier and mode selection
  - Contract negotiation for inbound, outbound, domestic, and international freight
  - Consolidation with foreign trade zone (FTZ) and customs compliance to minimize fines and penalties
  - Opportunities to reduce costs while increasing service
- Realignment of the logistics/DC reporting structure to improve communications
- Development of enhanced reporting to monitor and benchmark all logistics cost elements
- Integrating the SAP enterprise system with existing warehouse application software
- Development of a supply-chain strategy encompassing all U.S. warehouse locations

- For upper management, an assessment of the current DC manager's capabilities, and suggested guidelines for improving his effectiveness

Project results: The recommended reengineering initiatives produced annual savings exceeding $100,000. Other recommendations enhanced productivity and streamlined operations.

Project business: Various types of businesses.

Project description: We were retained by several different clients in a cross-section of industries to help them develop a process for handling special-purchase "deals." These situations occur when a buyer has a special opportunity to buy products at a great price, but must commit to buying large quantities. Such deals normally arise at the end of the quarter or year, when sellers are anxious to "make their numbers." They also commonly occur when the seller is trying to "stuff the channel" prior to the introduction of competing products by major competitors. Prior to implementing our process, we frequently found that our clients had as much as 40 percent of their inventory composed of these special deals. This often put a real strain on both warehouse space and cash.

We undertook the following actions:

- Interviewed key Purchasing, Finance, and Sales personnel, plus selected suppliers
- Developed a financial model (of the economic trade-off between the added profit from buying at the special price and the cost of carrying the additional inventory) that generated an optimal buy quantity recommendation
- Designed a process that assured that Finance personnel were involved in seeing whether these special buys met their cash constraints

(if any) as well as their return on investment targets
- Trained the buyers on the use of the model, the new process, and negotiation tactics, as well as how to use the model and the process as a negotiating tool to get the suppliers to "sweeten" their deals even further to satisfy the model's targets.

Project results: All clients reduced their purchases and their inventory associated with these special deals, while increasing the total money obtained via special discounts. They also achieved greater control and consistency through the new process, and all were assured that special deals met the target ROI and overall cash constraints.

One client decreased quarterly special deal purchases and inventories from $90 million to $15 million, and increased gross profit from special deal discounts by $1,500,000.

The following example was contributed by Charles Cunningham.

Project business: Major tire manufacturer.
Project description: Change-over time reduction. I was working in a large tire factory in the early 1970s right smack in the middle of NASCAR country. We had a varied product line that included many different sizes and types of tires. The approximately 200 tire builders were individually tasked with changing over their assembly machines. It normally took at least 4 hours for an operator to change over because they did this somewhat infrequently. This practice resulted in lost productivity and extra labor cost. A proposal was made to train a designated change-over operator to assist with the process. If change time could be cut to 1 hour, it would pay for the extra labor unit. The productivity gain would be a bonus. The tire builders

were enthusiastic about this prospect because it would increase their incentive pay.

Project results: The tire builders far exceeded the 1 hour change-over goal by using the same concepts that they learned making quick pit stops (a number of them were involved in the local stock-car racing culture) and decreased the change-over time to less than 30 minutes. When the corporate industrial engineering personnel were told about this outcome, they said the process could not be completed in 30 minutes. The plant sent a video of the change-over being done in 25 minutes (yes, that one was rehearsed) so the corporate industrial gurus came for a visit to see how they were getting hoodooed. The plant responded with a sub-20-minute demonstration. The engineers were enthusiastic and helpful. They designed a very pretty aluminum carrier for the equipment to replace the wooden one the "pit crew guys" had knocked together. Then they went back to corporate headquarters.

Later, the carrier was delivered. It was too big to fit in the space available, so the "pit crew guys" went back to using the wooden box on casters they had originally made. Besides, it was easier to modify the wooden box as the change-over process evolved. As the process was perfected, 15-minute changeovers were achieved and the average was less than 20 minutes. The concepts spread to other plants, was applied to other processes, and is still in use today improving productivity.

The talents of employees often show up in their outside activities. Creating a climate that enables them can let an organization "tap" into the talents of the hands-on experts. We often do this much better today than in the past, but it needs to be a part of any business plan to reevaluate how well we use this resource. I have seen this approach fall out of favor, only to then be revived with significant results several times over the years.

Following are examples of results emanating from Kaizen projects managed by Jerry Feingold. Many seem repetitive; however, the examples give you a good idea of the types of results that can be achieved.

Project business: Aerospace industry.
Project area: Low-profile actuators.
Project results: Reduced labor standard 34 percent, for a savings of $91,146 per year; reduced WIP value from $32,000 to $4,000; reduced line stock $117,000; reduced floor space from 775 square feet to 139 square feet (82 percent reduction).

Project business: Aerospace industry.
Project area: Switch assembly cells (#132 and # 232).
Project results: Reduced lead time from 2.4 days to 1 day (59 percent improvement); reduced standard time from 40 minutes to 25 minutes (37 percent improvement); reduced WIP from 127 pieces to 26; reduced floor space from 1,086 to 360 square feet (66 percent improvement); reduced conveyance distance from 425 feet to 106 feet.

Project business: Aerospace industry.
Project area: Switch assembly cell (#3).
Project results: Reduced lead time from 3 days to 1 day within the cell; reduced WIP from 129 to 43 (66 percent improvement); reduced assembly time by 25 percent; reduced conveyance distance from 432 feet to 60 feet; reduced floor space from 800 square feet to 560 square feet (30 percent reduction).

Project business: Aerospace industry
Project area: New employee orientation packages.
Project results: Reduced time to assemble package from 27 minutes to 1 minute 19 seconds.

Project business: Aerospace industry.
Project area: Combine valve assembly and test areas.
Project results: Reduced WIP from 265 to 21; reduced assembly and test times by 23.5 percent; created 1,892 available square feet of assembly floor space; reduced conveyance distance from 770 feet to 12 feet.

Project business: Aerospace industry.
Project area: Switch assembly cell (# 40).
Project results: Reduced processing time from 8 days to 3 days (63 percent improvement); reduced WIP from 524 units to 195 (63 percent improvement); reduced lead time from 20 days to 11 days (45 percent improvement).

Project business: Aerospace industry.
Project area: Gate valve assembly and test integration.
Project results: Reduced WIP from 160 to 51 (68 percent improvement); reduced assembly and test time by 23.5 percent; reduced conveyance distance from 775 feet to 48 feet.

Project business: Aerospace industry.
Project area: Gate valve cell.
Project results: Reduced standard time 27 percent; setup reduced from 4.2 hours to 2.4 hours.

Project business: Aerospace industry.
Project area: Machine shop-switch cell.
Project results: Reduced setup time from 1 hour, 38 minutes to 1 hour, 11 minutes.

Project business: Aerospace industry.
Project area: Machine shop improvement—mill valve.
Project results: Reduced setup time on a key part number from 3.1 to 0.56 hour; reduced walking distance from 5,200 feet to 258 feet.

Project business: Aerospace industry.
Project area: Butterfly and ball valve area.
Project results: Reduced 8 weeks of machining lead time; reduced WIP from 700 to 60; reduced overtime 517 hours; obviated the need to purchase a $225,000 machining center.

Project business: Aerospace industry.
Project area: Switch assembly cell (#1173).
Project results: Reduced time from kit completion to final test from 30 days to 5 days (83 percent improvement); reduced time from etching to test from 30 days to 2 hours (99 percent improvement); reduced WIP value from $65,7645 to $18,194 (72 percent improvement); reduced conveyance distance from 3,250 feet to 985 feet.

Project business: Aerospace industry.
Project area: Machine shop—ATA cell.
Project results: Reduced total process time from 37 days to 11 days; reduced conveyance from 6,471 feet per day to 1,731 feet per day; reduced WIP from 1,875 pieces to 400 pieces; eliminated $34,000 per year in overtime.

Project business: Aerospace industry.
Project area: Machine shop grinding department.
Project results: SMED (single-minute exchange of die) resulted in reduction of setup times on selected parts from

4.9 hours to 25 minutes; reduced cycle time from 16.3 hours to 1.9 hours; TPM (total productive maintenance) resulted in rationalization and organization of all grinding tooling. The *APICS Dictionary* describes TPM as "Preventive maintenance plus continuous efforts to adapt, modify, and refine equipment to increase flexibility, reduce material handling, and promote continuous flows. It is operator-oriented maintenance with involvement of all qualified employees in all maintenance activities." A synonym for TPM is "total preventive maintenance."

Project business:	Bicycle component manufacturer.
Project area:	Oil soaking process.
Project description:	Bicycle components were previously made in batch sizes of 1,100. All components needed to be soaked in oil. The oil was in a 1,000-gallon tank. Parts were collected and brought with forklift trucks to the oil bath and then redistributed throughout the facility after the oil treatment.
Project results:	Reduced batch sizes from 1,100 to 60, and each factory location was given a small plastic tub for the small amount of oil now required; eliminated the large oil tank; eliminated forklifts; reduced the travel time.

Remember that the best time for a cost-cutting and productivity-improvement program is now. It is much better for you to initiate such a program than have it imposed on you.

Thank you for reading this book.

Contributors

Evan Ackerman, BA, BS, CMC, of South Miami, Florida

James Ayers, BS, MBA, MS, CMC, of Playa Del Rey, California

John Bryan, BA, BS, MBA, PHD, CMC, of San Diego, California

Carlos Conejo, BS, CSSBB, of Thousand Oaks, California

Peter A. Crosby, BS, MS, Engr., CMC, of Pacific Palisades, California

Charles Cunningham, MA, MS, of Dry Fork, Virginia

Jerry Feingold, BS, MBA, of Ventura, California

Index

Absenteeism, in employees, 59, 61, 73
Accountability, 165, 180
Accounting Department, 80, 130
Accounts Payable area, 188–89
Ackerman, Evan, 185
Acquisitions. *See* Consolidations
Activity-based costing, 80–81
Advertising costs, 7–8, 56, 87, 101
Advice, free services and, 38–40. *See also* Consultants
Aerospace industry, 20–21, 226–29
Airline industry, cost cutting by, 5
American Production and Inventory Control Society, 69–70
APICS Dictionary, 19, 20, 70, 194, 229
"Ask for it" (axiom), 51–52
Assignments list, 180, 183
Association for Retarded Citizens (ARC), 131
Automobile industry, 5–6
Axioms, for cost cutting. *See* Common-sense axioms
Ayers, James B., 18–19, 80–81

Bar-coding system, 2, 42, 52, 139–40, 143; for warehouse management, 2, 110, 112, 140
Bicycle component manufacturer, 229
Billing and collection, 8. *See also* Invoices

Bill of material (BOM), 42
Blind reverse auction, 57
Bottlenecks in work flow, 74, 77, 173, 174
Bottom line, cost cutting and, 6–9
Bryan, John, 186
Budget expenses, 27–30, 79–85, 170; across-the-board cuts in, 153; activity-based costing and, 80–81; cash flow and, 84–85; expenditure approval levels, 81; expense history, 27–29; general ledger chart of accounts, 29–30; managers and, 14, 16, 79, 80, 81; nicety or necessity, 81–85, 174; organizational structure and, 91; reduction, by percentage, 15–16; responsibility for, 14–15; service and maintenance agreements and, 89; variable expenses, 27; zero-based budget concept and, 79. *See also* Freight expenses
Business-to-business (B2B) portal, 185–86
"Buy *versus* make" decisions, 100, 175

Cash flow problems, 7, 8, 52, 60, 84–85
Cellular repeater manufacturer, 194
Change, managing, 151, 179
Change over, in manufacturing, 224–25
Chrysler Corporation, 5
Collaboration, 18–19

Committees, forming, 11–12, 22
Common-sense axioms, 51–78; "Ask for
  it," 51–52; competitive bids, 54–55;
  consistent policies and procedures for,
  57–59; eliminating bottlenecks, 74, 77;
  "High volume equals high opportunity," 65–68, 134, 135; improved productivity and, 69–73; Internet and
  technology, 56–57; "Keeping eyes and
  ears open," 59–64; reducing unproductive time, 73–76; return on investment
  and, 52–54; "Time is money," 68–69;
  "Trust your instincts," 64–65. See also
  Cost cutting
Communication, 24, 116–17, 127–29; of
  basic concepts, 51; email, 57, 117, 128;
  facsimile (fax), 117; memoranda, 116,
  117; teleconferencing, 56; telephone,
  39, 68, 113, 127–28
Communications equipment
  manufacturer, 204–5
Competitive bids, 54–55, 56–57, 82, 171
Competitors, 2, 7, 61
Computer hardware distributor, 217–18
Computer software distributor, 219–20
Computer technicians. See IT
  (Information Technology) Department
Conejo, Carlos, 190
Confidentiality, consultants and, 34
Consolidations, 198–99, 200, 209, 212;
  acquisitions, relocations, and, 105–14;
  examples of, 106–11, 218; open-ended
  planning guide, 111–14
Construction company, 209–10
Consultants, 12–14, 53, 104, 170;
  contingency basis and, 39, 40;
  employee interviews and, 34
Consumer products companies, 203–4,
  206–7, 221–23
Cost cutting, 1–9; alternative approaches
  to, 11; areas to avoid, 25; in automobile
  industry, 5–6; bottom line and, 6–9;
  consultants and, 12–14, 34, 39, 40, 53,
  104, 170; establishing objectives, 9;
  free advice on, 38–40; importance of,
  4–6; incentive programs, 16–17; key
  questions, 183–84; paper usage
  reduction, 114–18; potential benefits

from, 1–3; setting goals for, 14–15;
  teams and committees, 11–12, 22; value
  engineering and, 42–43; as "whack-a-
  mole" game, 90–91. See also Budget
  expenses; Suppliers, cost cutting and
Cost-cutting programs: evaluating results
  of, 162–65; getting started, 21–23;
  objectives in, 169; planning worksheet,
  181–83; potential benefits of, 1–2; top
  management and, 21–22; weekly
  report, 166
County Department of Health
  Services, 188
Crosby, Peter A., 194
Cunningham, Charles, 224
Customer complaints, 87, 133;
  overreacting to, 89–90
Customer focus group, 86
Customer service, 108, 122, 137, 197;
  consolidation of, 199; order processing
  and, 101–2, 196; product liability and,
  86–87; shipping costs and, 124–25
Customs broker service, 104, 120

Dairy products company, 202–3, 212–13
DCs. See Distribution centers
Delivery service, 57, 68, 76, 220. See also
  Freight expenses; Shipping costs
Distribution, 141, 204–5, 214; costs in,
  197; direct store delivery, 220;
  marketing and, 195–97. See also
  Shipping costs
Distribution centers (DCs), 64–65, 206,
  212, 222–23; relocations and, 106,
  108–9, 114
Drugstore chain, 220–21

Education. See Training and education
Efficiency, productivity and, 69–73
Efficiency experts, 62. See also
  Consultants; Industrial engineers
Electrical products manufacturer, 207–8
Email communication, 57, 117, 128
Employee morale, 2, 32, 37, 78, 160
Employees, 171–72; absenteeism and
  tardiness in, 59, 61, 73; cost cutting and,
  23–24; early retirement of, 149, 178;
  exit interviews for, 154, 179; flexibility/

cross-training of, 71–72; game playing
by, 129; hiring mentally challenged,
131, 177; management and, 190–91;
managing change, 151; new hires and
replacements, 148; overtime (OT) pay
for, 62, 64, 132, 148, 177; performance
standards for, 44, 53, 73, 150, 153,
155–61, 171; productivity analyses and,
43–49; recruiting, 56, 104, 152–53;
reducing unproductive time and, 73–76;
reductions in force, 15–16, 153–54,
163, 179; relocations and, 111; retention of, 147–48; rewards and incentives
for, 16–17, 36, 38, 52, 73; rules of conduct for, 58–59; shortened work week/
hours, 148, 178; suggestion programs,
34–38; supplier gratuities and, 151–52;
survey interviews with, 31–34, 170;
temporary and part-time, 61–62, 108,
149–51, 178; transfer of, 23; unions
and, 108, 150–51; work logs and,
48–49, 69. See also Human Resources
Department
Employee training. See Training and
education, of employees
Energy savings, utilities and, 39
Entertainment, travel and, 129–30, 176
Equipment, 88–89, 103, 111, 203;
replacement of, 53; safety in operating,
93–94; selling excess, 114, 176, 210
Ergonomics, safety and, 94
Exit interviews, 154, 179
Expenditures. See Budget expenses; Cost
cutting; Freight expenses

Facsimile (fax) transmissions, 117
Feingold, Jerry, 20–21, 226
Five Ss (sort, simplify, scrub, standardize,
sustain), 194
Food and Drug Administration
(FDA), 60, 61
Food products company, 197, 205–6
Ford Motors, 5–6
Forecasting, 207–8
Freight All Kinds (FAK) agreement, 121
Freight expenses, 28–29, 102, 113,
119–25, 198; "drop and switch," 41–42;
employee morale and, 78; high-volume

discounts and, 65; inbound shipments,
120–21; internal shipping policies,
123–25; less than truckload (LTL), 119,
120, 121, 125; outbound shipments,
121–22; post-auditing of, 39; pre-
auditing, 40, 104; reverse auction
method and, 57; small packages,
122–23, 124, 126. See also Shipping
costs
Frozen food manufacturer, 199–200
Full truckload (FTL) shipments, 119, 121.
See also Freight expenses

Gain sharing (incentive program), 16
General ledger chart of accounts, 29–30.
See also Budget expenses
Generally accepted accounting
practices, 80
General Motors (GM), 5–6
The Goal (Goldratt), 77
Goldratt, Eliyahu, 77
Grocery products company, 198–99,
215–16

Head counts, reduction in, 15–16. See also
Employees
Health products company, 216–17
"High volume equals high opportunity"
(axiom), 65–68, 99, 134, 135, 173
Hotel chain, 189–90
Housekeeping, safety and, 92
Human Resources (HR) Department, 73,
130, 147–54; employee morale and, 78;
employee retention and, 147–48, 178;
recruitment and, 56, 104, 152–53, 179;
reductions in force and, 153–54;
temporary workers and, 149–51; union
negotiations and, 150–51. See also
Employees

Inbound shipping, 8, 28, 29, 120–21. See
also Shipping costs
Incentive programs, 16–17, 96, 160–61;
piecework, 74, 135–36, 160. See also
Rewards, for employees
Indonesia, outsourcing from, 106,
107, 108
Industrial engineers, 43, 44, 225

Industrial plastics manufacturer, 209
Information technology. *See* IT
    (Information Technology) Department
*In Search of Excellence: Lessons from
    America's Best Run Companies* (Peters
    and Waterman), 7
Insurance, 86, 140; for small packages,
    122–23
Internal auditing, 12
International suppliers, 28, 100
Internet, 56–57, 128, 129
Interviews. *See* Survey interviews
Inventory, 113, 177–78, 215, 218; bar-
    coding systems for, 139–40, 143; car-
    rying costs, 8, 18, 68, 219; control and
    accuracy in, 110, 141–45; obsolete, 145
Invoices, payment of, 60, 68
IT (Information Technology) Department,
    42, 103, 125, 129, 179; paper usage
    reduction and, 114–15

Janitorial functions, 100
Japanese methodology, 192. *See also*
    Kaizen projects
Job functions: productivity analysis of,
    43–49
Job search websites, 56
Just in time (JIT) manufacturing, 18,
    19–20, 65

Kaizen projects, 20–21, 170, 182, 193,
    226
"Keeping eyes and ears open" (axiom),
    59–64

Labor costs, 8, 107; relocation and, 108,
    110. *See also* Employees
Labor unions, 108, 150–51, 157, 178
Landscaping and gardening, 101, 112
Lean training, 193, 194
Legal assistance, 104
Less than truckload (LTL) shipments, 119,
    120, 121, 125. *See also* Freight
    expenses
Liability insurance, 86. *See also* Product
    liability
Lifting safety, 92. *See also* Safety
    concerns

Logistics network analysis, 213–14
Logistics reengineering, 215–16
Los Angeles Times (newspaper), 5, 117
Lost (unproductive) time, 73–76

Magnetics and electronics manufacturer,
    193–94
Mailings and mailing lists, 103, 125. *See
    also* U.S. Postal Service
Maintenance, 103; preventive,
    88, 174, 229
Maintenance agreements, 88–89
Managers and supervisors, 41, 71, 90, 100,
    170; accountability of, 165; bottlenecks
    in work flow and, 74; budgets and, 14,
    16, 79, 80, 81; collaboration and,
    18–19; consultants and, 13, 14;
    employee morale and, 78; employee
    relations and, 190–91; evaluation
    reports and, 162; goal setting by, 14–15;
    Kaizen event and, 20; leadership role
    of, 21–22; performance standards and,
    157, 158, 189; printed reports and, 115;
    problem-solving courses and, 135;
    productivity analyses and, 43, 71;
    quality-related issues and, 134, 135;
    relocation and, 112; responsibilities of,
    173; sourcing and, 220; teamwork and,
    192; workforce empowerment
    and, 193
Manufacturer's representatives, 102–3
Marketing costs, 7–8, 87, 101, 195
Material-handling equipment,
    93–94
Materials costs. *See* Raw materials costs
Medical equipment manufacturer, 106–8,
    127, 208–9
Mentally challenged workers, 131, 177
Morale, employee, 2, 32, 37, 78, 160
Municipal school district, 201–2

National Motor Freight Classification
    (NMFC), 121
Negotiation, 110, 176; with employees'
    unions, 150–51, 178; with suppliers, 31,
    99, 100, 170
"Nicety or necessity," 81–85. *See also*
    Budget expenses

Observations, 171; productivity analyses and, 45–48
Occupational Safety and Health Administration (OSHA), 40, 91, 94, 95, 175
Offshoring, freight costs and, 28
OSHA. *See* Occupational Safety and Health Administration
Outbound shipments, 8, 29, 121. *See also* Shipping costs
Outsourcing, 19, 28, 101, 102, 107
Overtime (OT), 62, 64, 132, 148, 177

Package carriers, 102, 110, 120, 126; insurance for, 122–23. *See also* Shipping costs
Packaging, 39, 66–67, 126–27, 134; customer complaints about, 89–90; reuse of, 117–18
Paper products distributor, 194–95
Paper usage reduction, 114–18, 127, 176
Paperwork, 210
Payroll processing, 101
Performance review process, 167, 180
Performance standards, 16; auditing and revising, 162; for employees, 44, 53, 73, 150, 153, 171; management and, 189; setting fair, 156–61, 179–80
Peters, Thomas, 7
Petroleum company, 202
Pharmaceutical manufacturer, 60–61
Piecework incentive system, 74, 135–36
Plant shutdowns, 105, 176
Policies and procedures, 57–59, 172–73; security, 97–98, 100, 112, 113, 175; shipping, 58, 123–25; supplier gratuities, 151–52, 179; travel, 130; warranty policy, 58–59, 85, 133
Polyester processing business, 186–88
Preventive maintenance (PM), 88, 174, 229
Printed reports, reducing, 114–16
Printing needs, 101
Product design, 42; development and, 85–86
Productivity, definition of, 4, 69–70
Productivity analyses, 43–49, 71, 74–76, 153; bottlenecks in work flow and, 74, 77; functions list and observation record, 45–46; random periodic observations and, 47–48; unproductive time and, 73–76; work logs, 48–49
Productivity-improvement programs, 4, 7, 8–9; consultants and, 13; cost savings in, 35–36; efficiency and, 69–73; free advice on, 38–40; goal setting in, 14–15; Kaizen and, 20–21; main objective of, 9; planning worksheet, 181–83; potential benefits of, 1–2; top management and, 22; training with, 24; weekly report, 166
Product liability, 86–87, 174
Product packaging. *See* Packaging
Profitability, 6–9, 209
Protective coatings manufacturer, 213–14
Purchased materials and parts, 99–100, 211. *See also* Raw materials costs
Purchase orders, 56, 101–2
Purchasing Department, 40, 60, 65, 211, 218

Quality assurance, 12, 67
Quality-related costs, 107, 133–45, 177; doing things right in the first place, 138–41; inventory control and, 141–45; piecework incentives and, 135–36; portion control, in restaurants, 136–37; prevention and identification of, 135, 138; scrap and rework, 130–31, 133, 139; understanding, 137–38. *See also* Inventory

Random periodic observations, 47–48
Raw materials costs, 8, 66, 117, 134, 137; purchased parts and, 99–100, 175
Recruitment, of employees, 56, 104, 152–53
Recycling, 117–18, 176
Reductions in force (RIF), 15–16, 153–54, 163, 179
Relocations: acquisitions, consolidations, and, 105–14; examples of, 106–11; excess equipment and, 114; open-ended planning guide for, 111–14
Research and development, 2

Restaurants, 200–201; portion control in, 136–37
Return on investment (ROI), 2, 52–54, 140, 182, 224
Reverse auction methodology, 56–57
Rewards, for employees, 36, 38, 52, 73; incentives, 16–17, 74, 135–36, 160–61; safety concerns and, 95, 96
Rework costs, 130–31, 133, 176
Rice mill, 190–91
RIF. *See* Reductions in force
ROI. *See* Return on investment
Router cards, 131
Rules of conduct, for employees, 58–59

Safety concerns, 85, 91–97, 114, 175; employee training and, 95–96; ergonomic risk and, 94; general safety rules, 91–92; housekeeping and, 92; lifting safety, 92; lost work-time injuries and, 96–97; material-handling equipment and, 93–94; rewards and, 95, 96
Sales and salespeople, 8, 41, 68–69, 87; forecasting, 207–8; manufacturer's representatives and, 102–3
Scrap and rework costs, 130–31, 133, 139, 163, 176
Security policies and procedures, 97–98, 100, 112, 113, 175
Service agreements, 88–89
Services, inside versus outside, 100–105, 175. *See also* Customer service; *specific services*
Shipments, tracking, 57
Shipping costs, 18, 41, 89; freight analysis, 28–29; inbound, 8, 28, 29, 120–21; negotiating lower rates for, 110, 176; outbound, 8, 29, 121; packaging and, 39, 126–27; performance report, 156; raw materials and, 137; warranty replacement and, 133. *See also* Freight expenses
Shipping policies, 58, 123–25
SKU (stock-keeping unit), 142, 143, 219–20
Small Business Administration, 40

Small-package shipments, 122–23, 124, 126. *See also* Package carriers
Soft drink manufacturer, 211, 214–15
Sourcing, 100, 220. *See also* Outsourcing
Special purchase deals, 223–24
Stack train trailers, 41–42
Statistics, maintaining, 161–62, 180
Steel products distributor, 210–11
Stock-keeping unit. *See* SKU
Suggestion programs, 34–38; rewards in, 36, 38
Supervisors. *See* Managers and supervisors
Suppliers, cost cutting and, 30–31, 40–42; competitive bids and, 55, 82, 171; free services from, 39; freight costs and, 41; gratuity policies and, 151–52, 179; high-volume commitments to, 65, 67; interviews with, 32; negotiation with, 31, 99, 100, 170; paying of invoices and, 60; quality issues and, 137; reverse auction methodology and, 56–57
Supply chain partnering, 17–19
Supply chain strategy, 203, 216–17
Surveillance systems, 97. *See also* Security policies and procedures
Survey interviews, 25, 31–34, 170

Tardiness, of employees, 59, 61, 73
Teams and committees, 11–12, 22, 192
Teleconferencing, 56
Telephones, 39, 68, 113, 127–28
Temporary workers, 61–62, 108, 149–51, 178
Thermo forming/food packaging plant, 192–93
Third-party logistics/distribution company, 104
"Time is money" (axiom), 68–69; lost (unproductive) time and, 73–76
Tire manufacturer, 224–25
Total productive maintenance, 229
Training and education, of employees, 24–25, 53, 116, 147, 151; 172; cross-training, 71–72, 173; government funding for, 40; group seminars, 66; interview guide, 32–34; Lean training, 193,

194; online, 56; portion control and, 137; safety rules and, 95–96
Transportation costs, 205. *See also* Freight expenses
Travel, sales and service, 68–69
Travel and entertainment (T&E), 23, 129–30, 176
Travel Office, 23
Truck fleet lines, 102, 213
"Trusting your instincts" (axiom), 64–65

Unions, 108, 150–51, 157, 178
University of Michigan, 14
U.S. Postal Service (USPS), 5, 125, 126
Utilities, 39, 82

Vacation policy, 73
Value engineering, 42–43
Vehicle fleet planning, 201–3

Volume sales. *See* "High volume equals high opportunity" (axiom)

Warehousing, 104, 142, 195, 196, 216; bar-code-based system for, 2, 110, 112, 140; costs of, 213, 214; distribution strategies and, 206–7; stocking strategy, 219–20
Warranty policy, 58–59, 85, 133
Waterman, Robert, Jr., 7
"Whack-a-mole" game, 90–91
Wine and spirits wholesaler, 212
Worker safety. *See* Safety concerns
Worker's compensation claims, 96–97
Work flow process, 193; bottlenecks in, 74, 77, 173, 174
Work logs, 48–49, 69, 174

Zero-based budget expenses, 79. *See also* Budget expenses
ZIP codes, 124

About the Author

Fred H. Neu is a Certified Management Consultant with more than 35 years of international experience in consulting and executive management. A University of Michigan graduate, he managed the Cost Reduction/Productivity Improvement consulting group in Los Angeles for what is now Price-WaterhouseCoopers. Fred has helped a variety of businesses be more successful by saving them tens of millions of dollars annually and by increasing areas of measurable performance to all-time highs.